No Profit
but the Name

THE LONGFORDS AND THE
GATE THEATRE

'We go to gain a little patch of ground
That hath in it no profit but the name.'
Hamlet, Act IV, Scene 4

No Profit but the Name

THE LONGFORDS

and the

GATE THEATRE

JOHN COWELL

THE O'BRIEN PRESS
DUBLIN

First published 1988 by The O'Brien Press Ltd.
20 Victoria Road, Rathgar, Dublin 6, Ireland

British Library Cataloguing in Publication Data

Cowell, John

No profit but the name: the Longfords and the Dublin Gate Theatre

1. Dublin.Theatres: DUBLIN GATE THEATRE, to 1960

I. Title

792'.09418'35

ISBN 0-86278-175-2

Illustration page 1: Logo of Longford Productions, a symbolic
Shakespearean stage, designed and drawn by Edward in the old Imperial
Hotel in Cork during the company's first tour.

Illustration page 2: Christine and Edward after their wedding at St
Margaret's Church, Oxford, 18 July 1925.

10 9 8 7 6 5 4 3 2 1

Typesetting: The O'Brien Press

Book design: Michael O'Brien

Printing: The Bath Press, Bath.

Acknowledgements

In the preparation of this book I am deeply indebted to Lady Mary Clive for permission to use copyright material left by Christine Longford.Christine's unfinished memoir dealt only with the period between 1918 and 1939. I have quoted liberally from this memoir. In doing so I hope I may have preserved something of Christine's delicious sense of humour, always expressed in her own inimitable style. Again, I am grateful to Lady Clive for so generously assisting me with her own reminiscences of a unique childhood as a daughter of the fifth Earl and Countess of Longford, and as a sister of Edward, the sixth Earl, the saviour of the Dublin Gate Theatre.

I am indebted to Thomas and Valerie Pakenham for their help and encouragement from the moment this project was first mooted on the lawn at Tullynally Castle one sunny morning in October 1980. Incidentally, Tullynally Castle was known as Pakenham Hall throughout the period covered by this book. I am particularly grateful to Thomas for the trouble he took in locating and providing family photographs from the 1920s.

There were others, many others, who helped in so many ways: Rachel Burrows; Mary Cannon and the Hilton Edwards Estate; Richard Clery; Brendan and Sheila Ellis; Alice Grattan Esmonde; Fr Pancras Fanning CP, archivist, Mount Argus Monastery; Anthony Farrell; Liam Gaffney; Eileen Healy; Michael Johnston; Cormac Kavanagh; Anna Manahan; Kay Mullen; John O'Dea; Colm O'Doherty; Desmond Rushe; Phyllis Ryan; Fr Daniel Shields SJ; Mary Smith; Patricia Turner; Dr Moira Woods; Brigid Dolan, librarian, Royal Irish Academy; the librarians and staff of the National Library and the Royal Dublin Society; R. Russell Maylone, curator, Special Collections Department, Northwestern University Library, Illinois; the National Gallery of Ireland and Bord Failte.

John Finegan, drama critic of the *Evening Herald*, kindly allowed me to use as an appendix a list compiled by him of 151 plays presented by Longford Productions in the twenty-four years of their existence. The list represents an amazing achievement by a privately financed theatre company when State and commercial subsidisation were still unknown.

My special gratitude goes to those one-time members of Longford Productions who reminisced so patiently and generously, sometimes sadly, sometimes wistfully, sometimes laughingly, but always with a deep sense of admiration for their beloved Edward and Christine: Jean Anderson; Christopher and Kay Casson; Cathleen Delany; Aiden Grennell; John Izon; Margaret Lawlor; Iris Lawler; Charles Mitchel; Ann O'Connor; Deirdre O'Meara; Alpho O'Reilly; Dan Treston; Dermot Tuohy and Eve Watkinson.

Without the expertise of Michael O'Brien and the staff of the O'Brien Press this venture wouldn't have been possible. I am grateful to Máiréad FitzGerald, Liz Meldon, Ivan O'Brien and Íde ní Laoghaire.

Left: The refurbishment of the Gate Theatre in 1957-58 called for strenuous efforts to raise the necessary funds. Edward resorted to every means of fundraising, including walking the streets with a begging-box.

Right: Christine outside the Gate Theatre in 1946.
Opposite: An exterior view of the Gate Theatre in 1941. As shown by the posters, *Macbeth* was being presented by Longford Productions. Rarely noticed, the sculpture on the portico is particularly beautiful.

CONTENTS

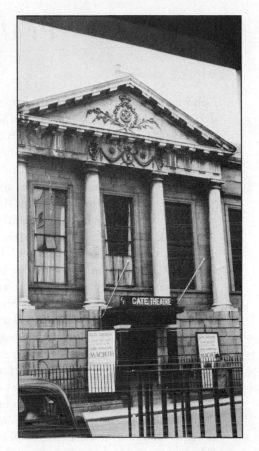

Prologue

Echoing to every footfall, the huge, empty room was cold and dim and dirty. Festooned with cobwebs and the tattered paper chains of some long-forgotten Dublin hooley, high above the chill and grime there arched a Georgian ceiling of great beauty. Two young men poked about in the rubble, one a little dreamily, the other with great energy. They were trying to see this ghastly ruin as a future theatre.

'It's so dark and empty,' said Micheál Mac Liammóir, the handsome, curly-haired actor who had recently made his mark in some *avant garde* plays at Dublin's Peacock Theatre.

'What the hell do you expect? Buckingham Palace?' retorted Hilton Edwards. He was the one with the trilby and the walking stick with which he poked vigorously in the nooks and crannies. Edwards it was who had just enraptured intellectual Dublin with his productions of *Peer Gynt, Anna Christie* and *The Power of Darkness*, also on that tiny Peacock stage.

The cold cavern they were exploring had once been the Rotunda Concert Room where Handel was said to have played. In Dublin's golden age it had provided an income for Dr Bartholomew Mosse to run his famous Lying-in Hospital, the first of its kind in these islands. Now it was 1929, and the two young men — 'The Boys', as Dublin would come to know them — had just seen their dream come a little closer to reality: their own theatre in Dublin. Afterwards from Groome's Hotel across the street Edwards surveyed the façade of the graceful Georgian building.

'We'll have the name up there in lights,' he said. 'Just the one word — GATE.' The name was taken from Peter Godfrey's Gate Theatre in Villiers Street under Charing Cross Station in London. Edwards had planned an exchange-of-plays scheme with Godfrey.

In that same Groome's Hotel, on Christmas Eve 1929, a lease was signed for the Rotunda annexe, the one-time 'Upper Concert Hall'. A young man called Michael Scott was recruited. He was the actor/architect destined to become Dublin's greatest builder of theatres. Soon the dank room in Parnell Square swarmed with carpenters and painters. Meantime, the Dublin Gate Theatre Company Limited was formed and registered, and a board of directors appointed. Mac Liammóir commented: 'Fate, with her sleeves maliciously rolled back, a smart spit in her hands and a demoniacal gleam in her eye, was preparing for us.'

Money was raised through the launch of an impressive shareholding scheme. Buying shares in the Gate Theatre Company became the fashion with a coterie of genuine theatre-lovers. The trouble was the coterie was too small. Not all the shares were taken up.

Their enthusiasm in no way diminished, Edwards and Mac Liammóir recruited a cast and rehearsals began. In another month their Dublin Gate Theatre had taken shape, its decor a striking use of black and red and gold. Four hundred seats faced a black proscenium, its curtain bearing a great, symbolic, golden gate painted by Mac Liammóir. On 17 February 1930 that curtain first opened, to present Goethe's *Faust*, with Mac Liammóir playing Faust and Edwards Mephistopheles.

The weather was arctic, with frozen snow piled high in the gutters and the streets like glass. The atmosphere within the theatre was hardly better. At the critical hour of eight o'clock the heating system failed. By the first interval there were those who felt ill-done-by, who knew it was silly, to say the least, to open a theatre in Dublin's latitude without proper heating. It boded ill for the theatre's future. There were others — those who appeared to be better informed. Of course there was a heating system, they argued. The fact that it had flopped was just a little setback, in the true tradition of first-night accidents. Indeed, it might be taken as a good omen.

With the final curtain, the icy air of the Gate auditorium had been forgotten. After a last act commanding rapt attention the applause was tumultuous. Still not recognising it for the historic occasion it was, that first-night audience left the new Gate Theatre, some in a frenzy of excitement, some in a trance-like ecstasy. Dublin would never be the same; something like a theatrical cataclysm had occurred.

Faust, of course, lost money, as did *Berkeley Square* and *Back to Methuselah* and some twenty other classics which followed through the year 1930. The board of directors — or some of them — became concerned. As Chairman, Hilton Edwards was the financial figurehead. But, like Micheál Mac Liammóir, he was already committed, conjuring up unique presentations of non-commercial plays never before seen in Ireland. Each was produced on a tightly-stretched shoestring, yet each was more visually exciting than the last.

The other directors were Madame 'Toto' Bannard Cogley, who ran a cabaret in Dublin; Gearóid O'Lochlainn, who had acted in Irish and English, and even in Danish at the National Theatre in Copenhagen; and Norman Reddin, a solicitor, who came from a family with a long theatre-loving tradition, and whose mother never ceased to plague intellectual Dublin in her fund-raising for the Gate. Probably the one member of the board with some real financial insight was Gordon Campbell, otherwise Lord Glenavy. A one-time member of the

Parliamentary Bar in London, he had come home to the new Ireland and served as Secretary of the Department of Industry and Commerce from 1922 to 1932. His wife was Beatrice Elvery, and his son, Patrick, was to become the famous comic journalist and television personality.

Gordon Campbell was the first to realise that the income from the Gate box-office simply wasn't enough to pay the theatre's way. Through those early months he warned repeatedly of imminent bankruptcy unless the remaining shares were bought up. This was the last thing The Boys wanted to hear. Hilton found finances a bore, and Micheál called Campbell 'a pessimist of brilliance and as depressing as a dromedary'.

But the situation worsened. At the first annual general meeting of the shareholders, on 12 December 1930, it was announced that unless the remaining unsubscribed shares, a matter of £1,200, were taken up, the Gate Theatre would be forced to close immediately. It was already £700 in debt, a considerable sum in 1930.

Rising from his seat in the audience, a pink-faced, rotund young man began struggling out of his overcoat. In an Oxford accent he announced that he would very much like to buy all the shares on offer, adding, 'and my cheque is ready whenever it is wanted'. The Gate Theatre was saved. But who was its saviour? Who was this carefree young man for whom money seemed no object?

Micheál Mac Liammóir didn't know. Nor did Hilton Edwards. As usual, it was the practical Gordon Glenavy who helped out. 'It's Lord Longford,' he said.

Thus it was that the death of the infant theatre was prevented. Lord Longford had saved the Gate as effectively as Annie Horniman had earlier saved the Abbey. Forty years later, Longford's widow, Christine, Countess of Longford, remembered that 'the moment of drama was unrehearsed. He knew that the Gate mustn't close, it was a necessity of life in Dublin and Ireland.' And so, on 12 December 1930, Lord Longford wrote the first of his many cheques, always written so willingly, in favour of the Gate Theatre. Unfortunately, the occasion also marked the beginning of a love-hate relationship.

That isn't to say the love and the hate were always apparent. It was a case, perhaps, of familiarity breeding contempt rather than of time being the great healer. Time in fact was the destroyer. After a startlingly artistic honeymoon, the relationship passed through the cooling processes of stress and strain, eventually ending in mutual and naked enmity.

The rights and the wrongs of the situation have never been fully revealed. But on reflection, and with hindsight, it is all too apparent that no artistic movement requiring dedicated cooperation could have ever

DUBLIN GATE THEATRE CO.
LIMITED

This is to Certify that

Dr Bright Thornton

of 8 Herbert Street, Dublin

is the Registered Proprietor of _one_

Fully Paid _____ Shares of £1 _____ each

numbered 2031 to _____ inclusive in the above-named

Company, subject to the Memorandum of Association and the

Rules and Regulations thereof.

Given under the Common Seal of the Company

the 1st day of November 1930

Hilton Edwards

T. Norman Reddin

SECRETARY

DIRECTORS

A Dublin Gate Theatre share certificate. Buying these shares had a certain snob value. However, it helped to save the theatre from extinction.

contained, for any length of time, three men of such dynamic character, each with such fixed and diverse views as Hilton Edwards, Micheál Mac Liammóir and Edward Longford — as the chubby young man became known. True, between them they endowed Dublin with an arts theatre whose reputation spanned the world. But, regrettably, the animus generated by their effort lasted for the lifetime of all the participants.

11

Chapter 1

'That's Lord Longford'

IN WRITING OF THE SIXTH EARL of Longford and of his wife, Christine, Countess of Longford, one must be correct on the subject of their birth dates. Accuracy on this point was demanded by Christine, who, from the moment she met Edward, was acutely conscious of her chronological seniority. 'We must make quite certain to be candid,' she said. 'He was two years and three months younger than me.' It had an important bearing on her married life. Also, she had a neat way of locating herself in time and place: 'I am as old as the century,' she would tell you,'and I was born in Cheddar where the cheese comes from.'

She was born Christine Patty Trew on 6 September 1900, at Cheddar in Somerset, the only child of Richard and Amy Trew. The family was not in Burke's Peerage. In fact, they were not gentry. According to Christine her family was not well connected. Indeed it was 'quite disconnected like the Bennets in *Pride and Prejudice*, middle class, though my mother would never admit it.Uppermiddle if you like, but certainly middle, with the claim to gentility that is so common in England.'

She had both English and Irish ancestry, though, like her husband,she detested the expression Anglo-Irish. 'My English grandmother was said to be connected with an extinct baronet, but he cannot be found in a book. I had my private *Who's Who* of people who counted. Intelligentsia versus the Others, that was my class war,and very pleasant it was.' Throughout her life she maintained that same class war.

From childhood Christine had a passion for Ireland. It was so intense as to induce the occasional telling of lies.'Sometimes,God forgive me, I pretended to be Irish.' The feeling probably originated with her Irish grandmother who came from Youghal,County Cork. As a young woman she had gone to England and had married an Englishman. In time he had left her stranded.So it was in England that she had brought up her son, Richard Trew, with no help from her husband.

History repeated itself. The marriage of Christine's father and mother broke up when she was three. Her father was the cause. A naval officer by profession, it was said he drank heavily. For whatever reason, he was eventually despatched by her mother.Though she didn't really remember her father, Christine bore her mother some resentment for her lack of feeling for even the memory of her husband. A Freudian thing, no doubt, and a little girl's desire to be like other little girls with loving fathers. Christine summarised the situation: 'I was the result of two bad matches and I claimed to be Irish on the strength of a half-Irish father whom I had barely known by sight.'

Her memory of her father came principally from photographs. Many years later when Longford Productions were on tour,a strange woman, a Miss Smart, approached Christine in Cork,claiming to be a cousin. While she had never heard of her,Christine felt convinced there must be some relationship because of the striking resemblance of this woman to her father in his photographs. On another occasion there was a similar incident in Limerick. Christine laughed, saying perhaps she should keep quiet about her long-lost Irish relatives.

Her first novel, *Making Conversation*, was published in 1931. She described it as 'the kind of first novel anybody can write,based on funny stories of childhood and youth'. On her own admission it is thinly-veiled autobiography, so transparent indeed that little is changed but the names. The life of the heroine, Martha Freke, matches almost exactly that of her creator. Even the same month and year, October 1918, marks the date when the creator and the created went up to Oxford.

Martha Freke also came from a broken home. Her father, Major Freke, 'had written too many cheques and disappeared. He was now thought to have become nautical, and to be interested in salvaging ships.' For whatever reason, Richard Trew left his home and family in Cheddar. He was eventually drowned at sea during World War I. Significantly, he wasn't mourned by his wife.

Being an only child, Christine Trew had to combat loneliness. But she was soon to learn self-reliance, something that was to last her for life. In old age she would tell you she loved nothing better than her own company. Reading became an early and a lasting passion. By the age of fourteen she had read far more widely than the prose and poetry prescribed for her age group. Tennyson, Longfellow and Macaulay she took in her stride. As a child, recitations took priority over music. Again in old age, she could quote pages of poetry without pause.

Mother-daughter friction was inevitable. As a one-parent only child Christine was at a singular disadvantage. Here the situation was worsened because the relationship involved an embittered mother and a strongly self-opinionated daughter. The former resented the loss of a husband, whatever the reason, the latter instinctively missed the protective presence of a father. Had he still been around, and been possessed by even the smallest admiration for precocious intelligence,

Christine would undoubtedly have been the apple of her father's eye.

Always a rebel, she showed her tendencies early on. Dress was one of the first sources of contention. School uniforms she accepted — there was no alternative. But when it came to white dresses, especially the concoctions worn for children's parties, Christine had deeply rooted objections. Her mother was equally strong-willed. Frequent rows ensued. Naturally, Mrs Trew wanted her little girl to conform with what Edwardian England expected little girls to look like: lacy white dresses with broad sashes and floppy bows of matching ribbon were *de rigueur*. To Christine this picture was revolting. Any old thing was preferrable to those shroud-like frocks.

Living in the small village of Coombe, Martha Freke attended the Adderbury High School, making the journey by waggonette in all weathers. Living in Cheddar, Christine Trew attended the Wells High School, travelling the eight miles to that cathedral city every morning by train. This helped at an early age to boost that sense of independence which was to be a lasting characteristic.

The school was situated over a cloister in the precincts of the cathedral. Gifted with an extraordinary memory, Christine soon became an exceptional pupil. Though she favoured history and languages, her greatest delight was of course English literature. As might be expected, mathematics held no attraction for her. She was a spirited child, entering into practical jokes and the nicknaming of her teachers. But this girlish side of life was confined to the school day. It was left behind when she came home. No permanent school friendships are recorded, nor did school girls visit her at home. This may well have had to do with home circumstances: to make ends meet, her mother had to take lodgers. As Christine grew older this became a subject of embarrassment which she tried to smother with her sense of humour.

Apart from the mother-daughter friction her home-life was happy, if sometimes lonesome. Yet she never yearned for brothers or sisters. It meant she had ample time for reading and she compensated by making good use of it. Also, the Somerset countryside was as attractive as any in England. Through the year the seasonal changes made real the images in the prose and poetry she read. In their turn came Wordworth's daffodils and Keats' seasons of mists. In summertime it was particularly thrilling to walk in the Mendip Hills, because it was from here the mummers with their masked faces came down in midwinter, on Boxing Day, and frightened the life out of an imaginative little girl.

And then there were the occasional trips to the seaside at Weston-Super-Mare. Christine didn't share her mother's enthusiasm for music, even popular music, nor did her mother try to push her into learning to play the piano as so many mothers did. Nor had Christine any antecedents who were interested in the theatre, except as spectators. Her own interest was aroused by occasional visits to see Sir Frank Benson's Shakespearean Company in Bristol, and West End successes on tour in Weston-Super-Mare and, of course, there was the annual pantomime, something which she found as silly as she was eventually to find opera.

She remembered seeing a production of Ibsen's *Ghosts* once when she was about fourteen. Billed 'For Adults Only', Christine, her curiosity whetted and with her usual independence, put her hair up and went in unchallenged. She was disappointed. She confessed she had little idea what it was all about. But in due time, Ibsen was to become a passion.

While still at Wells High School, she was given a prize by the Bishop of Bath and Wells for scripture repetition. She greatly valued that prize until she met her husband and discovered that at Eton he had won, not once but twice — two years running — an infinitely more prestigious distinction, namely, the Wilder Divinity Prize. Ever after, she bowed to his superior religious knowledge. 'I was not a good church-goer as he was, but I was well brought up and had an aunt an Anglican nun.'

The comparison with Martha Freke is again inevitable. When the Freke's favourite vicar went away they stopped going to church, and Martha was never confirmed, 'so she ceased to be an Anglican, except when filling in forms'.

Mrs Trew had four sisters. One married a wealthy South American. Two never married, and the fourth became Sister Grace, the Anglican nun. To her great advantage, one of Christine's maiden aunts acted as her personal teacher. She even taught her Greek and Latin, laying the foundations for the hoped-for scholarship to Oxford and all that followed. Her relationship with her Aunt Dodo lasted through the years. Her letters always amused Christine, reflecting as they did the innocence of an age that was gone for ever. Aunt Dodo would complain of how awful the world had become when people would eat ice-cream cones in the street. Also, she was saddened that the taste of strawberry jam was no longer what it used to be; even the butterflies, she felt, had lost their former brilliance.

In 1914 Mrs Trew moved to Oxford. There were reasons. First it would provide greater educational opportunity for her daughter, whose cleverness had already been recognised — and Mrs Trew was ambitious for her daughter. Thus Christine became a pupil at the Oxford High School. But second and more important, money was scarce and Oxford overflowed with graduates and undergraduates in search of living accommodation. It was agreed that the niceties would be observed: in

Oxford they would take 'paying guests', not lodgers. Once when a schoolgirl enquired of Martha Freke, 'You let lodgings, don't you?' she replied, 'Oh no, we only take in paying guests.'

Whether she liked it or not, Mrs Trew was accepted by undergraduates as another of Oxford's many landladies. Perhaps it was her socialistic outlook that made her a resilient woman, untouched by the pangs of empty pride. Indeed, she was sustained by the company of young people, and while her home became a home for some, it also became a popular meeting-place for many. She became a sort of universal mother. Her young men were devoted to her, all the more because she played the piano with gusto, anything from ragtime to the music-hall ditties in which the company could join. Indeed, her young men were so devoted, they vied for the privilege of standing beside her to turn the pages while she played. In summer they took the Trews on picnics and camping holidays.

Often her residents included colonials and, of course, Oxford had its homosexuals. Mrs Trew seemed to have an unusual understanding of these lonely people. Her maternal instinct reached out to them in a special way. She bequeathed to her daughter that same sympathy towards sexual deviants. Capable of making a spot diagnosis of lesbianism or homosexuality, Christine always retained a special understanding of these people's plight. It was for so diagnosing two of her teachers that Martha Freke had been expelled from Adderbury High School.

Life in Oxford soon broadened the vision of both mother and daughter. Mrs Trew's preoccupation with her paying guests and their friends was matched by Christine's immersion in the activities of the Oxford High School. The mother-daughter friction faded to a mutual indifference. To a teenage girl with an abiding interest in English literature, the air of Oxford was stimulating. Her ambition — and her mother's — was that she should matriculate to Somerville College — with a scholarship of course. Meanwhile she edited the High School magazine and made the momentous decision to become a writer. Such distractions took up more time than an academically ambitious girl should give them. Her associates were mainly the daughters of well-heeled fathers to whom money was no object. There were times when Christine became panic-stricken: how could one become a writer without a degree, and how could one fail to become a writer with an Oxford degree. For however long, these ruminations never failed to get her back to some serious study.

Christine's romantic passion for Ireland, a country she had never seen, continued to flourish, principally through her reading. In 1918 her passion was fomented by a meeting with a scion of a patriotic Irish family who was then an undergraduate at Balliol. Osmonde Grattan Esmonde,

16

a flamboyant young Irish extrovert, became infinitely more Irish and more extroverted whenever he found himself in England. He was the son and heir of Sir Thomas Grattan Esmonde of Ballynastragh, County Wexford. Christine remembered him singing Irish rebel songs at her mother's piano; 'The West's Awake' particularly thrilled her.

Ossie Esmonde might have been a missionary singing hymns to make conversions. Christine puts it another way: 'He always sang with great emphasis "Fleet as deer the English ran", and not "the Normans ran", to make it clearer for me; and he solemnly admitted me as an honorary Irishwoman to his tea-parties for oppressed nationalities, which included Indians and Egyptians and Serbian refugees.'

Until now her whole life had been geared towards getting into Oxford University. It was like trying to get into heaven on a free ticket. She had to get that scholarship for it was taken for granted that her mother could not afford the fees. True, she had been told she was clever; she had worked reasonably hard, but in the academic world one could never be certain. Yet as she swotted in the throes of exam fever, her better judgment told her she had the academic edge on many of her contemporaries, girls of place and fashion — flappers, more concerned with their romantic dreams than with the twilight philosophy of Pythagoras.

And so, Christine wasn't too greatly surprised when the news arrived that she had been awarded a classical scholarship to Somerville College. After her initial jubilation, and a summer of relaxation, she accordingly went up to Oxford in October 1918, taking Greek, Latin, ancient history and philosophy. Everywhere there were autumn leaves. There was mist at the end of every street, and in another month there would be Armistice Day and an end to the destruction of the flower of England's manhood.

The change in her status from schoolgirl to undergraduate brought intellectual compensations. Oxford for Christine, as for Martha Freke, was now to become 'a nursery of independent thought and intellectual aristocracy, of brilliant young men of every race and advanced young women who asserted their equality with them'. Intellectualism was to be the only class distinction she would recognise for the rest of her life.

Her social horizons too soared far beyond the confines of her mother's music room. Oxford became crowded with hopeful and high-spirited young men recently demobbed from the muddy hell of trench warfare. Theirs was a gut-hunger for freedom from fatigues and barrack-square bashing, from the thud of bursting shells and the scream of falling shrapnel. Oxford was to be a rest-cure in which these jaded young men might rehabilitate their spirits, might recapture something of the youthful years they had missed out on. They sought the adventure of its brilliant social circle, with the liberty to exchange intellectual ideas. As well, they sought a belated education on the strength of their hard-earned gratuities. They were older than the average entrant, and the Oxford proctors had to modify their regulations — undergraduates were no longer required to wear, but still had to carry, gowns at night.

In the years following the armistice a galaxy of literary stars brightened the Oxford firmament. It was a sort of incubation period of a disease that can only be described as contagious inspiration. In all its history Oxford had hardly ever housed at the same time so many budding writers of exceptional promise. It was as if the years of slaughter on the Western Front had stifled all self-expression and now, in its accumulation, it was to burst forth in profuse strains. Harold Acton, himself as bright a star as any of the period, the epitome of the Oxford aesthete, believed 'the arts which had been chloroformed awoke and asserted themselves so aggressively that the Philistines were made to tremble'.

Undergraduates of those years who were to become well-known writers include Robert Graves, Louis Golding, Leslie Hartley, Graham Greene, Evelyn Waugh, Vivian Pinto, Maurice Bowra, John Betjeman, Christopher Hollis and, of course, Harold Acton, who was already a myth before he came down from Oxford.

In due time Christine Trew was to know most of these men. Many became her life-long friends — but not immediately. Women had only recently been allowed degrees at Oxford. Their companionship with male undergraduates was controlled by strict rules. Besides, the males of the time had no great wish for female company. Homosexual friendships flourished in the Oxford of the post-war years. For all that, in the celibate quadrangles beneath the dreaming spires any woman was bound to be conspicuous. If she was intellectually articulate, that was an added bonus, ensuring her acceptance in the rarest aesthetic circles.

Christine Trew fulfilled the requirements. She could even out-manoeuvre the proctors. Her home was in Oxford, and her mother enjoyed the company of young people, especially young men. And so the house rang to the melody of Gershwin's 'Rhapsody in Blue' and to all the tunes of Tin Pan-Alley that added up to the transatlantic neurasthenia of the time. Years later, Martha Freke was to put things into perspective: 'Men can enjoy themselves without women, but women can't enjoy themselves without men.' That, broadly speaking, was also Christine's philosophy. She never made secret the fact that she preferred male company, principally because she believed men to be intellectually better developed.

Flora Grierson, a Scot, was Christine's closest woman friend. They were in the same year and they worked together in feverish fits and starts. Together too they dreamed of their futures in the world outside college — which inevitably meant London. Flora's father was Professor of English at Edinburgh University. He had edited John Donne and knew more about English letters than any Englishman. 'I was lucky to have Flora for my companion in college,' Christine recollects. 'She told me about seventeenth-century poets and more besides. She sang songs of the Hebrides, and that was how I first heard the Gaelic tongue.'

Nor was Christine's education in Irish republicanism being neglected by Ossie Esmonde. On St Patrick's Day 1920, he and his sisters took her to a concert in the Queen's Hall in London. There she heard strange, emotional Irish songs. 'Astra Desmond sang "Aghadoe", and I burst into tears. A man called Francis FitzGerald did Irish dancing, and the Esmondes told me he was a brother of Desmond, who had been out in 1916.' Francis FitzGerald was the uncle, and Desmond the father, of Garret FitzGerald, one-time Taoiseach.

After that concert the little party became caught up in an Irish patriotic procession, the object being to become involved with the police. Christine was disappointed that nothing happened. 'I was determined to be oppressed,' she writes, 'and not an oppressor.'

It was with Flora Grierson that Christine Trew first visited Garsington, the home of Lady Ottoline Morrell, reputed to be a temple of the Muses. This speaks volumes for Christine's standing as a highly intelligent undergraduate, for an invitation to Garsington represented a move from the entrenched safety of middle-browism to the explosive front line of intellectual bombardment.

China tea and cress sandwiches on Sunday afternoons with Lady Ottoline and her husband, Philip, was an educational ordeal of a gruelling order. Many an undergraduate failed the social test on a first visit and was not seen again. Never overawed by Lady Ottoline's exotic appearance and behaviour, Christine remained a regular visitor, and sometimes introduced suitable friends. Harold Acton described Lady Ottoline, with Lytton Strachey, 'aureoled against the terrace, like two early saints in a window of Chartres Cathedral'. This rare composition alone he considered worth the six-mile trudge from Oxford.

Once a monastery, Garsington Manor, an Elizabethan stone building, stood on a hill above a lake with a sculptured group on an island and statues round its edges. It was usual, especially in winter, to take a bus from Oxford to Cowley village, and to walk the remainder of the way. The road wound past farms and cottages before rising steeply to the tall

Italian gate. At the end of an avenue of ilexes, the first view of the mansion was always a delightful surprise.

Like Mrs Trew, Lady Ottoline revelled in the company of young people — but at Garsington it wasn't sing-along music. It was conversation, often of a high order. For as well as scribbling cubs, Lady Ottoline relished literary lions. For instance, when W. B. Yeats moved to Oxford in 1919 he became a regular visitor. She became the original of many characters in novels of the time: Hermione Roddice in D. H. Lawrence's *Women in Love* and Priscilla Wimbrush in Aldous Huxley's *Crome Yellow*. And the ambience of Garsington is never far removed from the atmosphere of *Brideshead Revisited*.

Christine Trew saw Lady Ottoline Morrell as a great chatelaine, an eccentric and patroness of the arts. 'I use the word "eccentric" as a term of the highest praise; and her husband, under the guise of a country gentleman, was at least as eccentric as she was. Nobody could have been more patient as we discussed our careers and our problems and our views about life. They were very kind to the young, and I wonder how they ever put up with us.'

Garsington teemed with people of genius at weekends. It was well worth a country walk from the bus-stop in any weather. Christine describes a typical Sunday afternoon with a pride of lions present: 'Tea at a long table. Then Turkish cigarettes and bulls' eyes, woodsmoke and incense in a room with Venetian mirrors and Omega Workshop lampshades. Or we might sit in the garden, among peacocks and statues, and listen to Bertrand Russell, Lytton Strachey, E. M. Forster or W. B. Yeats. My favourite was Bertrand Russell. We did not interrupt them, or ask them for jobs, but we knew it was the kind of conversation we liked.'

Lady Ottoline's politics particularly appealed to Christine: 'She was against wars and empires, and all in favour of the Irish and the Indians and the Egyptians. Her heart, in her amazingly elongated and chalk-white body, was in the right place.'

Christine had a friend called Charles who was an accomplished classical scholar. She does not identify him more accurately. One dark wet evening in the autumn of 1921, when she was twenty-one, she was walking round the big quadrangle of Christ Church with Charles. They had been to a lecture on Roman Gaul. In front loomed the shape of a big boy in an Etonian overcoat with a velvet collar.

'That's Lord Longford,' Charles said.

'Oh! Is it?' Christine replied off-handedly.

She had no special feeling for or against lords. She knew some who were intelligent, and as a self-confessed intellectual snob, that was what mattered to her.

Charles went on: 'I hear he has come up with quite a good reputation from Eton.'

'Oh, really?' said Christine.

Clearly, as this woman didn't seem interested in hearing any more about a bright young man up from Eton, Charles resumed their discussion about Roman remains in Provence.

Chapter 2

From the Shires to Sinn Féin

Edward Arthur Henry Pakenham was born on 29 December 1902, at 14 Curzon Street in London's Mayfair. He was the first son, and the heir, of Thomas Pakenham, fifth Earl of Longford. In due course Edward would enjoy the company of a brother and four sisters. Being a scion of the privileged class didn't necessarily entitle him to a happy childhood. Even less happy was that of his brother and sisters.

The family's natural attachment to their mother was marred by social, psychological and physical circumstances. Eventually her rheumatic illness played its part. Her sheltered upbringing as a daughter of the Earl of Jersey had made Lady Longford a highly sensitive and over-conscientious worrier. A frustrated woman with many contradictory characteristics, her autocracy extended even to her children. She could not glimpse any one of them without saying 'no' or 'don't'. Her maternal instinct was torn between her well-meaning sense of duty and her insistent avoidance of any demonstration of affection. Kissing, for instance, was out. Even Edward — her first born and the very apple of her eye — was never kissed. There were inhibitions and complexes, some perhaps inherited, others arising from her disappointment at having four daughters, three in sequence. In fact, time proved six children to be five too many for her.

As was the custom of the time, much of their infancy was spent in the charge first of nannies and then of governesses, housed in nurseries and schoolrooms well removed from the reception area, thus adding to the Victorian void between parents and children. Yet at an early stage Lady

Longford managed to sow literary seeds. The children were brought downstairs regularly. Apart from prayers, hymns and readings from the Bible, she read them Dickens, a delightful experience they agreed, because she read well, making the characters live, and of course these occasions meant release from the nursery and the schoolroom. Sometimes card-games were allowed: donkey, newmarket, bridge — though never on Sundays and never for money. Often they turned to solitary pursuits, like scribbling stories, or drawing or painting. Edward, already showing aesthetic tendencies, claimed the most beautiful part of the garden.

Lord Longford spent much time away from home, usually with his regiment, the Life Guards. 'His passion was for the army,' says Lady Mary Clive, his second daughter. 'Pansy, Frank and I thought the army very romantic but I have been told that when Edward was small he screamed at the sight of a soldier and when he grew older he certainly seemed to have a vendetta against the British Army, though he liked the idea of classical battles and killing, and the *Lays of Ancient Rome*.' Edward showed his individuality at an early age.

'In the Life Guards Dada was considered eccentric,' Mary Clive continues, 'but at home he behaved quite conventionally. He was a quiet, kindly, indulgent, easy-going man, who read a lot and went out hunting and smoked a pipe in an armchair and liked children around and took us walks on Sundays.' An enthusiastic polo player who liked to read Latin and Greek, Lord Longford's name as an eccentric probably arose from his reputation as a haphazard dresser. Once he was described as the worst-dressed man in England.

He was strongly anti-Home Rule and didn't particularly care for Ireland, nor indeed for Pakenham Hall, his ancestral home in its sylvan setting beside Lough Derravaragh, the centrepiece of a sixteen-hundred-acre estate near Castlepollard in County Westmeath. Its greatest attractions for him were its informality and the sense of duty he felt towards the Westmeath Hunt of which he was master.

His indifference to his inheritance was strange because Pakenham Hall had a long family history behind it. Several generations of Pakenhams had been in Ireland before the outbreak of the Civil War in 1642 between Charles I and his parliament. At first a Royalist, Henry, the Pakenham of the time, became a Cromwellian officer in charge of a troop of dragoons after the execution of Charles in 1649. The English parliament paid its post-war debts to its soldiers with gifts of Irish land. Accordingly, in 1655 Henry Pakenham was awarded land in County Westmeath, where Pakenham Hall was later to be built.

The nucleus of the house was a seventeenth-century stronghouse called

Tullynally Castle. About 1740 and again in 1780, this edifice was enlarged and up-dated in the Georgian style. In the early 1800s it was castellated and embellished in the Gothic manner by Francis Johnston, Ireland's greatest architect of the time. In 1839 Sir Richard Morrison restored the Great Hall, and a cousin, the much-married inventor, Richard Lovell Edgeworth, father of the celebrated Maria, conferred a distinguishing feature on Pakenham Hall by installing the first-ever central heating plant in Ireland.

Variations were made throughout three hundred years of residence by ten generations of squires, barons and earls of the Pakenham family until the castle became a forest of towers and turrets occupying two acres in area and containing some 120 rooms. When in 1899 Thomas, the fifth Earl, brought his bride there, she had never seen the place before. Nor did she greatly take to it, then or ever. Yet it was she who planted many of the trees, made new paths and cut terraces — perhaps to occupy her lonely hours, for as a young married woman she had to share the house with her mother-in-law while her husband was either hunting or serving overseas in the Boer War. Perhaps because of unhappy memories, she was never to be completely at her ease in County Westmeath, nor indeed in Ireland. Maria Edgeworth, a regular visitor in the nineteenth century, once described Pakenham Hall as 'a nest that only needed a bird'. Mary, the wife of the fifth Earl, was never likely to settle on that nest.

Nevertheless, in duty to her family, Lady Longford enthusiastically organised a vast bi-annual pilgrimage across the Irish Sea to County Westmeath. At Easter, and again in the summer, a party of anything up to twenty would move like a well-trained little army: children, nannies, governesses, a cook, house- and kitchen-maids, man-servants, and a lady's maid. In the teeth of storms and swells the sea-faring endurance of the various young Pakenhams became well-known to the stewardesses on the Royal Mail steamers plying between Holyhead and Dun Laoghaire, or Kingstown as it then was. All that, of course, was in the halcyon pre-war days that were to end all too soon.

Before 1911, life for the family alternated between summers in Westmeath and furnished country houses in England, taken for the winter for the convenience of Lord Longford's military commitments. Then they purchased North Aston Hall, a large unglamorous mansion. Within touching distance of a church, it overlooked the Cherwell Valley in North Oxfordshire. There were other advantages. Its proximity to the Bicester and the Heythrop hunts meant that Lord Longford could indulge himself more conveniently, for, like his army career, he took his duties as a master of foxhounds very seriously.

But even more important, for his wife coming to North Aston was almost like coming home, for six miles away stood Middleton Park where, as the daughter of the seventh Earl of Jersey, she had grown up. 'That most endearing stately home,' as Mary Clive describes it, was still remembered by Lady Longford as the most solid background of her childhood, 'a hallowed place of memories'. It stood in gentle Bicester countryside which she liked better than the wind-swept bogs and lakes of County Westmeath.

For those of the Longford children old enough to remember the pre-Great War years, it was Grandma Jersey's massive Christmas house-parties at Middleton which made the most lasting impressions. Mary Clive recalls that 'Edward was allowed to put on plays in the drawing-room before an audience of relations and servants (said to number sixty). Mama and her maid made the dresses. Edward was always the hero and killed a lot of people, shouting, "Wretch! Villain! Traitor!" None of us were much good at acting and the cousins, who were pressed in, did not even want to; perhaps the best that could be said for the plays was that they were extremely short.'

Short or no, unrecognised, a future man of the theatre was already in the making. But Edward had a long hard road ahead. As her favourite, his mother spoiled him. He had privileges denied the others, like the freedom to approach her in her sitting-room. When the time came to leave the nursery school there were difficulties. He had to be removed from his first prep school, a fashionable one at Stonehouse, Broadstairs in Kent. This failure on first meeting the outside world probably left a scar. His next school was Fursie Close, New Milton in Hampshire, where he fared better. He had to begin to learn the rough-and-tumble of schoolboy life. While his cleverness wasn't in doubt, his marked individuality was liable to be taken as a bold rebelliousness.

North Aston Hall never exactly found favour with the Longford children who always held lingering memories of the joys of Middleton Park. With visiting cousins they made the best of its woods and gardens. Edward wrote more plays for family production. He edited newspapers for family reading. He favoured charades and delighted in designing costumes, sometimes putting them into effect, like the opera cloak and the purple scarf with which he dressed a statue as a bishop in the hall. Perhaps here one can discern the influence of his ancestor, the theatrical costumier at Queen Elizabeth's court, or the stirrings of the future theatre designer.

There were, of course, childish rows and jealousies, and sometimes boyish scraps. Edward's likes and dislikes were carefully seen to by his mother. Those of his brother, Frank, later to become Lord Longford the politician, were of less consequence, and in the post-Victorian scheme of things the girls — Pansy, Mary, Violet and Julia — well, they were girls and not expected to have serious feelings, much less the cheek to express them. Frank liked vigorous, competitive games, like hockey and tennis. Edward too liked games, but he wasn't good at them. Inevitably, these activities could lead to youthful violence. Edward already had a temper that could flare frighteningly when he was obstructed — another shadow of the future man, whose sudden outbursts were to become occasions of deep embarrassment. Their sister, Violet, describes one such boyish scrap which 'ended in Edward brandishing a chair over Frank's head, while four sisters strove to hinder him from fratricide'.

As the shadow of war mantled the world, North Aston Hall could not escape its darkening dreariness. Christmas 1914 brought only memories of better times. Naturally autocratic with her children — all but one, that is — Lady Longford's temperament was not improved by her aggravating illness, a progressive form of rheumatism, a tragedy which beset her married life, and something which she tried to hide from her family. The boys were away at school for two-thirds of the year, and the girls, now growing up, had time enough on their hands in which to take stock of themselves. There was a sense of bewilderment, a crisis of identity. Who were they? And where did they fit in? In England they were taken for Irish; in Ireland they were taken for English. It was an old and well-recognised problem amongst the Anglo-Irish. Elizabeth Bowen was another victim and she found it a disturbing emotion.

'As we grew older,' says Mary Clive, 'we thought North Aston very dull and longed to meet more interesting people.' But for these girls, life at North Aston in rural Oxfordshire presented little opportunity to socialise with others of their age. When they did, they felt gauche. It required an effort of will to make conversation. Even Edward never learned to be a good mixer. Only Frank, the irrepressible extrovert, younger son though he was, seemed assured of a place in the world. As the family grew up it contained the makings of a palace revolution; but before it could break there occurred a world revolution.

As a colonel in the Life Guards, Lord Longford was with his regiment when war broke out in 1914. He had always been an enthusiastic soldier. Once he had told his younger son he would give ten years of his life to take part in a charge. On 21 August 1915 that opportunity came at Gallipoli. With his aide-de-camp, the Marquess of Hartington, brother of Lord Charles Cavendish of Lismore Castle, and later Duke of Devonshire, Longford led the 2nd Brigade of Yeomanry in an abortive attempt to take

Scimitar Hill, held by the Turks. At the end of the engagement nothing had been gained territorially, but all the officers and most of the men were missing.

Although Lord Longford was officially posted as 'missing', his death was feared. Month after month of waiting for news made for an uneasy atmosphere at home. Aged thirty-eight and already crippled, Lady Longford, as best she could, assumed the role of father as well as mother. The younger children missed the father who had always shown them loving patience and understanding. Their mother's disposition towards them didn't compensate. If anything, the relationship worsened, except, of course, in Edward's case. To his mother he became even more precious, while she continued to overlook her younger son.

'My mother', wrote Frank, 'came of a family, a world and a generation where the distinction between the eldest and the younger sons was drawn very sharply. A psychologist might discover ways in which this affected me subconsciously. But I grew up thinking her perfect.' Two of his sisters expressed other views in their biographies. 'My mother doted on Edward,' wrote Pansy. 'She always took his side, and we all felt she was unfair to the rest of us.' Mary confirmed: 'Other people's mothers liked us but she didn't. We couldn't get through to her at all.'

Still hoping against hope, they hardly dared mention their father's name. Mourning, and in chronic pain, their mother's passion for privacy increased. She desperately wanted to keep her illness secret. Even her children had difficulty in seeing her. An interview would have to be arranged through her personal maid. Then they would find her in a cold room in circumstances ideal for the worsening of her disease. Good fires she considered as a self-indulgence. 'A wicked waste of fuel and undesirably relaxing,' she maintained.

Contradictorily, perhaps in an effort to make up to them for the absence of a father, Lady Longford would occasionally attempt to join her children in their games. Perhaps this was a sick woman's subconscious fight against the relentless progress of an incurable disease. Usually in pain, and no longer ever seen without a stick or crutches, her attempts to participate in outdoor games only emphasised her tragic incapacitation. Her children remember these scenes. 'Mama liked games,' Mary Clive remembers. 'She liked tennis, but the racket fell out of her arthritic hand and she could not run, and we used to coax her to play goal at lawn hockey, with a crutch in one hand and a hockey-stick in the other.' Violet Powell, remembers that her mother 'only abandoned striving to defeat her children at tennis when it became clear that they were embarrassed by having to conceal the ease with which they were winning'.

One year elapsed before definite information about Lord Longford came from the War Office. 'When Mama told us', says Mary, 'that hope had been given up it seemed a pity but was not exactly a wrench. We did not discuss Dada's death, in fact, his name became too holy to mention, but we were very conscious of Gallipoli and perhaps were rather bored by it.'

As the elder son of the Earl of Longford, Edward had carried the courtesy title of Lord Silchester. When their father's death was finally announced, the younger Pakenhams were sent for by their mother. With a certain awe she explained that their elder brother was now the new earl, implying that he might be due a greater degree of respect. The ravages of the Great War often led to the inheritance of titles by boys of tender years. Accordingly, aged fourteen, Edward Pakenham became the sixth Earl of Longford. He was still at Eton, where Harold Acton remembered him as 'dear Edward, painting pictures of St Patrick in the drawing school'. Yet his mother became deferential to him. She behaved as if he had become a mature adult overnight. Mary Clive remembers the new relationship: 'Mama made efforts to treat Edward in a way which she wildly imagined was suitable to a peer. Even we could see that she was being absurd. It helped to make him uncertain of his place in the world.'

As Edward had now inherited the Longford estates, he was encouraged to learn something of the activities carried on at Pakenham Hall. In her own way, Lady Longford tried to groom him for the role his father and his forebears had played in County Westmeath. During a summer holiday she mustered some ponies on which the children were to learn to ride. They were a bit flighty, and nobody took the exercise too seriously, least of all Edward. He had no balance on a horse and wasn't very interested anyway.

But Lady Longford wasn't amused. Whatever about the others, Edward's future would most likely lead him to the mastership of the Westmeaths, like his father. Not alone therefore must he ride properly, but he must also learn to hunt. She hired a professional coach from Dublin, but he was no more successful than the local grooms in making a horseman of her son. 'Although no good at riding,' says Mary Clive, 'he rode with the rest of us long after many boys would have given it up as a bad job.' Lady Longford was disappointed, but the fact was that Edward wasn't the least interested in horses, let alone in riding them. As a girl she had adored outdoor activities, including riding, until she had been savaged by a wicked horse.

If the Westmeath grooms had failed in teaching her son to ride, their whispered political gossip taught him something about Ireland, the real Ireland, the seething Ireland beyond the high walls of the Pakenham estate. He was an apt pupil, a good listener, and adding two and two — what he read and what he heard — he cultivated an admiration for Arthur Griffith and Sinn Féin. Moved to action, he appeared one morning at the breakfast table and announced to his family that from now on he was a Sinn Féiner. Horrified, his mother appealed to her eldest daughter, only to be told that Pansy supported her brother. Lady Longford's distrust of political Ireland swelled alarmingly.

The family was at Pakenham Hall for Easter 1916. They were marooned by the Rising in Dublin. News of the reality trickled through slowly. Violet recalls that the Irish question made the luncheon table 'hideous with its repercussions'. A traditional Unionist, Lady Longford was furious at the outbreak of another Irish rebellion, this time one in the middle of which she found herself. Usually she was good at arguing her point, but really, her family was becoming too much for her! Violet continues, 'Edward and Pansy presented a more-or-less united front as nationalists, while Frank, supported by Mary, brought off the difficult feat of arguing against Edward without siding with my mother.'

At first Violet thought the whole thing a laughing matter — until she was banished from the table. She soon learned to retain her composure, even when Edward 'arguing as to whether killing was or was not always murder, rose from his chair in his rage and went stamping round the dining-room table'. The word 'rage' is noteworthy. With time such irrational outbursts from Edward were to increase in frequency and intensity.

Lady Longford's realisation of Edward's and Pansy's new devotion to Sinn Féin and to Irish nationalism gave her serious pause in which to wonder what sort of a nest of vipers she had reared. As soon as it was possible she found it advisable to take Edward and Frank back to England to resume their schooling. Of lesser importance, as usual, the girls were left behind in County Westmeath. Afterwards, Edward was sufficiently moved to write an account of their passage through the wreckage of Dublin, where the fighting had so recently ceased. Frank, apparently, remained detached.

The masters at Eton appreciated Edward's cleverness. He was getting on better there than at his previous schools, and had even made some friends. In spite of being a bad mixer he was gregarious. But occasionally the rebel in him surfaced. When it became known that he now subscribed to Sinn Féin he was ragged. He became very annoyed, refusing one day to parade in his uniform of the Officers' Training Corps. On being threatened with expulsion he compromised, turning up on the parade ground wearing his suit and his top hat, making himself a conspicuously absurd figure in a parade of uniformed boys. The headmaster told him, 'You are too dishonourable to remain an Etonian.' But that didn't bluff Edward. It had merely added grist to the mill of his growing and defiant Irish nationalism.

Another glowing interest was writing poetry. But it was poetry alien to the tradition of Eton. In 1920, when he was seventeen, his adoring mother had his schoolboy poems printed by Bumpus, all nineteen of them in a green cover, the colour no doubt chosen by the poet. It was dedicated to Pansy, his ally in Irish nationalism: 'A Book of Poems by L. Dedicated with kind permission to my eldest sister.' Thoroughgoing Unionist as his mother was, unwittingly she had paid for the printing of curses on Strongbow and Cromwell and Orange, and such sentiments as 'When shall the Saxon flee, and his bloodsucking host be confounded?'.

Notwithstanding his new-found nationalism, Edward had never let up on his classical studies. Indeed, he had distinguished himself as a promising scholar. Also, with only the aid of O'Growney's Grammar, and entirely on his own, he had taken to studying the Irish language. Come what might, he meant to be a thorough Irishman. By the time he left Eton, aged eighteen, and went up to Oxford in the autumn of 1921, he was already signing himself Eamon de Longphort.

Chapter 3

'Your Lasting Friend'

In the autumn of 1921 Christine Trew was twenty-one, and beginning her last year at Oxford. She knew she should be working harder, but there were distractions. She could delude herself into believing they were distractions with an educational value. Besides, she was trying to plan a career. She looked forward to earning a living and never doubted her ability to help her mother by making money. A job in publishing was what she wanted — for the time being. 'Writing was my line, so I had decided when I edited the school magazine; and in time I would write books myself.'

She got an interview in London with Horace B. Liveright, of Boni and Liveright, the ace of American publishing. It was rumoured that he was starting an English branch to his business. He never did, but at the interview he asked Christine's advice on the English ritual of the tea-party. She obliged. Indeed, she helped. 'We bought masses of cakes, and I poured tea for Rose Macaulay, Sinclair Lewis, Michael Arlen, Noel Coward and many others. There was one familiar face from Oxford, the scintillating orator, Leslie Hore-Belisha, already moving on London.' He it was who introduced the Belisha beacon pedestrian-crossing, now so familiar that even unaccompanied dogs use it.

She discussed the advantages and disadvantages of a college education with Sinclair Lewis. Having read his masterpiece *Main Street*, she told him he had done pretty well without one. Then he confessed how, in poverty, he had sat on a seat in Central Park and dreamed of Oxford. 'I took to him instantly,' Christine remembers, 'and we became great friends, and slid down the stairs on tea-trays.'

When Sinclair Lewis came to have a look at Oxford, Christine found some representative undergraduates for another tea-party. This was a function one had to perform occasionally for people who wanted to capture a glimpse of life at Oxford.

'It's a remarkable thing,' Lewis said, 'in London I was just about as much mangled shaking hands with people as the Prince of Wales. And none of these lovely lads here ever heard of me.'

Presently he spotted another kind of lovely lad, with mauve eye-shadow and Russian ballet gestures. They explained that he was one of the type then known as the aesthetes, in contrast to another type, known in Oxford as the hearties. The hearties played rugger and beat one another up; they were intolerant, athletic philistines. 'Never marry a man like that, my dear,' Lewis advised, as he looked at the aesthete. 'He's doomed to failure.' She was grateful for American wisdom, but, in general, she stood up for aesthetes — as long as they were intellectual. That was the criterion that mattered.

Examination results in 1922 for both Christine and her friend Flora Grierson, were not brilliant: 'A third class in Greats for us both, but we should have done better. We had been given a better classical education than most girls, and thought ourselves any man's equal, but we simply hadn't worked hard enough. It didn't matter, we said, as we weren't going to be schoolmistresses; and we had learned a great deal from miscellaneous reading, talking, dancing, play-going and the cinema. An intensive secretarial course, and we would be ready to seek our fortunes.'

Flora went to London, but as her mother lived in Oxford, Christine remained and found a commercial academy over a shop. The proprietor, polite and obsequious in the shop, became a principal upstairs and a fierce one, because most of his pupils had left school at fourteen. They threw things at the enlarged photograph of Sir Isaac Pitman. A sensible woman taught shorthand and said it came with practice. A young man taught elementary book-keeping. He had favourites among the girls. Christine wasn't one, but she didn't mind. It was amusing, it wasn't hard work, and she was convinced it was the right road to London and a career in publishing.

With Ossie Esmonde she shared the friendship of Marie Beerbohm, niece of Max, the famous novelist. Christine has described Marie: 'A wit and a patron of artists and an ideal nineteen-twenties beauty, tall and slender beyond belief. Her clothes came from Lanvin and Poiret, and she often handed them over to me when I was hard up.'

One evening Marie was showing off Oxford to an American poet. 'Is there anyone we can call on?' she enquired of Christine. 'Not a soul,' she replied. 'All my friends have gone down.'

Then she remembered a friend called Herbert. He would be deep in esoteric studies in his lodging in St John Street. But he was definitely of the intelligentsia and he could be relied on to make conversation. When they found him he was accompanied by a blond young man called Lord Longford, whose back view Christine had once seen and forgotten. 'We had dislodged him from the fireside,' she remembers, 'and he sat on the edge of a hard chair and eyed us with resentment, rather than interest.'

'Conversation started about Oxford poets,' Christine continues. 'It moved to T. S. Eliot, whom I was just beginning to worship. I had met him with Marie in London and was inclined to show off about it. Herbert deflected us to W. B. Yeats, having listened to him at Garsington and in Oxford. Then came portraiture and Augustus John. Marie knew Augustus, and I wished I did. Somebody mentioned the King of Spain. Herbert was a monarchist. Longford and I were republicans. He thought I was a Londoner, and said he avoided London. I was too anxious that the discussion should be a success. I talked too much and he talked too little.'

As they walked back, the American asked Christine, 'Who is the lord? Is it himself, or is it his father?' 'I haven't the faintest idea,' she replied.

Marie thought him marvellous to look at. 'So he was, with golden hair and a radiant complexion, heavy-lidded blue eyes, a straight nose and curling lips. I entered him on my waiting-list of intelligentsia, a probationary member.'

On his first arrival at Oxford, Edward Longford soon selected the societies he would support. The Oxford Irish Society was high on his list. Higher still was the Union, where the debates fascinated him, particularly if Ireland happened to be the subject.

Yeats had brought that most formidable of audiences cheering to its feet with his oratory on the wrongs of Ireland. Later, at Wadham, he spoke of his hopes for Ireland. Superciliously, a don enquired if his hopes weren't a bit unrealistic and remote from life. Yeats replied in a flash: 'No sir. Too many of my friends have been shot.'

Longford was less fortunate when he bravely defended Ireland by opposing a motion at the Oxford Union condemning as murderers the nationalists who had assassinated Field-Marshal Sir Henry Wilson in London. Wilson had been responsible for the pogroms of Catholics in Belfast in 1920. At that same meeting Maurice Bowra of New College said the assassination was a good thing, as Wilson was a diplomat and 'soldiers who are good diplomats should always be murdered'. But Edward Longford ended his speech with high passion, calling on all loyal Irishmen to leave the house in protest. That night a large crowd of undergraduates waited for him and on his return to Christ Church he was manhandled and hurled into the pool called 'Mercury'.

When Christine next met Herbert, Longford was with him again. Ireland turned up in their conversation and they told her how Longford had been ducked in 'Mercury' for expressing Irish sentiments about that mischief-maker, Wilson. That did it! First Christine expressed fuming indignation, then her sympathy: 'The young man, Longford, explained that he had not suffered much in the pond as it had been a warm night, and he had been dining and drinking no less than his enemies. But they had wrecked his rooms and cut up an Irish kilt, and defaced all the books in which he had written his name in Irish. They included a Protestant prayer book and several volumes of Yeats. I cursed his enemies.'

Longford then talked about the Irish Players: Sara Allgood and Maire O'Neill, and Lennox Robinson's brilliant comedy, *The Whiteheaded Boy*. Christine had seen them on tour, but Longford had actually met them. He had been to a party in their rooms in Paradise Square, and Sara had given him a signed photograph. Then he enthused about the Oxford Irish Society, which had just been reconstituted on respectable lines, with a special rule banning the song 'When Irish Eyes Are Smiling'.

Christine concluded that Longford was really a decent chap, doing his bit for poor old Ireland. She decided she'd invite him to her next evening coffee-party. It meant writing him a letter, because the telephone barely existed in college. He sent his regrets.

Christ Church
Monday
Dear Miss Trew,
I am very sorry I cannot accept your invitation for Friday. I feel
much inclined to, but alas! The Irish Society holds its first meeting
that night and duty seems to draw me there, especially as I am a
member of the Society's committee. It is most regrettable, as I was
unable to meet you on Sunday, for which no doubt Herbert conveyed
my sorrow to you. But I hear you did not go to Garsington. I hate to
think of you shivering over my pogroms. I appreciate the
compliment, but it is only I to be distressed.
Is mise do bhuan-chara
Eamon de Longphort

Re-reading that letter fifty years later, Christine asked herself: 'Was I
making advances? No, I often asked people to coffee. But I was definitely
taking an interest. Ossie Esmonde was in Oxford, and we were trying to
get Longford to Garsington, to show him to Lady Ottoline, but he was
holding off. I knew no Irish except *céad míle fáilte* and *O'Donnell Abú*,
but Ossie translated Longford's leave-taking in Irish as "Your lasting
friend".'
Next time she asked Longford to coffee, he came. Ossie was there, and
they all sang rebel ballads, and Longford roared louder than any.
Christine's mother 'thought him "a nice boy, but rather too noisy and
badly dressed". It was true, he wore baggy ill-fitting tweeds, and under
stress of emotion his collar and tie parted company.'
His next letter is dated 5 November 1922, and it marks an advance in
their friendship:

Dear Miss Trew,
Having so badly lured you into parting with two shillings, I feel
impelled, having discovered the sum in a remote corner of my purse,
to refund it with all possible speed, hoping that I have not seriously
inconvenienced you, and that you will forgive my borrowing it.
Mise do bhuan-chara
Eamon de Longphort

Christine comments, 'So I had lent him two shillings. It looks like a
confidence trick. It was the price of a tea or a seat in the cinema.' Herbert,
with somebody called Mildred, Longford and Christine, had taken to
going to the cinema as a party, and afterwards to tea in The George café.

Soon Longford and Christine took to going on their own: 'Harold Lloyd, Buster Keaton and Charlie Chaplin, any or all of them, brought Edward and me close together, helpless with laughter, and we began to use Christian names. He had a splendid, resonant laugh, and spontaneously, simultaneously we laughed at the same jokes and sometimes made the same comments. Our reactions were exactly identical.'

They talked about their relatives and agreed their mothers had characteristics in common: 'Both of them argued, both used no face-powder and drank nothing stronger than water, and both were tigresses in defence of their young,' according to Christine.

Before facing a stuffy Christmas in the bosom of his family at North Aston, Edward decided at the end of term on a quick trip to Ireland. Despite the Civil War and the horrors of the Irish Sea in mid-winter, he considered a glimpse of Ireland worth the risks.

He had arranged to meet Christine on his return journey through Oxford. They lunched on strong coffee and buns, and went to Blackwell's bookshop in Broad Street for last-minute Christmas presents. Christine remembers: 'That day Edward and I exchanged our first presents; he gave me a pocket Keats and I gave him the *Golden Asse*, which was classical reading, though not set for examinations. His spirits revived over tea and cakes, and he took the train to what he called "darkest Oxfordshire". On the station platform we kissed each other goodbye and wished each other a happy Christmas.'

That night he wrote:

Dear Christine,
I must thank you for a most enjoyable day and the complete cure of my *mal de mer*. I fear I must have been rather doleful company. However I hope that I shall be flourishing next Wednesday. Will you meet me a short while before one at the corner of George Street? I hope no answer will be necessary. I tried to read the *Golden Asse* in the train, but the G.W.R. light their carriages vilely. *Nodlaig sona dhuit*, (which means all the Compliments of the Season).
Mise do bhuan-chara
Edward

A nice letter, Christine thought, 'such as he might have written to his tutor'. They lunched in The George on omelettes and meringues. 'My taste in food was no more sophisticated than his at the time. We were far below the standard of the cosmopolitan Harold Acton, who deplored the tepid white wine and the melting pat of butter.' Her friend, Harold Acton, the most sophisticated aesthete in all Oxford, had become a myth in his own time.

While Edward was no athlete, he would hardly have considered himself an aesthete. On the other hand aesthetes reckoned conversation a worthy attribute, and Edward revelled in conversation. He and Christine talked, on their walks, over meals, at the pictures. They never stopped. Once on the railway platform at Oxford, the guard blew his whistle just as Edward was refuting Christine in an argument about Moses. He had to leave off and run to catch the train.

His devotion to religion often manifested itself unexpectedly. Once he asked Christine, 'Have you ever lived with a man?' 'Oh no, of course not,' she replied. 'Why not?' 'Because I haven't wanted to.' 'Would you think it wrong?' 'Not particularly,' Christine answered. 'But I've never been tempted to.' 'I think it's a good thing,' Edward said, 'to have a religion that stops you doing what you don't want to do.' Christine then confessed she was a sceptic in religion. He took it quite well, then and ever afterwards.

He was twenty on 29 December 1922. He didn't mention it to Christine until later. He felt melancholy. He had days of black depression. He wanted to do something about the wrongs of the world. Education was good, but discipline a curse. Dons, examinations, England and family life were a bore. He was unhappy about Ireland and its Civil War, and the loss of its leaders, Michael Collins and Arthur Griffith.

With her age superiority of two years and three months, Christine adopted the little mother role. She doled out some pep-talk: he should work hard, at regular hours. He needn't reform the world until he left Oxford. He was intelligent, healthy and good-looking. He had been to a good school and had enough money to live on. Then she came perhaps to the nub of his discontent: 'Of course it was a bore to translate Cicero and Demosthenes when he preferred the Greek poets and Catullus; but he would be doing philosophy soon and would like it. I begged him to read his set books, and then came off my tutorial high horse.'

They walked together everywhere around Oxford, to the Hinkseys and Boar's Hill and Headington, Port Meadow and Godstow. And at last she got him to go to Garsington. 'He had a moment of terror, as the front door opened on the smell of incense and the sound of the Pekinese barking.' Once inside he liked it, and Lady Ottoline found him promising.

Flora Grierson came down from London and took a look at Edward. 'She thought him very young, and she said I was staying in Oxford too long. Her training was more methodical, more intensive, and she thought I should follow her. I swore I was coming in no time.' But Christine continued her commercial course in Oxford, graduating with 'a dubious leaving certificate and a genuine typewriter'. Then she received a letter in Flora's typing. It said: 'I hope you are not falling in love with Edward, he is much too young.'

Somewhat indignantly, Christine replied that she certainly wasn't in love. He was only twenty. Besides, he couldn't dance — wouldn't even try — hated it, and she couldn't imagine love without dancing.

Lady Longford took Edward and Pansy to Paris for the Easter vacation in 1923. One morning there was some excitement when a great cortège came by. It turned out to be the funeral of Sarah Bernhardt (1844-1923), whom Edward regretted he had never seen perform. Now he lingered so long that when he returned to their hotel lunch was over — a small sacrifice for the privilege of seeing 'divine Sarah' making her last exit. Christine too had missed seeing her in Bristol because, at ten, her mother thought her too young.

A family confrontation arose during that holiday in Paris. Some young man from Oxford had told Lady Longford about Edward and Christine being continually seen together. In a locked room, Edward was confronted by his mother. He told her the truth, as far as he knew it. He always told the truth. Yes, he was in love. She regretted his falling in love so young. No answer to that. She said he was too young to get married. He said that was obvious. She said he must see the world, have a profession, learn to manage a large estate.

With truth and loyalty, he wrote all this to Christine. Promptly she replied: 'I said I was not in love, I knew better, I was experienced. Of course he must see the world, I said, so must I. I was very anxious to see the world. He must have a career. So must I, and I was rather nasty about it. He had two and a half years of Oxford ahead of him, and anything could happen to either of us. We could fall in love with other people. He must meet more young women, I said, and I wouldn't stop dancing with other young men. Anyway, why worry until 1925? We would promise to tell each other no lies, and that was all about it.'

That letter was hardly posted when Christine suffered agonising regrets. 'Poor Edward, I was really angry with him for telling his mother the truth, when I should have admired his courage. I ought to have been grateful, or at the very least flattered by his declaration.' Adding to her suffering was the fact that he had sent her an Easter present, a black silk bag 'in perfect taste'. She had sent him a batik handkerchief in a letter, knowing well that Paris was full of better handkerchiefs.

'I wrote another letter to say I was sorry for being so angry. He wrote back that he was ashamed he had made me angry, and he was drying his

tears in the batik handkerchief, and what was batik anyway? I was happy
to explain the process, and I couldn't pretend I had cried over the
handbag, it was much too nice.'

Lady Longford dutifully advised her son not to meet Miss Trew in
Oxford on his way back to North Aston. He ignored her advice. He kept
the appointment they had already made, at the usual spot, the corner of
George Street. When Christine appeared, there he was, waving a
bottle-green hat with one hand, and holding a pile of French books with
the other. As Christine records: 'We were friends as before.'

Chapter 4

Enchantment on the Woodstock Road

Horace Liveright offered Christine a job in New York. It wasn't what she
wanted, nor did Edward want her to take it. Then Horace sent her a
female pupil, another American who had dreamt of studying English
literature at Oxford. At their first meeting the girl struck what she
believed might be an appropriate attitude for an English literature
student. 'Tread softly because you tread on my dreams,' she declared.
Christine had reservations. 'I feared the examiners would tread on her
dreams and they did; it was very sad. She was not one of my successes.'
Tutoring Edward was more rewarding.

As a first step in seeing the world, he went again to Ireland. He stayed
with his Uncle Eddie, Lord Dunsany, the dramatist. Dunsany was
married to Edward's Aunt Beatrice, Lady Longford's sister. Lady
Dunsany was the one and only person with whom Lady Longford had a
rapport — a greater devotion and understanding by far than she ever had
with her children.

The young Pakenhams had been great favourites with their Uncle
Eddie, though they had their reservations about him. He was
well-meaning, but odd. His games could become so boisterous that he
frightened the lives out of them. His redeeming feature was his generosity
at Christmas. There would be gifts of books for everybody, each with a

humorous inscription in his enormous writing.

The Dunsanys took Edward to Tara and to Punchestown Races — Ireland ancient and modern. At Tara Edward sketched the Stone of Destiny and sent it to Christine. He couldn't believe the High Kings of Ireland had sat on it; it was a phallic symbol, 'though in this holy and pure country no one could dare say so'. At Punchestown he watched the 'new rich' rubbing shoulders with the 'old Ascendancy'. His letters became torrents of Anglophobia, but he made allowances in her case: 'I don't mind in the least if you are largely English. I may not be wholly free of such blood myself.'

From Dunsany Castle he went to Pakenham Hall. The more he saw of the place, the more he loved it. In Castlepollard he bought stamps and bootlaces and admired the many shades of red hair of the local girls. His tour concluded with a stay in Wales. His paternal grandmother had been a Rice of Dynevor Castle, and he was more proud of his Welsh than of his English blood.

Back in Oxford, with the strains of the Easter vacation forgotten, Edward and Christine were idyllically happy. They met John Cournos, a romantic Russian-American novelist. From delivering newspapers as a boy in Philadelphia he had clawed his way upwards and eastwards to the centre of London's literary glare. Christine remembers him as 'the first man who told us about *Ulysses*, and we borrowed a copy. This was the year 1923, when 499 copies were burned by the Customs at Folkestone.'

Though not an aesthete in the current sense, Edward Longford had reason to be on their side against the hearties. In Oxford it was the great Harold Acton period, and Edward had to agree with Christine about Harold, who was exceptional. 'He was a new and original kind of aesthete,' she explains, 'who disliked mauve eye-shadow, scrubbed his face clean and pink, wore a grey bowler-hat and black whiskers and collected Victorian *objets d'art*. He recited his poems through a megaphone, like the Sitwells.' Acton's individuality brought a breath of fresh air, in the form of his Florentine sophistication, to a dour post-war Oxford. His friend, Evelyn Waugh, he called a little faun, never guessing the monster the little faun was to become.

Like most past summers, 1923 was remembered as fine. The King of England invited Edward to a garden-party at Buckingham Palace. How was the King of England to know the Earl of Longford was a die-hard Irish republican? 'It would be against my principles,' he told Christine, 'to go anywhere near the place. I gather these things are broadcast pretty freely among the idle rich about this time of the year, as well as among Labour leaders and other people they want to convert to the monarchical principle. As nothing will convert me to such a footling principle, and as I am not proud of being idle, I should not think it decent to eat the poor old gentleman's ices or trample up his lawns. And if they put me into the torture-chamber for high treason, I'll go to the rack shouting "God save Ireland".'

To escape the London heat, Edward went to a hotel on Dartmoor to study Plato's *Republic*. He loved the very word 'republic'. Christine posted him an English translation with tutorial advice. He decided he didn't like the aristocracy any better than the monarchy, and that Plato's aristocrats were impossible, because their way of life was founded on lies and slavery and maintained by intellectual stagnation. 'What a great thing an aristocracy could be,' he said,'if it were either possible or right. It is, I think, neither.'

He moved to Ireland. She posted him Tawney on the *Acquisitive Society*. That made matters worse. He felt guilty about living on ground rents. Property was theft. 'A poor penitent rentier,' he called himself. 'Without my dishonest and uneconomic gains, I become a highly inefficient farmer with a lot of profitless land, a house too large to use or sell, and an annual deficit of vast proportions.' At the time he wasn't even a fully-fledged landlord. Still under twenty years old, he was in the hands of trustees.

A Castlepollard committee asked his trustees for the loan of a field for a 'sports day', to be held on a Sunday. They were refused. Edward was furious. Though he never missed church, and though he was no athlete, he favoured entertainment, even on a Sunday. He may have been a minor, but he was a man entitled to his opinion, so he made an impassioned defence of Sunday games. His younger brother, an active athlete, joined him. He was even ready to take part in a race. Together they won their point. The committee got their field; the field became the 'sports field' and the Castlepollard Sports became an annual event.

Meanwhile, Alice Grierson, Flora's sister, had invited Christine to Holland to join her in a holiday job in a small museum in Veere in the province of Zeeland. 'Alice met me,' Christine recalls 'and we sat outside a café and drank coffee from Java and smoked gold-tipped cigarettes, and I became a travel-snob on the spot. Then we drove in a golden light along a perfectly straight cobbled road between Hobbema trees and houses with criss-cross painted shutters and people dressed by de Hoogh.'

Still life and seventeenth-century scenes were everywhere. In haste she wrote to Edward telling him he must see it. He replied that she must see Fore Abbey and Clonmacnois and Lough Derravarragh. Then she was jerked back to reality by young Alice Grierson. 'One night, after music and a walk in the moonlight, Alice asked me "Are you in love with Edward?" "No, no, no," I said. "Nothing of the sort," and she laughed a great deal. Though she was younger than I was, she had more sense.'

Of their meeting at the opening of the Michaelmas term 1923, Christine writes: 'Separation had done its work, and we were more pleased with each other than ever.' She still refused to acknowledge that she was, at least as much in love with Edward Longford as he was with her. Yet she had already admired his naive acknowledgement of the truth to his mother. With no apparent past experience, she had quickly acquired the wiles of the woman in love.

For some time she had successfully played the tutorial matron. The advantage was hers, both in age and in academic ability, and Edward willingly acquiesced. But the day would come when he would outstrip her in the worldly wisdom of men, in the knowledge that goes beyond the confines of academe. In their peculiarly mother-son type relationship, would she, like any sensible mother, prepare herself for the day when she would have to accept that her son was already a man? Soon there were to be indications of an answer — in the affirmative.

Christine records happily the first of the important events of that Michaelmas term: 'Edward moved into lodgings in Beaumont Street with Jim Byam Shaw, of whom I approved tutorially as a suitable friend. Jim was a young classical scholar whom my contemporaries found promising, and he was a wit, an accomplished dancer and already a connoisseur of art. He was also well dressed, which Edward was not. Edward was untidy, though always well washed.'

Those were the days of Oxford bags, very wide trousers in pastel shades, sailor-like, and hiding the shoes. They had been popularised by the redoubtable Harold Acton, and the fashion spread far beyond the shores of England.

Critical of Edward's sloppy dress and rumpled collars, Christine considered herself tidy enough, with her Eton crop and short sack-shaped dress, its waist near the thighs. The whole was set off by a pair of red silk stockings. Edward ruined everything. 'He told me the stockings were a mistake. I was angry. I did not surrender an inch before saying goodnight. But then I went to a mirror, and found it was true. I was beginning to take his advice.' His superior knowledge of pictures was the next thing to be acknowledged. 'Slowly and with reluctance I realised that Edward knew more than I did. He had seen more Old Masters; he could tell me about the pictures in Dublin, and he could remember the National Gallery in London, with names and dates. He had a very exact visual memory, better than mine.'

The second important event of that term was the opening of J. B. Fagan's Oxford Playhouse at the end of the Woodstock Road. The Playhouse was small and gimcrack and uncomfortable, and the buses shook its fabric as they passed. Its foyer was the footpath outside, where you conversed in the intervals, and ate bars of Cadbury's chocolate. But for Edward and Christine it became an Aladdin's Cave wherein they first encountered the magic that is called non-commercial theatre.

A charming Irishman, born in Belfast and educated at Clongowes Wood College, James Bernard Fagan (1873-1933), in weekly repertory, produced everything that could be called classic, from Sophocles to Shaw, including Shakespeare, Congreve, Sheridan, Wilde, Ibsen and Chekhov. Armed with season tickets, they never missed a first night. Born play-goers, both, their excitement mounted with every new production. And they had no notion that at last their education had begun for what was to become their mutual careers — 'the theatre of the arts, plain living and high thinking', as Christine summarised it.

Fagan opened with *Heartbreak House*. A group of aesthetes walked out in protest, screaming that Shaw was *vieux jeu*. Next came *The Rivals, The Master Builder* and *The Importance of Being Earnest*. Christine never forgot the judgment of John Cournos on *The Importance*: 'In graveyard tones he pronounced, "This is a very interesting little comedy of manners, and *will live*"; which was not nearly so obvious in the twenties as it is now.'

She thought 'the best of all was our first sight of *The Cherry Orchard*, with the young Gielgud playing the student. It had never been done in England before, though it had been in Dublin. Ossie Esmonde once came back to Oxford and spread the news: he had seen an extraordinary play by a Russian, in Edward Martyn's little theatre in Hardwicke Street, a play in which the characters really spoke their minds.'

In discovering this horde of treasure on the Woodstock Road, they also discovered a new source of life itself: discussion of the drama became never-ending; they made new friends, and the itch of inspiration even moved Edward to composing a ballade of which the refrain was 'There is enchantment on the Woodstock Road'.

Not for the first time, Edward had taken to writing poetry — 'quite absurdly so-called heroic couplets', as he said himself. He did a philosophic 'Defence of Truth' which Christine liked very much, particularly these lines:

Go bait with sprats, and catch a whale,
Distil a storm-cloud in a vat,

Stir up the oceans with a flail
Or wear a mountain for a hat!

To dust the mountain grinds your head,
To dust the Truth would grind your heart,
If in mind's wisdom it were said
Or dwelt at one with human art.

In 1923 he wrote a patriotic poem about Ireland, because, as he said, he didn't see why he shouldn't, and he hadn't written one since Eton:

Green magic glass no more in vain
Will show us where dead antique things reflect
Themselves in half the lustre of a star
At a well's bottom. Eire shall expect
Great things and soon: I hear the hosts afar.

Christine's comment is characteristically pointed and typical: 'Maybe the great things did not happen so soon as he expected, but never mind.'

Leslie Hore-Belisha, by then a Liberal Member of Parliament, offered Christine a job in London in the autumn of 1923. 'I did not take it, I let my career go hang. I was not an English Liberal, so I went on typing for Edward, who was my genius of the moment. I was gradually turning into his secretary instead of his tutor.'

In his book, *Green Memory*, L. A. G. Strong, a contemporary at Oxford and Garsington, calls Christine 'an extremely lively and witty girl who had captured the heart of Lord Longford', who was 'stubbornly devoted to her'. He recalls the incident when Edward refused to move along the bus in which he was standing beside Christine as she sat, with the result that other passengers couldn't get by. 'Requests, even objurgations, produced no effect except to make him crimson with resentment, and only a word from Christine overcame the difficulty.'

Commenting fifty years later, Christine said: 'Leonard Strong is dead now and not to be questioned. If he saw that happen, it must be true. He often took the same bus as we did.' But fifty years later Christine knew it was true, and furthermore, that it was an early instance of many similar occurrences in her life with Edward, when, repeatedly, she had to play the ministering angel with the soothing balm.

The third memorable event of 1923 was when Edward decided that Christine should meet his mother. Before Christmas a dinner was arranged. A ground-floor restaurant was chosen because Lady Longford still suffered badly from rheumatism. 'It was an alarming occasion for her,' says Christine, 'and for me and for Edward; but young Frank was there, and he contributed brilliantly to the conversation.'

Lady Longford was informed on the situation. She knew how often her son and this girl were to be seen together in the Woodstock Road, and she was charming about it. 'Lady Longford, I was relieved to find, was not Lady Bracknell. She was then only forty-six, very fair, tall and pale, with beautiful regular features, but she looked ill and did not dress up to display her beauty. She invited me to North Aston for the weekend after Christmas, and I thanked her as well as I could.'

Next day, Edward wrote from that address: 'How delightful yesterday was, in spite of the formidable nature of events. My mother undoubtedly likes you, and even my brother says he cannot perceive any defects in you. And of course, though younger than me by three years, he is really much cleverer and nicer in every way.'

The weekend came, and was hardly formidable. Lady Dynevor was there, Lady Longford's sister, a dark, lively lady with an easier charm. North Aston was beside a church and a graveyard. The house was dark and gloomy, excepting the drawing-room where white paint and chintzes and the beauty of the young Pakenhams lit everything up.

Saturday, 29 December was Edward's twenty-first birthday. He said he felt no more grown up than he had the day before, but it meant much to his mother, as Christine realised later on: 'She was proud of the way she had brought him up. Then she was thinking of estate business, and of the celebrations that would have to be organised at Pakenham Hall. That was his house, and now it was really his, and he was determined to live in it. He could not properly "come of age" out of Ireland. He did not love Oxfordshire as his mother did.'

In the evenings they played charades. As she lay on the floor, acting dead in a macabre scene, Christine thought how funny it was: 'I was exposing myself to a pretty thorough examination in my second-hand Poiret dress; but nobody seemed to be curious, they were too kind, or too well brought up. Nobody asked me my intentions, which was a good thing, as I didn't know them myself. I was older than Edward, but he said it didn't matter. I was English, and he said that didn't matter either. I was socially unsuitable, but he said there had been a revolution in Ireland, and social distinctions didn't matter anymore. Anyway, it was too soon to think of marriage, and our situation remained the same.'

Early on Monday morning there was a shock. Lady Longford's brother, Lord Jersey, had died suddenly. Breakfast with the young Pakenhams was full of gloomy forebodings about the funeral. Christine packed in haste, and offered her confused thanks and condolences to Lady Longford.

She remembers the next day: 'Edward came into Oxford to buy a top hat, but couldn't find one big enough. All he could find was some black gloves, which made him feel like *The Importance of Being Earnest*.' So, cheered by Christine's effervescent sense of humour, he left to fulfil his first duty of the New Year, at his uncle's funeral at Middleton Park.

Chapter 5

Sunshine and Showers

Hamlet was the play produced by J. B. Fagan for the Oxford University Dramatic Society in the spring of 1924. Odd though it seems, Edward was never a member of the OUDS, nor was he enthusiastic about its work. When he heard about *Hamlet* he remarked, 'At least they have a good play.' Christine says: 'He was surprised and amused and still critical when I was invited to walk on as a lady-in-waiting. But I said "At least it's a good play", and I was glad of the experience.'

So for the first time she saw life backstage: rehearsals, costumes, make-up, crowds sitting around talking, gossip tempered by discipline. Then the girl playing the queen objected to the big black hats worn by her ladies-in-waiting: 'Those girls can't wear those hats. They look pure Piccadilly.'

'But it was a good production,' says Christine. 'Edward came every night, not for my performance, but for Shakespeare. We discussed it excitedly every night in the Woodstock Road. Of course, everyone in the audience felt like Hamlet; Edward did. But no, he was not Hamlet, I made him understand. He was a man of action — but what kind of action? I told him he would find out in time. He was not meant to be an extra, a walk-on, like me. That play made him think about producing Shakespeare, and started something that lasted a lifetime.'

Come the Easter vacation and the whole Pakenham family was *en route* for Ireland for the official celebration of Edward's coming of age. On the arrival of three cars at the gate of Pakenham Hall, an army of men from the farm was waiting to drag the first car, occupied by Edward, to the house. On the doorstep, he made a speech promising a wonderful party.

Then the oldest employee — a well-known local nuisance — made an eloquent speech about Edward and his noble father and grandfather and great-grandfather, who 'found me a young gosoon spinnin' me top on the road and took me in and made a man o' me.'

Regarding the magnitude of the celebrations, the oldest employee, with his usual blarney, issued a sort of challenge to Edward and his mother by remembering too clearly that the feasting for Edward's father had lasted a week, with fireworks and bonfires, and a dance that started at tea-time and went on till 3 p.m. next day. And that was described in the press as 'a modest ceremony by force of the depressed condition of the times'. The year was 1885, after a minor revolution, the triumph of Parnell and the Land League.

In 1924 things began with the presentation of an illuminated address. Next was the luncheon for the male estate workers, Lord Dunsany, Edward's Uncle Eddie, presiding, with Edward on one side and Mr Stewart, the family banker-trustee, on the other. The parish priest, the rector, the doctor, the solicitor, the steward and the head-gardener were placed in accordance with correct protocol. Violet, Edward's sister, then a little girl, remembers the occasion: 'The ladies came down after luncheon to listen to the speeches and applaud the drinking of Edward's health.' The family was eulogised by Mr Stewart, first their late father, then 'my mother, her son, and finally her daughters, whom he referred to as "those four bright girls". I felt that only engulfment by the cobbles and sawdust beneath our feet could assuage my embarrassment.'

Next day, sports were held in an arena marked out with flags on the front lawn. The Artane Boys' Band played throughout the afternoon, ending with 'The Soldiers' Song', at Edward's special request. That night a dance was held for the workers in a barn over the saw-mill. Lady Longford was apprehensive about the results of too much drink, but Edward insisted that nothing should be spared. 'I want them to enjoy themselves thoroughly, as rural life doesn't include much diversion. And even if they get a trifle boiled, they will only be following the noble example of cultured Oxford undergraduates and big business men and writers.'

A bigger headache for the family was the ball given in the house for their neighbours. Lady Longford had spent so little time at Pakenham Hall that, apart from the Dease family, their nearest neighbours, she knew very few of the local county folk, and she was diffident about people she didn't know. Edward favoured tradition, which meant asking as many as possible — it was only a question of how many the house would hold. Parties in the country were rare, and it would be worse to offend people by leaving them out. 'Nobody is *select* here in practice,' he told his mother, 'though everybody is in theory.'

She worried again about drink: how much to provide and how to avoid noisy drunkenness. Edward hated dancing, and didn't like over-drinking, but he enjoyed an occasional bit of rowdiness. He assured his mother that some exuberance would be inevitable among one hundred guests. She gave in with a good grace and didn't regret it. There wasn't a hitch from the moment the band struck up and Lady Longford, dutifully, put on her gloves and began to receive her guests. The sixth Earl of Longford's coming-of-age gave a lot of pleasure and left a lot of people with happy memories in and around County Westmeath.

Edward wrote telling Christine that his mother had, quite spontaneously, suggested that she, Christine, should be invited to stay in Ireland during that summer of 1924. 'So that will be very pleasant,' he added, 'though, like a Victorian, she is not quite sure of the advisability of letting girls know what they are in for.' Christine wasn't so sure herself that she wanted to be in for anything, 'especially after all this feudalism about his coming-of-age'.

And that summer Edward bought his first car, a grey five-seater Morris-Oxford. In fine weather he and Christine explored Berkshire, the Cotswolds and the Stratford Memorial Theatre. 'The Morris gave Edward the upper-hand over me,' writes Christine. 'I was no good with machines, I could do only what I was told, and not always even that. His ascendancy grew rapidly.' Gone already were the days when Christine's chronological seniority of two years and three months gave her the tutorial whip-hand. She was learning that the fair-haired boy up from Eton was developing a distinct and charming will of his own.

Both swallowed their anti-imperialistic principles and went to see the Empire Exhibition at Wembley. Afterwards, they went to tea with Edward's mother in Bruton Street, the house she shared with Uncle Bingo Pakenham, his father's brother. 'Lady Longford made explicit the invitation I had been led to expect,' writes Christine, 'and she spoke with such diffidence and nice feeling that I became diffident too, and could barely thank her. We discussed my journey. It would be crowded, of course, because I was going in the first week in August, Horse Show Week. She could not imagine I would reach Ireland without a sleeper from Euston. I said I would go from Oxford, change at Bletchley, Rugby, Crewe and anywhere else with pleasure; and she was gravely concerned, really shocked. Edward was sent out of the room on some pretext, and Lady Longford in terror begged me not to save money: if I was thinking of that, she would pay my fare. How good she was.'

Edward's first car, bought in 1924. Here Edward, her mother Mrs Trew and Christine are using the car as a grandstand at Castlepollard Show in September 1925.

With the Morris, Edward went ahead to Ireland, via Liverpool. From there he wrote amusing letters. For instance, he went to tea with some friendly 'squireens', a term used in affection and not in contempt. Their house was big, with a huge farm and two tennis-courts; they were first-rate tennis players, but didn't give themselves airs. Of these people he said: 'Devoted to piety and athletics and agriculture, they possess every solid virtue without being morose, and are not given to drink like most of their kind. All unmarried, yet seem contented. They are not handsome, more like horses than human beings.'

On 12 July he drove the Morris to the Border just for the hell of it. He looked over. There were no drums beating, no faction fights, no pogroms. It looked just like his own side, green fields, cottages and cows. His hope was the British Labour Party. Once the pro-Orange Tories were ousted, he believed, Labour would see justice done in Ireland regarding the Border. Christine has added a note which reads: 'That was written in 1924, and I am copying it out in 1971, and the Border is still where it was.

Edward was expecting "great things and soon".'

Another letter from Edward concerns W.B. Yeats and the Irish language: 'Yeats and Gogarty are attacking the language, apparently because Yeats thinks that a language he doesn't know is an insult to him on his railway ticket — as if he would ever have been heard of but for the 'Celtic Twilight', and as if there ever could have been such a thing but for the spadework of many excellent old men like Douglas Hyde who rediscovered everything. It is not for Yeats to turn on the Irish language now, unless he imagines that his position as the great interpreter of Ireland is likely to be impaired. I think very highly of him, but I don't see why even a Nobel prize-winner should have the monopoly of everything Irish.'

August came, and with it, Christine. As she stepped down from a Midland Great Western Railway carriage at Mullingar, Edward and the Morris were waiting. Ireland out-matched all she had dreamt of it. With every mile of the way, she was enraptured: past Lough Derravaragh, Knock Eyon and the Crooked Wood, to Castlepollard, 'a small town around a square, with a ruin in the middle of it, and "What did Barry die for?" painted up in large letters.' No doubt she had heard the Kevin Barry story.

'Pakenham Hall did not strike me as beautiful. It was certainly very big, like a terrace of houses more than a house, with improbable towers, and on the topmost a flag flying. Edward's mother was standing at the front door. I can guess what an effort it cost her, as she was crippled with rheumatism. But there she was at her post, expressing concern for me, as if I were tired or sick, instead of bursting with health and spirits. The front hall was enormous and panelled and Gothic, for which Edward apologised, and I was hurried upstairs to my room. Lady Longford apologised for it, as if I was used to pleasures and palaces. With extreme kindness she had put me on the top floor with Edward's sisters, and not in a big room far away.'

Between the sunshine and the showers, Edward showed off his estate. They walked to the pond called the Swanee River, which had an island and waterlilies and was shaded by willows. It was overlooked by a log hut, 'much used on Sundays and holy days by the boys and girls of the neighbourhood, who left inscriptions behind them; and Edward was glad to show me the proof that the Irish were normally sexed, which visitors sometimes doubted. The atmosphere was conducive to courtship, but Edward and I gave no scandal; we had been walking out for a long time now, and we were usually chaperoned by some of his sisters.'

For all their decorum, local rumour had sensed a romance. 'It was hard to prevent the oldest employee from making a speech prematurely to bless our union. He went down on his knees and became violent when interrupted; calling on heaven as his witness, he shook his fists and seemed nearer cursing than blessing us.'

One sunny day they climbed Knock Eyon, a hill high enough to deserve to be called a mountain. 'Then we looked around at what seemed to be all Ireland: mountains, woods, bogs and lakes.' The paradise that was Lough Derravaragh and its swans — the Children of Lir — reminded Christine of Edward's juvenile poem: 'Beside the wave of Dairbhreagh, beneath the cloud-soft sky.'

Back in Oxford, Christine taught Latin to a Mauritian and English to a German, and went on remembering Westmeath. She envied Edward, who had gone on a walking tour in Connemara with his Irish phrase books. To improve his knowledge he mixed and mingled with the locals, but not even for the sake of the Irish language could he get used to drinking Guinness.

Meanwhile Christine began to look at Chinese ornaments in antique shops. 'It was simply good luck that I liked a blue incense-burner mounted with a lion and dragons, and it turned out to be Ming.' Then she started collecting Chinese costumes. On his return to Oxford, Edward caught the disease. Under the tuition of a Mr Godfrey in St Giles, they learned to identify 'the more obvious Taoist immortals and Buddhist saints, marks on porcelain and the symbols for Happiness, Longevity and Wedded Bliss'. For both, Chinese art was to remain a lifelong interest.

If Edward ever proposed, Christine has not recorded the fact. It seems more likely that their relationship was gradually understood by all to be the prelude to marriage — even by the two concerned, neither of whom needed anything so old-fashioned as a formal plighting of their troth. However, Lady Longford took things in hand before Christmas 1924 when she said 'it was time to announce our engagement, and she was so kind, we hadn't the heart to resist'. That is Christine's version! As a celebration, Lady Longford sent them to a dance at the house of her friend, Lady Margaret Watney. 'If we could have looked at the house and the pictures, without any dancing, we would have been happy.' Christine's version again! The truth, of course, was that Christine loved dancing, but Edward loathed it. But because she thought he was the most wonderful man in the world, she was ready to pay the price to please him. The question of his learning to dance to please her wasn't even mentioned. It was early days, but Christine's sacrifices had already begun.

Their engagement announcement generated some absurd publicity. One newspaper called Edward 'the shy Earl'. Christine explains: 'Once he had made a joke about women in a Union debate. He was supposed to have said they were like fire, a good thing to have in a room, but dangerous if you burned your fingers, and as any remark about sex makes news, it stayed on the files forever.' It was also said he took after his father — 'the worst-dressed man in England'; that he had been educated under the influence of his uncle, 'the highbrow peer, Lord Dunsany', which was untrue, and that he owned five thousand acres of land, which was even more untrue.

Edward visited Dublin. There he met Mr Stewart, his former trustee. The Stewart family, old friends and relations of the Longfords, managed the estate from one generation to another. Mr Stewart took him round Dun Laoghaire, which he now owned jointly with Lord de Vesci: 'By the terms of a peculiar will they shared every stick and stone of it, and his half-share was what made Edward a guilty rentier.' Then a visit to Pakenham Hall provided a few pleasant surprises: the electric wiring of the house had been completed, and a new threshing-machine had been installed — the beginning of mechanisation. The oldest employee said he wouldn't stay in the place another minute if it wasn't for his lordship, and his lordship thought that was probably true.

By the end of the summer term Edward should have been panic-stricken. His degree examination was imminent, but he wasn't bothered. As Christine recalls: 'He worried less than I had worried, worked shorter hours, and came to the same result in the end.' Without fuss, and devoid of nerves, he passed his degree examination at Easter 1925. Now he was finished at Oxford. So what next? Why, of course! They would get married in July.

Chapter 6

Ireland For Ever

'Our wedding was eccentric, but properly blessed by the church,' Christine wrote, describing the event. 'Edward's mother couldn't believe that we wanted a quiet one, "very quiet, hardly a sound", we insisted, quoting a music-hall joke. My mother believed it quite readily, and said it would save her a lot of money and trouble. She knew how hard it had always

At Christine and
Edward's wedding:
Admiral Sir W.C.
Pakenham, Edward's
cousin; Lady Longford,
his mother; and
Christine's aunt, Sister
Grace, an Anglican nun.

been to make me wear white for a party.'

The result was that she allowed her guests to upstage her with their West-End-fashioned finery, while she made do in a ready-made muslin and a mass-produced twenties cloche. She may have thought to save her mother's money, but even maturity, wealth and the sophistication of later years never improved Christine Longford's sense of dress.

The wedding took place in Mrs Trew's parish church, St Margaret's. Only relations and a few friends were invited, and that by word of mouth. 'We had no bridesmaids or best man,' Christine relates, 'and my mother performed the office of "giving this woman", which we were surprised to find was a non-speaking part. Edward gave me a prayer-book to carry which was useful, and he took care of the ring himself. Our extreme quiet had an unexpected effect. The story spread that a really peculiar wedding was taking place, and it drew a crowd.

'It was a fine sunny morning, and there was good material for the cameras. The Pakenham sisters were radiant. Dunsany was magnificent in a grey top hat, and a particularly good grouping was made by Edward's cousin, Willie the Admiral, in a black top hat, and my aunt, Sister Grace, the Anglican nun, "enjoying a joke". My aunt's Mother Superior was not too pleased when the joke appeared in a social journal.

'And most important, a key-figure in the situation was the man from Ireland, Osmonde Grattan Esmonde, [now a] T. D., who had brought us our passport from the Department of External Affairs. He could not let it out of his hands until we were safely married, so he sat at the back of the church, a Roman somewhat detached from the Anglican service, and waited till we came out of the vestry.

'The party in Chalfont Road was extremely frugal, ices and lemonade instead of champagne. Our only concession to custom was a traditional cake decorated with Japanese toys. The topmost animal wasn't unlike Felix the Cat, so we carried him away with us as we left the poor wedding guests to fend for themselves.'

Mr White, Edward's family chauffeur, drove them to Folkestone from where they crossed to Flushing. What was more, Mr White was then taking the Morris to Ireland; both were to be part of their future lives at Pakenham Hall.

However temporarily, Christine's star was in the ascendant in Holland. She had been there before so she could show Edward round. They stayed in Delft 'in an enormous room with a balcony and plush-covered furniture where we could have given a party'. They saw the great pictures 'The Night Watch' and 'The Anatomy Lesson'. They bought household goods and furniture in Dutch taste for Pakenham Hall. And very soon Edward's star had once again soared away above Christine's: 'He was such a good traveller, he found more to see than I did, and soon he was guiding me.'

Interior decoration and furnishing at Pakenham Hall preoccupied them on their return. 'I didn't know how to manage a house, still less a castle,' wrote Christine, 'but it was made easy for me.' Mrs Cruickshanks, the housekeeper, was assisted by a staff of housemaids and kitchen-maids. Despite her assertion to the contrary, this army of minions trained in the ways of a Victorian mother-in-law, each bound by traditional duties, each jealously manning some nook or cranny of this vast pile, made nothing easy for Christine. Their very presence intimidated her, adding to her fears of what she had taken on. To her they represented a curtseying, forelock-pulling cohort of sycophants, as sneakily intimidating as those that greeted Daphne du Maurier's Rebecca when she arrived at Manderley to languish in the shadows as the second wife in that household.

It is said that Christine never had an easy relationship with the servants at Pakenham Hall, and that there were even times when the relationship broke down. This was quite uncharacteristic of Christine and one must assume that she invoked a defence mechanism in the face of superior numbers. However, she had taken Edward for better or worse and, with him, his castle and his retainers.

Nor was Edward very helpful in handling the staff at Pakenham Hall. He always distanced himself from his workers there, so that they never really knew him, nor he them. He was glad to leave all such responsibilities to his paid managers and agents. He even distanced himself from the people of Castlepollard. It was only when he became a theatrical impressario that he showed any capacity to cultivate relationships, and even then he largely confined them to members of his company.

Having substituted brightly coloured paint and Chinese banners for wallpaper in the hall and principal reception rooms, they explored the Dublin quays for attractive pieces. Osmonde Esmonde was their first guest, and expressed himself well-pleased with the castle. 'He was the first to teach us that sham-Gothic had points. It looked very well from the woods, a fine solid block nicely stuccoed, with battlements on the roof and towers at each end.' The next visitor was Christine's mother who was 'a severe critic, not of the castle but of what we were doing. She said we were ruining it with our paint, and our panelled hall looked like a third-rate cinema. She suggested we were copying the Morrells' red panels at Garsington, and there she had something; there might have been an unconscious influence.'

Edward's mother never visited them at Pakenham Hall. Indeed, she never came back to Ireland. She never liked the place. Christine found another reason for her refusal ever again to visit Pakenham: 'She was afraid to embarrass us, haunting a place that had once been her own. Also, she had often been ill there, and sometimes unhappy. She had stayed there with her mother-in-law when her husband was away in the army and wounded in the South African war. Anyway, she was not well now, and had five other children in England. But I believe that her delicate feelings came first. My mother was a brave woman too, but she had no such reasons for staying away; she was longing to see the place, and I was her only child, and she came very often.'

Eventually, they fixed up a flat for Mrs Trew in the old nurseries at Pakenham Hall, with a kitchenette and her books and her Oxford bric-a-brac. She was quite a character, impulsive, enthusiastic and with strong opinions and she didn't always hit it off with Edward. In particular, she criticised his eating habits, his lack of exercise and his resultant weight-gain. To keep her upstairs while she was in residence was one way of avoiding dietary lectures at the dining-room table.

The gracious old custom of county folk calling on the newly-weds was duly observed. There were the Deases of Turbotston, the Napers of Loughcrew, the Chapmans of South Hill, and many more. In returning these calls, Christine, the future writer, met interesting people in interesting situations. They were the foundations on which she based such plays as *Mr Jiggins of Jigginstown*, and such novels as *Country Places*, dealing with the extraordinary Pybus family of Castlepybus.

Edward and Christine were well settled in at Pakenham Hall by mid-September, when the second annual Castlepollard Agricultural Show took place. Mrs Trew was staying and watched the jumping events with frenzied excitement. 'That day I first attempted a difficult job,' says Christine, 'to present Edward's silver replica of the Ardagh Chalice to a man on a restive horse, and in addition, shake hands and be photographed. It was harder still for the horseman, but clearly, it wasn't the first time for him. I admired horsemanship as something miraculous.'

They continued their day trips to Dublin. Antique shops on the quays were their principal attraction. 'Abraham Cohen produced a cabinet that was a blaze of red lacquer, that looked like the Summer Palace, but had recently come from a fugitive Irish landlord. Then he found us two tall blue and white beakers, decorated with tall Chinese ladies called "Long Elizas", as good as any in Holland. Another treasure was a bronze deer, as large as life. When he came home to Pakenham Hall, he became, apart from the ceramics, our favourite thing.'

Some of the good pieces then in the antique shops had come from derelict houses, burned in the Civil War, or simply vacated. 'It was an ill wind...' says Christine. 'We were heartless, but we couldn't shed crocodile tears for the loyalists who went into exile, people like the landed gentleman who left a damp castle and settled in Wimbledon, because he enjoyed watching tennis more than anything else in life. The glorious Revolution seemed perfectly glorious to us, and the new Ireland was heaven on earth.'

Their first Christmas at Pakenham Hall was traditional. They allowed themselves to be guided by Mr Andrews. A Welshman, Mr Andrews was the butler who had come from the service of Edward's Aunt Markie at Dynevor Castle in Wales. Though he never became an Irishman, he loved Pakenham Hall enough to stay on for the rest of his life. The Christmas customs observed at Dynevor were good enough for Edward and Christine. Mr Andrews, therefore, 'dictated our timetable for meals, and unseen hands from the garden decorated the rooms with holly one dark morning before we woke.'

Christine was acclimatising to the 'last vestige of feudalism'. 'On Christmas Eve', she records, 'there was a ceremony in the farmyard, the presentation of beef: one of our own bullocks was divided among the employees in proportion to the size of their families, and some made speeches of thanks. The oldest employee was still there and still eloquent, on a peculiar footing between pension and working.'

Boxing Day in Ireland was St Stephen's Day, the day for the Wren Boys. 'Mr Andrews called them the Mummers, and I knew Mummers in England too; they came down from the Mendips with painted faces and rattled their boxes and frightened me as a child; but the Wren Boys were Irish, and collected their money with bare hands. The big fellows came early and netted the big money for punctuality and a big show; as the day wore on, the troops were smaller in number, the performers smaller and less accomplished, our enthusiasm waned and our change ran short.'

In February 1926 Edward and Christine stayed at the Shelbourne Hotel. They were the guests of Ossie Esmonde and his sisters at the Nine Arts Ball, the great fancy dress event of the year. Heavily disguised, they went in Chinese costumes. Dressing up reconciled Edward to dancing. Ossie was magnificent as a Byzantine emperor, and his sister, Patricia, was topical as a sugar-beet plant, representing the new Irish sugar industry.

At Ossie's party that night, everybody was talking about a new Sean O'Casey play at the Abbey Theatre. It was called *The Plough and the Stars*, and already it had caused riots. 'Some people, they told us, claimed to be shocked by the part of Rosie Redmond, the prostitute, but everyone knew there were prostitutes in Dublin. We could see them at night from our hotel window, women in black shawls who looked picturesque in the lamplight around the railings of St Stephen's Green.'

Edward and Christine saw the play, thought it marvellous, and couldn't believe that it caused riots. They admired Shelah Richards, and then discovered she was a daughter of their family lawyer, John William Richards, better known as Johnny Richards, a member of the firm of S. S. and E. Reeves, which is still situated at 51 Merrion Square. Johnny Richards impressed Edward and Christine by his wisdom, 'not only about the law, but also the theatre, and he was properly proud of his daughter'.

To relieve the boredom of life at Pakenham Hall, they increased their travels. During the General Strike of 1926 they by-passed England by joining a Hamburg-America liner from Cobh to Hamburg. They were raided by the police in their hotel bedroom and thought it was a case of mistaken identity. 'My phrase book failed me,' says Christine. 'But just as in the movies, the man put his thumb under his lapel and showed us a button inscribed "Polizei". He seemed to dislike our passport, particularly my photograph, and to doubt that I was the wife in question. We protested in pidgin German, but he never smiled or apologised.' Next morning they learned there had been a jewel robbery and all hotels had been searched. The incident spoiled Germany for them, and they left for Holland and another round of the favourite picture galleries.

Their house-warming at Pakenham Hall was an all-night party with dancing in the so-called Grand Hall. The floor was unyielding, but the guests were strong and hearty, and tireless till breakfast time. Traditional catering was done by the old-fashioned Dublin firm, now vanished, Mills of Merrion Row.

For an outsider like Christine, the attitudes to religion in Castlepollard in the pre-ecumenical days of the 1920s had a peculiarly amusing fascination. Edward was seriously religious and probably could not see the trivial absurdities of local sectarianism. With no such inhibitions, and with a fresh eye, Christine saw the situation for its comedy. Her record of an entertainment given to local schoolchildren is acutely observed in its sadly human and richly comic content:

'Another old-fashioned party was the school-treat, known as the "tay-party", a regular feature. This was a serious business, unassisted by Mills and organised by ourselves and Mr Andrews and Mrs Cruickshanks. We followed the method of Edward's mother, who brought it with her from her Oxfordshire home, and it was so popular that it couldn't be bettered. Tea and cake, presents and games, were provided for everyone, but there was an illusion of competition: races were run, and the winners had first choice of a prize; it might be a bigger hurley, a better French fiddle [Castlepollard's term for a mouth-organ], or flute or a sleeping dolly.

'Schoolmaster Coughlan and Mr Andrews started and stopped them with whistles and horns. Tickets were distributed beforehand at school, and great care was taken to ban gate-crashers and to prevent prize-winners from running again in disguise. At the signal for tea Edward and Mr Andrews planted themselves firmly at the door of one tent and checked the boys' tickets, while Mrs Cruickshanks and I did the same for the girls. Segregation of the sexes was taken for granted. Also, in one respect Lady Longford had adapted her method to local custom, and the sects were segregated as well. So the tea-party was for two days, not one: on the first came hundreds of Catholics, as it seemed (in fact about two hundred),and on the second twenty Protestants at the most.

'To the naked eye there was no difference between them. There were perfect stage-Irish beauties among the planters as well as the natives, and one submerged Protestant family about whom the rector told us scandalous stories. But the bigger party was bound to be noisier and more entertaining. They knew how to amuse themselves with games of the Gael, while the few little Protestants were inclined to be shy and to make a stickier social occasion. Edward told me that his mother had heard complaints in the past that "our dear little Protestants" of the second day were fed on stale cake and the crumbs from the Catholics' table; but it was clear he must have the main party first, and he always reserved a fair selection of prizes for the minority, neither better nor worse but identical.' Despite all these efforts at impartiality, local tradition has it that on their way home the little Protestants were often jeered by the little Roman Catholics triumphantly whooping 'Ye only got the lavings'.

The more Edward and Christine learned of Dublin, the more insistent became Dublin's call. They were tempted to drive there too often. In winter they frequently had to stop over in hotels. In 1927 Edward decided to find a home in Dublin, something more modest than the Georgian mansion in Parnell Square, once owned by the family, and in the drawing-room of which Kitty Pakenham had married the Duke of Wellington. They settled for 143 Leinster Road, Rathmines, a red-brick Victorian house in a terrace.

This house was another challenge to their ingenuity in furnishing and decorating, but this time there was no need for compromise with the past. They splashed the place with vivid colours, and on their next trip to the Continent they found furniture they couldn't resist in a most unlikely place: the museum-city of Bruges. And so from the summer of 1927 they led a double life, alternating between Rathmines and Castlepollard.

That summer Edward's nationalism took another forward stride. At Longford Feis he made his first speech in the cause of the Irish language, and presented a silver cup. He spoke in English, because he didn't yet dare speak Irish in public. 'I would be only insulting the language by trying it,' he said. 'But it is something to be proud of that we have a language of our own, and that is why I do my small best to help it by giving a small prize.' *The Leader*, the great Irish-Ireland weekly, welcomed Lord Longford's sentiments, and trusted he was a symptom of a tendency in his class.

A week later in Mullingar at the Midland Feis, he presented another cup, this time for Gaelic games. His prophetic speech was reported by the *Westmeath Examiner*: 'He feared the world in general, and Europe in particular, was in for a bad time, and he felt the League of Nations might as well cease its activities.' Christine remembers that often in that summer of 1927 'we sat on platforms with friendly clergy and Gaelic Leaguers, and watched Irish dancing and games in blazing sunshine with luck, and sometimes under umbrellas. My own performances were non-speaking.'

There is something sad about that last sentence. The time was already gone when Christine would be cast in speaking parts, in Irish or English. The blame was hers. There was no more diverting personality, yet, like a novice in a convent of elected silence, she took every step to have the limelight switched from herself and beamed exclusively on Edward, preferably centre-stage and alone. Her notes of their life together read remarkably, if for no other reason than their apparent absolute agreement on every conceivable subject. The words *we, our* and *us* predominate, and never once does she deviate. Never does she express her own opinion on any topic. The sparseness of the first person singular is remarkable. The development of this extraordinary relationship between two people of equal intellectual attainment makes a fascinating psychological study.

Here it is opportune to point out to readers of this book, and particularly to feminist readers, that every time Edward's name appears, Christine's, if not specifically mentioned must be understood to be implied. Statements, acts, decisions, even their very thoughts, although perhaps expressed by Edward, were most assuredly shared by Christine. Time and again, she has stated that fact. It cannot be said too often that this particular combination of husband and wife moved through life like two divine persons in one, living out their own extraordinary blessed unity.

One wonders whether, even in secret, she ever got bored with Edward's many interests. Could it possibly be that a woman could willingly cultivate interests quite so absurdly identical with those of her husband? From those early years there is only one recorded instance of a contrast, namely, the impact made by these two remarkable people on Yeats. He gave Christine an autographed book but whenever they met, Edward was struck dumb.

When he met intellectual equals Edward, in his shyness, went on the defensive, he refused to meet the other person's eyes, his demeanour became cold and distanced. Naturally, the other reacted accordingly, and so misunderstandings built up. In contrast, Christine's shyness was appealingly childlike. She spontaneously revealed her innately warm sincerity.

Chapter 7

A Peer at the Pictures

Christine's first book was published in 1928. For three years she had worked in a desultory fashion on her *Vespasian and some of his Contemporaries*. Nobody had greatly encouraged her — a Roman history isn't exactly a compulsive read. But she had set out to write 'a snappy biography of some Roman emperor'. She had chosen Vespasian because he amused her. Eventually 'he emerged as a slim volume published in Dublin by our friend Mr Figgis'. In fact, her Vespasian, in its easy style, is Roman history without tears. Feather-light and frothy on top, its lower layers reveal an amusingly malicious sense of fun.

Inevitably it contains many, many characters, and twice as many relationships. They are all etched in swiftly and humorously. Here is Nero: 'The spoiled child of an ambitious mother, he became a world emperor at the age of seventeen; but he would have done better in a college dramatic society... He spent an immoderate time with his hairdresser, who arranged his hair in layers of curls. His clothes were flamboyant and unconventional; instead of the natural woollen toga, he wore tunics in floral designs; and he never wore a garment twice.'

Edward, for his part, pushed on with his invasion of the rarefied territory of the nationalist movement. At a feis in Monaghan, Seamus O'Grianna, a speaker of Donegal Irish, recommended a teacher who was a native speaker. 'So a new significant figure appeared in our lives, Síle Ní Dhubhgáin. She was a small woman of infinite energy, very firm on irregular verbs, like the French woman who had taught me at school. At our first meeting, she said "So you want to learn Mr Green's Irish, do you?" and Edward said yes. She explained it was difficult, idiomatic and rich in local expressions, and he said all the better for that. We settled for Mr Green's Irish, and I was a long way behind, but that wasn't Síle's fault. I was careful and plodding, and wrote out my lessons from the *Bun-Chursa* in an exercise book, just like school. She let me down lightly with sudden bilingual jokes and gales of laughter. *"Tá* slave-mind *aige"* was her regular black mark.'

When they met Douglas Hyde, the patron saint of the language movement, he encouraged Edward's pursuit of Donegal Irish. 'He asked me,' says Christine, 'the easiest phrase-book questions, such as "Have you got a match?" and he shouted with pleasure to hear me say *"Tá"* in a Northern accent.' I have little doubt but that part of Hyde's pleasure was the novelty of hearing any Irish, let alone Donegal Irish, spoken with an Oxford accent. At that stage Edward and Christine could hardly have appreciated the elusiveness of that prized possession of the *Fíor-Ghael*, his *blas*.

My own first awareness of Lord and Lady Longford was on a winter evening in the early thirties around Christmas time on the Rathmines Road. The aroma of mince-pies came floating deliciously from a pastry-shop near the Town Hall. A penniless and hungry teenager, I got off my bicycle to admire the mouth-watering display through the steamed-up window. A stout man and a little woman stood beside me. They too were drooling with delight, but they...what was this? They were talking in seemingly perfect Irish, but in Oxford accents. But this was crazy! Hoping to entertain my family, I told the story at the supper-table. 'Better speak Irish with any accent than not at all.' That devastating remark came from my English mother, who feared for her dim-witted son in a Gaelic Ireland. Years later, that story gave Christine huge amusement.

His identification with nationalism sometimes brought Edward into strange situations. A memorial to 1798 was unveiled in Ballinamuck, County Longford, where Humbert's men had made their last stand. Edward was invited to speak. The platform party comprised local clergy and politicians. As Wolfe Tone would inevitably figure in the speeches, and was claimed as the patron saint of every political party, the parish priest warned Edward that he feared faction fights. Politics must therefore be kept out of it.

There were no fights. Instead, the occasion was just another stormy day in lonesome countryside, with a lot of wild men ready to whoop at the merest whiff of nationalistic rhetoric. French and Irish tri-colours flew and the Longford Fife and Drum Band paraded, largely composed of British ex-service men.

Inevitably, Christine was there too: 'Everyone had to shout to make themselves heard, and Edward shouted as loud as any. When his turn came he let fly about Tone and "break the connection with England, the

The Nine Arts Fancy Dress Ball at the Metropole Ballroom, Dublin, on 12
February 1926. The names recorded in Edward's album read, 'Mr Fitzgerald,
Edward, Mr Esmonde [Ossie Esmonde, their Oxford friend], Miss E. Esmonde,
Miss Annette Pilkington, Mr McGonigal, Captain Montague Stopford, Mr —,
Miss Cynthia Stopford, Miss Una (?) Green(e), Miss Patricia Esmonde,
Christine, and Mr Robert Green(e).

never-failing source of all our political evils". Quite non-political, as he
was only quoting verbatim. Then he pointed to the French flags on the
platform to raise cheers for Liberty, Equality and Fraternity.' Obligingly,
the cheers came, but whether the crowd had any notion what they were
cheering, or indeed, what the occasion was all about, isn't clear. It was a
day out and that was all that mattered.

There were two incidents, both in 1928, in which Edward's playful
nationalism earned him some less than dignified publicity. Indeed, one
of these incidents has passed into Dublin folklore. There are variants of
the story, even in print, including one in an English *Times* obituary, which
didn't please Christine. A top hat always figures prominently: Edward's
top hat or the top hat he is alleged to have rammed over the wearer's eyes
for singing the British national anthem in the Royal Dublin Society's
jumping enclosure during the Horse Show. Because she was on the spot,
it is best to give Christine's version:

'I must try to put down what I think is the truth, though it may not be
the funniest version. The teams in the international jumping competition

Opposite: Civic Week ball 1927 at the Mansion House, Dublin. From left: Oliver St.John Gogarty, Miss Hackett, Mrs James McNeill, wife of the Governor General, Edward, Marchioness MacSwiney, Mrs Kennedy, Mr O Briain, Mrs O'Sullivan and Mr O'Sullivan.

Left: Edward and Christine at the Dublin Horse Show in August 1926, escorted by Martin McLaughlin, an Oxford historian.

paraded, and their national anthems were played. At 'God Save the King' some people burst into song, which we thought very unpleasant and unkind to the horses. Still, I can't speak for the horses, but only for Edward and me. We had seats, but I think everyone stood for all the anthems, and I can't remember any hats, certainly no top hats. Cabinet ministers and official characters wore top hats in those days, but there were none near us, and of course Edward hadn't one. He hadn't even carried one since his uncle's funeral.

'I was on his right, and on his left was a man bawling into his ear; admittedly we were jammed close together. I heard Edward say or shout something like "Shut up" or "Will you shut up?" Yes, he must have shouted to make himself heard above the din; and he may have touched the man's elbow, but I wasn't looking. When I looked, they were both squaring their shoulders and elbows as if to fight. Then at once arms were stretched to restrain them, and it was all over in a minute. I did precisely nothing myself, and no thought of bloodshed occurred to me. That is what I believe happened, and I was there, but I know that an eye-witness may be wrong. According to another version Edward jammed a top hat over a

man's ears, and according to another, he sat down wearing his own hat and a man knocked it off. I deny both these stories.

'The parade ended and sympathisers collected, some for Edward and some for the singer. I remember that well, because a lady of the gentry came shouting around us "He ought to be turned out", and I shouted at her "You ought to be turned out yourself", which was rude and not clever.' The story is typical of two factors in their loving relationship. Firstly, Christine's version has defensive overtones, a muffling of the drums — and who could blame her? In every marriage there is always one who loves and one who is loved, and in defence of her Edward, Christine would have burned at the stake. Secondly, Edward's childish impetuosity, which on this occasion had got him into trouble in a very public situation.

The second incident took place shortly after Armistice Day, 1928. Christine considered it just another comic item for addition to Edward's biography. 'We were watching the newsreel in a Dublin cinema when King George V appeared on the screen, and some loyalists raised loud cheers. Naturally and spontaneously we joined in a counter-demonstration of booing and hissing; and when the Duke of York came on too, each faction repeated its performance, improving with practice. That was all about it, and nobody fought or was turned out.

'But next morning we read in *The Irish Times* a story called "A Peer at the Pictures". It described a remarkable scene, when a young "peer of the realm" booed and hissed the royal persons as they laid wreaths on the Cenotaph in London. But even if some people loved them, they needn't have whooped with joy at their mournful appearance. Of course *The Irish Times* took the line that most people cheered, and we were equally sure they did not. But you can't count heads in the movies. Of one thing I am certain and I put it on record: I never knew Edward to start a demonstration, but only to counter-demonstrate when provoked.'

That incident had a peevish little sequel for Christine. She had promised to speak at a charitable function of the Church of Ireland in a parochial hall. 'After "A Peer at the Pictures" my engagement was cancelled; a happy release for me and no less for the charity, as I was such a bad speaker.' A confused public indignation was running high at the time. It had resulted from a visit to their Portumna estate by Princess Mary and her husband, Lord Lascelles. She was the first royal person to visit Ireland since independence had been attained.

The *Irish Times* reference to a 'peer of the realm' raised an interesting point. Edward Longford was often criticised for the contradictions in his character: his form of nationalism, for instance, together with his continued use of his peerage. Nobody criticised Lord Ashbourne (known as Mac Giolla Bhríde), whose nationalism was of a much more flamboyant style. Not unlike a mournful Harry Lauder, he stalked the streets, with his flowing mane under a beret, wearing a saffron kilt, and carrying a gnarled walking stick. If current company was unable to converse in Irish, then his second choice was French. Indeed, he lived in Compiègne, to 'preserve a perspective' on Irish affairs. Could nationalism go further?

Edward's form of nationality was more simplistic. He lived in Ireland because he loved it. With money and two houses there was no hardship. And as to his earldom, that too happened to be Irish. It had come, not from Westminster, but from College Green, in the golden days of Grattan's Parliament, when in 1785, the widow of Thomas Pakenham, the first Baron Longford, was created Countess of Longford in her own right. There was, therefore, never a first Earl of Longford. Her son, Edward Michael, the second Baron, pre-deceased her in 1792. On her death in 1794, her grandson, Thomas, the third Baron, inherited the title, becoming second Earl of Longford.

Now spending more time in Rathmines than in Castlepollard, Edward and Christine were well-poised to keep abreast of anything new in theatrical Dublin. They would have gone to a theatre every night had it been possible. They had out-grown the Paul Twynings and the Cartneys and Keveneys at the Abbey Theatre. The Gaiety was commercial, and the Royal and Olympia were music-halls. Hence the peer at the pictures!

The first-ever performance of the Dublin Gate Theatre took place on 14 October 1928 at the old Peacock Theatre. The play was *Peer Gynt*. This historic photograph shows Hilton Edwards as Peer with Bridie Folan as Solveig. For Micheál Mac Liammóir that first night remained 'for all time the most poignant and profound, the funniest and by far the most moving.'

It was therefore the occasion of some excitement when the rumour spread that a new *avant garde* company was about to open a season of international plays at the little Peacock Theatre beside the Abbey. The tiny Peacock Theatre would be a more accurate description. Christine said of it: 'The seats tipped up and were better than in our old Oxford Playhouse, but it was up a nasty steep staircase, and the stage was minute.' Rumour had it correctly. On 14 October 1928, under the style and title Dublin Gate Theatre Studio, two almost unknown actors, Hilton Edwards and Micheál Mac Liammóir presented Ibsen's *Peer Gynt* on the Peacock's little stage.

About the Abbey Theatre's early financial difficulties Yeats had said 'Poverty is the mother of genius', a poetic version of necessity being the mother of invention. Either way, never was the point more truly made than by the famous Edwards-Mac Liammóir production of *Peer Gynt* at the Peacock. Years later, Edwards revealed how they managed the miracle in so small a space. The illusion of infinity was quite simply

First produced in June 1929, Denis Johnston's *The Old Lady Says 'No'* mesmerised theatrical Dublin. Micheál Mac Liammóir as Emmet and Meriel Moore as the flower seller meet in College Green at the foot of the Grattan statue.

created by painting the back wall a neutral blue-grey, and flooding it with white light. Two sets of steps were used. As required, they were placed back-to-back to make a peak, and then in the opposite direction to make a valley. The result? *'Peer Gynt'*, says Christine, 'took us by storm.'

In this fantasy taken from Asbjornsen's *Norwegian Fairy Tales*, Ibsen moves his hero, the ebullient Peer, from the Norwegian mountain tops to the coast of Morocco, to a ship at sea, to the Sahara Desert, to the Cairo Lunatic Asylum — a tall stage-management order in 1867 when the play was written, and no less tall in the Peacock Theatre of 1928. Yet Con Curran, reviewing the production for *The Irish Statesman*, could write that 'the freshness of the mountain farms, the dark encounters of the night, the grotesque horror of the Trolls' hall within the hill...filled with the vileness of creeping things were treated in stage scenes of great skill.'

Under the spell of the youthful Edwards, the audience had little difficulty in suspending its disbelief as it witnessed a master-actor's dissection of Ibsen's greatest character. Layer by layer, from the surface to the source, Peer Gynt's nature was exposed: reckless, ruthless, bullying, self-pitying, sometimes odious beyond belief, but always warm with well-intentioned humanity. An 'agonising enchantment', as Micheál

Mac Liammóir called it.

It was a watershed in Irish theatre, an event long-awaited in Dublin, like the coming of a theatrical Messiah. If Edward and Christine Longford were never stage-struck before, the alchemy and inspiration of two young men had now permanently enchanted them. Grateful beyond belief, they went home spell-bound.

If confirmation were required that something theatrically momentous had struck Dublin, it came with the programme of fifteen further international plays produced in the Peacock Theatre in the eight months to June 1929. Perfection was aimed at, if not always achieved. The contrast between accents, for instance, could irritate, but could not be helped. Professional actors made all the more obvious the adenoidal accents of helpful Dublin amateurs, without whom the Gate Theatre could never have survived.

The locals came into their own in Irish plays, of course — in Micheál Mac Liammóir's *Diarmuid and Gráinne*, for instance, first written in Irish for Taibhdearc na Gaillimhe, and then translated. Hilton had promised he would produce it on a Dublin stage if it was the last thing he did before dying of starvation in Ireland. It became the third play done at the Peacock by the Dublin Gate Theatre in 1928, with Micheál and Coralie Carmichael as the tragic lovers.

An exciting event was the first production in these islands of Oscar Wilde's *Salomé*. The play had been banned in England, and besides, 1928 was only thirty-three years after the date of Wilde's 'disgrace'. There might be titillation: Christine records that 'Coralie was Salomé, Micheál The Baptist, and Hilton was Herod, when they presented a gorgeous, exotic production...and Dubliners poured in to see it.' In filling a Dublin theatre, nothing succeeds like the bush telegraph. True, the Dublin Gate was already being talked about. It was highbrow, some said. Others thought it decadent. There were even those who found it unintelligible. But most were agreed it was worth a visit, if only for its curiosity value. *Salomé* changed all that. It became a must. It was being played with the entire cast half naked. *Salomé* demanded exotica, and as exotica couldn't be afforded, they had to settle for the next best thing, the human body, with only elaborate head-dresses and loin cloths. For whatever reason, *Salomé* was a huge success.

But the greatest sensation of that first year came in June 1929, with Denis Johnston's first play, *The Old Lady Says 'No'*. Here was the new expressionism applied to an Irish theme. Here was satirical drama, a send-up of ould Ireland's cherished pipe-dreams. Here was a drumbeat of vocally orchestrated clichés, a cacophony of familiar sounds in unfamiliar places. Dublin was mesmerised, struck dumb. Dublin wasn't ready for such advanced ideas. But open-mouthed, awe-inspired, and possessed only by confusion, Dublin packed the theatre and tried to rationalise an experiment in purposeful confusion.

Edward and Christine saw the play — how many times? But every time, they saw another aspect: like a Jack Yeats circus picture — another horse here, another rider there. Christine concluded that *The Old Lady* proved the Gate was a serious business. No, not a business, but a serious idea; the Studio needed a home of its own.'

Chapter 8

Country and Town

With Solveig's Song still ringing in their ears, Edward and Christine set off for another foray into Europe. This time it was Poland and Czechoslovakia. Edward felt that, since new hope had returned to the world, a free Irishman should see how the Poles were using their freedom. He was already aware that they had saved their language in a way the Irish had not.

Like good tourists, the Longfords used phrasebooks for their immediate needs. But to enjoy to the full these exciting new countries, they made a decision — one may be forgiven for suspecting that Edward made the decision. He would teach himself Polish, and Christine would tackle Czech, and she should be passably fluent by the time they reached Prague. 'In fact I was not,' Christine records. 'On that trip I was forced to admit Edward could beat me at languages. I was lagging behind him in Polish and Czech as I had been in Irish.'

Her notes of their ever-changing cross-country journey read like history in an age when we take for granted a two-hour trip in the belly of a Boeing: 'How delightful it was to sit in a train and look out of the windows at Europe, to eat and sleep well and to guess where we were when we woke; we had never slept in a train before, except between Euston and Holyhead.'

She goes on to describe the Warsaw of 1929, a Warsaw now gone for ever: 'Our first impression was of cream stucco, bright in the sunshine, the style they called Empire, with statues and trees. The Hotel Europejski was grander than any we knew, and there were armies of people to help us and carry our bags. They weren't alarming, they smiled and knew what we wanted before we spoke.' But there was a jarring note in the dining-room. They were disappointed to hear English spoken, especially as it might have spoiled Edward's enjoyment of a favourite food: 'An Englishwoman was raising her voice to complain "This is too big. Much too big. I've told you before." It was pastry smothered in cream, and we made it clear to the waiter that we didn't agree with her. Some women of striking beauty and elegance were eating the same thing.'

After Poland, Czechoslovakia was an anti-climax. They realised they should have gone there first. The Czechs lacked the warmth of the Poles; the validity of their passport was questioned by a tetchy railway official; and to their great disappointment Prague's National Theatre was closed. To make matters even worse, a new play by Capek was billed for its reopening. No, Czechoslovakia was an anti-climax.

Consequently, on their return to Dublin, Edward's enthusiasm for Poland glowed with a new warmth. He was continually struck by the analogies between Poland and Ireland, countries with so much in common, yet greatly different in their capacity to display their culture, their folklore and their language. There was much Ireland could learn from Poland. He had said they must go back. Now he knew he wanted to go back as soon as possible.

'We did that in August,' according to Christine, 'and stayed in Poznan to see the General National Exhibition, celebrating ten years of Polish freedom. The white Polish eagle perched on a big "X" for ten was its symbol, and the national colours, crimson and white, were splashed everywhere. There were pleasure-dromes and palaces, courtyards and colonnades, flowers and fountains, but more important, there was a theatre specially built for national music and dancing. We saw new ballets based on folklore, and the costumes and settings were gorgeous. And the agricultural park at Poznan was like Ballsbridge glorified!'

Edward and Christine returned to Ireland, Edward bursting with energy and ideas. If Poland could muster her nationalism to such good effect, why not Ireland? If Poland could speak her own language so proudly and so naturally, why not Ireland? He remembered that good Polish woman with a historic name who had kissed him on both cheeks in some museum and said, 'We are brother and sister — Ireland and Poland.' It was true. Poland and Ireland ... sisters under the same skin. But one thing was certain: his Polish experience had convinced Edward that Ireland must be Gaelicised.

Edward's first political activity was the preparation of propaganda for the Cumann na nGaedheal Party, now Fine Gael. This reception at the Metropole Ballroom, Dublin, shows from left: Christine; Mrs W.T. Cosgrave; Mr W.T. Cosgrave, President of Dáil Eireann; Edward; Miss Murphy; Mr Rowan; Dr Desmond Reddin and others.

Unlike his younger brother, Frank, Edward Longford was not a politician. His interest in politics was perfunctory, but such as it was, he gave it to Cumann na nGaedheal. He had not forgotten, nor forgiven, the unnecessary Civil War and the damage it had done to Ireland. For some time he had been sufficiently active politically to write propaganda for the Cumann na nGaedheal party. Now Poland was to loom large in these writings as well as in his speeches.

In 1929, he was a young, energetic and imaginative man, with a solid family background and a good education. While his interests were multifarious, they were mostly transitory: writing, painting, the theatre, and languages of course, particularly Irish. Consciously or not, he was thrashing around in search of some form of self-expression which might promise aesthetic satisfaction. Christine once described Edward's many enthusiasms as eccentricities. In 1929, helped by his Polish experience, his current eccentricity was the Irish language. And so, with new-found zest, he set himself towards the Gaelicisation of Ireland. As for Christine, she quietly fell in and followed, whatever the current eccentricity might happen to be.

Lords in Ireland were popularly associated with hated landlordism. They were the upper-crust who wouldn't be found dead speaking anything but the best King's English. A lord who spoke Irish was therefore unique, the more so when he had the courage to parade in Gaelic costume, like Lord Ashbourne. Ashbourne was a polyglot, but the Gaelgeoiri were interested only in his capacity in Irish, and for that they promoted him to the dizziest heights of Gaelic Ireland: president of the Gaelic League.

Now another Irish-speaking lord had appeared in their midst, this time a handsome young scion of an ancient Irish house. True, he spoke his Irish with an Oxford accent, but for that alone he was a novelty. His propaganda value was instantly recognised. Thus Edward became irresistible to the Gaelgeoiri. Invitations poured in asking him to speak at Gaelic functions all over the country. At Tullamore, Longford, Mullingar, and Athlone he raised many a lusty cheer for an ancient nation lately loosed from slavery.

When the Abbey Theatre made a knowledge of Irish compulsory for their new young actors, Roibeard O Faracháin published a humorous poem in *The Irish Times*. In passing, he remembered Edward's latest eccentricity:

Then Longford, too, bad cess to it, can talk the Gaelic tongue;
We used to have aristocrats that sooner would be hung!

As president of the Gaelic League, Lord Ashbourne was guest of honour at the Longford Feis. Edward invited him to stay at Pakenham Hall. Christine saw the humorous side of it: 'He spoke Welsh to Mr Andrews (the Welsh butler), who refused to respond, we believed from perversity, though he said lack of practice. Mr Andrews took a keen interest in his lordship's costume, which he wasn't allowed to press, the brogues, which he wasn't allowed to clean, and the traditional Gaelic shirt used for sleeping. His lordship spoke Irish and French to Edward and me, but my mother was there and one couldn't control her. She made him speak English. She liked him very much, and referred to him privately as "The Mac Gilly Cranky".'

At the Longford Feis Edward spoke Irish in public for the first time. His performance was approved by Dr MacNamee, the Bishop of Ardagh and Clonmacnois, the first Catholic Bishop Christine had met. He struck her as being 'very live and amusing with a voice from the north wind'. Afterwards he gave the two lords, and Christine, a sumptuous dinner, but the attendant clergy found things a bit confusing. They were calling three people 'my Lord' which to Christine 'sounded excessive'. The bishop had made a rousing speech at the Feis. He told parents they mustn't say that children couldn't learn English properly if they had to learn Irish. On the contrary, if you know only one language, you know no language. You must learn a second language, to get to know the first from the outside. 'What do they know of English that only English know?' The Longford public looked blank.

The Longford Leader recorded laughter when Lord Ashbourne said he would attempt to speak English. 'But the Irish,' he went on, 'have never at any time spoken English. They have only attempted it. When they try to speak English, they say many things the English don't understand'—which seems to be as true today as in 1929! Edward told the audience that Gaelic wouldn't frighten the tourists, nor would it mean less bread and butter. He had been a tourist in Poland, where they spoke their own language and there was no shortage of bread and butter. Then he called for three cheers for Poland, and got them, presumably on the grounds that Ireland had already had more than its share of cheers for one afternoon.

His invitation to a language meeting at the Coliseum Cinema in Cork presented Edward with his greatest challenge yet. It would test his fluency in Irish, as well as the strength of his political allegiance, for the other lion in the Coliseum was to be none other than Eamon de Valera himself, the generally accepted personification of everything that was Gaelic Ireland. The prospect was daunting. For all his seeming self-assured arrogance, Edward was essentially a shy man.

Politically, he had never seen eye to eye with de Valera, and besides, the man was still slightly suspect. He had yet to prove his sincerity, as well as his political dexterity, as prime minister of a democratic parliament. Edward decided to tread warily in Cork.

As it turned out, the lion lay down with the lamb. Mr de Valera couldn't have been less fierce or more reasonable, and there were no party politics. Christine witnessed the proceedings: 'Edward said the language was greater than politics, and that was why he could come on the same platform as Mr de Valera. He also said that Irishmen owed no allegiance to any country but their own. Mr de Valera said his heart went out to Edward, and Edward had to sit and smile, without the right to reply. Then de Valera said the bigger political cause was the national cause, and went on to discuss the teaching of Irish, the poverty of the Gaeltacht and the urgent need for home industries. Edward could only mime agreement.'

The Cork meeting ended amicably, but there was no fraternisation. Edward and Christine left immediately for Waterford. There was nothing exciting in next day's Irish newspapers. It was different when the English

Edward and Christine at a fête in Dalkey accompanied by Rev. C.S. Collins. With his enthusiasm and his Oxford Irish, Edward became the darling of the Gaelic Leaguers, attending their meetings throughout the country.

newspapers arrived. A peer was still news in the English press, and as Mr de Valera was always top news, the combination was too good to be missed. The Longfords were first alerted to the sensation when they saw a poster outside a shop: 'Peer Joins de Valera'. Christine kept press cuttings:

'From Liverpool, Manchester, Oldham, and Birmingham, from *Punch* and from *Truth* came cuttings about the peer's eccentricities, sometimes coupled with those of Lord Ashbourne. "Irish Peer Supports de Valera", "Irish-Speaking Peers", "Young Peer's Outburst", "Young Peer With Fiery Views". *The Morning Post*, to be fair to that enemy of Ireland, said only "Lord Longford's Outburst", and didn't say he had joined de Valera. But by the time the news reached India, the *Madras Mail* had "Convert to Fianna Fail" and more still: "As was only to be expected, the Fianna Fail leader, who spoke immediately afterwards, playfully welcomed Lord Longford as a distinguished convert." It couldn't be helped, and Lord Longford continued to write voluminous articles for Cumann na nGaedheal.'

Poland, particularly the visit to the General National Exhibition at Poznan, had unleashed another of Edward's eccentricities — home industries. He had noticed some beautifully hand-woven woollen scarves in a Dublin shop. He was told they had been made by a man working in his own home. Edward sought him out, and thus met Mr Copithorne, shortly to become his partner in the homespun business.

White-haired, elderly, and decided in his views, Mr Copithorne claimed he knew hand-weaving from 'A' to 'Z'. He knew how to pick weavers, where to find idle looms, where to buy yarns. There was nothing he couldn't make, from tweeds, light or heavy, to decorative wallpieces like those from the East. All he required was a little capital and bigger premises. And that was how Edward became involved in the Leinster Hand-Weaving Company, and later the Hand-Loom Shop.

All that Mr Copithorne had said was true — he was a strict Protestant. Even stricter, he was a Plymouth Brother. Indeed, so strict a parent was he that his children had fled and left him alone. So he wanted to start in business again — in a small way. It was another chance for Edward to indulge his creative urge. So they installed two looms in a small place in South Richmond Street, and Mr Copithorne promptly elected himself managing director. 'One of our French friends,' says Christine, 'thought him "centrifugal", an ominous word. "Very likely," said Edward, "and you might say the same of me."'

In no time, Mr Copithorne had three looms going and was making real tweeds in classic designs and 'conservative' colours, heather mixtures, checks, and herring-bones, and planning to export them all over the world. Christine recollects the occasion when Mr Copithorne 'told us with hoots of laughter that some makers put the smell into tweeds on purpose. They lit turf fires to give them a whiff of the cottage industries, indeed he could do it himself if he had more room. He would like a lot more room to expand. He knew a good tailor and I knew a dressmaker. We could make model garments. But where could we show them? Not in a back lane in South Richmond Street. Edward agreed, we needed a showroom.'

Meanwhile, Edward and Christine had met the famous Reddin family: a mother and father and four artistic sons, who produced plays in their drawing-room in Fitzwilliam Square. Just then the Reddins were industriously collecting funds for the new Gate Theatre, planned to open in the new year in an annexe of the Rotunda. Edward helped by purchasing some shares in the Dublin Gate Theatre Company Limited.

The share certificates were impressive, handsome documents bearing the now famous theatre design by Mac Liammóir.

The most important artistic event of the year 1930 was the opening of the Gate Theatre. Christine recalled the event: 'It opened on a freezing night in February 1930, with Goethe's *Faust*. We had no idea of what the actors suffered backstage, or how the heating had failed, we simply sat and admired. This was a real theatre, with a beautiful black and gold curtain painted by Micheál MacLiammóir. We were in an eighteenth-century hall of the Rotunda, with Georgian plasterwork on the ceiling. But in a moment the world became German and Gothic. The stage seemed enormous after the Peacock Theatre. It was a great night for Dublin. After that we never missed a show at the Gate.'

Edward insisted on going back to Poland in 1930. Remembering Mr Copithorne, he studied Polish folk-art with a new interest. 'The shops made us jealous,' said Christine. 'We had to stop loading our bags with embroidered shirts ... From Zakopane I carried home a dressing-gown in the local style, which Mr Copithorne tried to copy without success; it was eventually turned to better use on the stage.'

At Tatra they admired the richly embroidered white homespuns worn by the mountaineers, the whole costume topped off with shallow black hats with peacock feathers. It was usual for tourists to buy a costume. Edward had to desist because, as Christine said, 'he wouldn't have found one to fit him. It must have been about then that he was putting on weight. But what harm? We were very greedy in Poland. I have yellowing snapshots of both of us, dressed in Mr Copithorne's tweeds, lying on a hillside at Sucha and eating wild strawberries and Borowki, eating in the Babia Gora and eating at Ojcow under fantastic rocks.'

Edward's mother spoke about his weight next time she saw him. She advised Christine to make him take exercise, to make him run round the wood every morning before breakfast. 'But she hadn't done it to him herself,' said Christine, 'and I knew I wouldn't.' Never, even for his own good, could Christine bring herself to deny Edward food of any kind, and as much as he fancied.

Refreshed, if a bit more rotund, Edward returned to Dublin with a few non-edible imports. First there was the Polish national anthem. He was proud to be word-perfect, and it turned out to be a tremendous asset as a rousing party-piece. Then there were the lantern-slides: scenes in Poland, costumes of different regions and their customs. Edward began to use them for lantern lectures in aid of the Gaelic League. This eccentricity faded out quite soon, despite a good local press.

Finally, there was the foundation of the Irish-Polish Circle. 'There were friends of Poland in Dublin,' said Christine. 'Our most constant and patient listeners were Desmond and Mabel FitzGerald, who let us come to their house in Bray every Sunday, and talk our heads off about Poland and Ireland and the state of the world.'

Desmond and Mabel were the parents of Garret FitzGerald, Taoiseach of the coalition government. They were highly intellectual and travelled liberals, who had both been in the GPO in 1916, without making any particular fuss about it. As Minister for External Affairs, Desmond FitzGerald, amongst other historic acts, signed the application of the Irish Free State, in April 1923, for admission to the League of Nations. Having lived in France, he was as friendly with French poets and philosophers as he was with the Irish writers of his time, including W. B. Yeats.

Christine greatly admired the FitzGeralds: 'They looked young and charming, and entertained guests of all ages all over their house and garden. Mabel was a woman of independent mind, a "new woman" and friend of Shaw. Though Desmond was a cabinet minister, she would not play the official part of a minister's wife, she wouldn't take sides on the Treaty, and political discussions were on a higher plane. So were religious discussions; Desmond talked Thomism to Edward, and Edward talked Anglicanism to Desmond, and they got on well. Desmond lent us piles of French books, philosophy, poetry, novels, and plays, and kept us firmly attached to the Free State and Cumann na nGaedheal.'

The summer of 1930 saw a lot of holiday arrivals and departures at Pakenham Hall. For all that, Christine occasionally went into hiding: 'At odd times I stayed indoors and wrote the first novel that anybody can write, stories of my past life; and here I must say in praise of Edward that he neither stopped it nor censored it. I showed it to him in sections and waited to see if he laughed at the jokes, but I didn't ask for advice and he gave me none, and I showed it to no one else. Lennox Robinson came for a weekend and guessed my secret. He told me to persevere, I was doing no harm, and I liked doing it, didn't I? Yes, I certainly did.'

This, of course, was *Making Conversation*, her first novel, which got rave notices from every newspaper and periodical in London and Dublin. 'I have been going about lately,' said Compton Mackenzie in the *Daily Mail*, 'reading extracts from this delicious book to anybody who would lend me his ears.' First published by Victor Gollancz in 1931, *Making Conversation* was to be republished forty years later by Faber & Faber with equal success.

As a novelist, Christine Longford was blessed with a natural facility.

Her writing flowed so freely that she was inclined to neglect it. True, there were two more novels: *Country Places*, published by Gollancz in 1932, and *Printed Cotton*, published by Methuen in 1935. Both were set in Ireland. The secret of her success as a novelist lay in her aptitude for telling dialogue, as well as her avoidance of tortuous introspection. Also, she set her first novel in England, and her second and third amongst the Anglo-Irish, thus avoiding the pitfalls of so many English authors writing about the Irish: the use of a bastard form of Synge-like dialogue never heard in this world, let alone in Aran or Ireland.

The publication of her novels was the culmination of a youthful ambition which had been agitating her since her Oxford days. More than anything she had wanted to be a writer. After *Making Conversation* she quickly gained confidence as a novelist. Had she continued in this *métier* her novel-writing might well have proved to be her greater achievement. But Edward saw the pungency and wit of her dialogue as potential for successful playwriting. And anyway, once she became familiar with the Gate Theatre, she *wanted* to write plays. As she observed: 'Dubliners go to plays more than they read books, and write plays more than they write books.' And so it was with her second play, *Mr Jiggins of Jigginstown*, that she made her mark as a playwright.

Thus encouraged by Edward, it was as a playwright that Christine continued to write. She churned out plays, almost to order, and always under pressure from Edward. They came so fast the Longford players reacted tiredly, 'Oh no, not another.' Capable of infinitely greater heights in the drama than she ever attained, Christine's talent was neglected, undisciplined, wasted. In old age she was well aware of what might have been achieved had she lived a settled life and been given the opportunity to concentrate on serious writing.

As we have noted, Edward stood in shuddering awe of W. B. Yeats. There is no known reason for this, beyond the arrogant poise with which Yeats was capable of intimidating lesser scribes. But then, the poet had a weakness for titles, so perhaps the void was due to misunderstanding. At any rate, it is certain that in 1930 Edward would not have dared to invite Yeats to Pakenham Hall. As it turned out, he didn't have to. Christine recalled what Oliver Gogarty told Edward he must do: 'There was a railway strike, and Yeats had to be brought to Renvyle, the Gogartys new hotel, where Augustus John was waiting to finish his portrait. John had painted a young, black-haired Yeats years before, and now he was painting him white-haired, a greater and handsomer man and a major poet. Yeats had been ill at Rapallo, he must be treated with care; Edward must bring him from Dublin to spend a night at Pakenham Hall and drive him the next day to Renvyle. It was a royal command.'

Yeats was tired on arrival at Pakenham Hall. After dinner he discussed Wyndham Lewis and went to bed early. But the household was still terrified. Flora Grierson, Christine's Oxford friend, was also staying. She should not have worried for Yeats had stayed with her father in Edinburgh. Edward decided to take them all to the west. 'We had a bigger car now, an Armstrong Siddeley. Taking care to avoid the bumps, and anxious to listen to the poet sitting beside him, Edward missed several turnings near home. He missed some more later on, although he knew the road to Galway perfectly well. We were late and worried at lunch at the Great Southern Hotel in Galway. We were really shaken up by the time we reached Renvyle.'

Yeats wanted tea. It was brought immediately. Recovering his spirits, he had launched into a monologue on some subject of rare erudition, when suddenly he paused. With all the shocked accusation he could muster he boomed: 'Edward, you are drinking my tea.' In picking up the wrong cup, Edward had made his biggest boob of the day.

As a memorial of that journey Christine had two books 'that are not to be lent or sold. *Selected Poems* and *Coinage of Saorstát Eireann 1928*, given to me and inscribed by W. B. Yeats, July 22 1930. When the Cuala Press published his *Pages from a Diary Written in 1930* this was the entry for Renvyle, July 23: "I have talked most of a long motor journey, talked even when I was hoarse. Why? Surely because I was timid, because I felt the other man was judging me, because I endowed his silence with all kinds of formidable qualities. Being on trial I must cajole my judge." The other man was Edward, and as I have said he was terrified.'

Despite his honesty as a diarist, Christine puzzled as to how Yeats could possibly have been timid or found Edward formidable. Edward was 'a young man worried about the car and the road, that was why he was silent. He was sure Yeats was a major poet, the greatest then writing in English. But he was also a magician; nothing escaped him. He may have sensed a resistance. Edward was not his disciple in some things, religion or politics, and he didn't believe in ghosts or Toryism or Anglo-Irish ascendancy. He wouldn't and couldn't have argued, but was he daring to judge?'

Here Christine displays her defensive concern that Edward and Yeats, as travelling companions, hadn't exactly hit it off. She converts Edward's foolish fear into a resistance against the poet. As his greatly-loving wife, she could never have believed that Edward had any shortcomings, least of all that, conversationally, he could be forbidding and devoid of geniality. When he was ill-at-ease, his big blue eyes stared beyond you into a space where you were not included, or he looked at the top button of your waistcoat, but never at the level of your eyes. Edward had inherited something of his mother's inability to relate to people. Yeats was right in feeling he was being judged.

Edward's sister, Pansy Lamb, brought her remarkable husband, Henry Lamb, to Pakenham Hall. A medical doctor with a distinguished record in World War I, he later became far more distinguished as a painter. He was twenty years older than Pansy, something which Lady Longford had felt was unworthy of her pretty and talented twenty-three-year-old daughter. It was during these summer holidays that Lamb began painting the series of family portraits which now hangs in Pakenham Hall. The first, of course, was of Edward, wearing a Fair Isle jumper and a red carnation.

Then Frank brought a friend. His name was John Betjeman, afterwards the Poet Laureate. Christine loved him from the start. 'If friends could be marked by arithmetic in a marking game, as we used to do in the evenings, I would mark John up as the greatest: he gave Edward the most and the longest pleasure, either by his company or by letters and books for thirty years.' I can testify to the pleasure Sir John Betjeman's poetry brought to Christine in her old age, when, word perfect, she could recite page after page.

Betjeman went with Edward to Lough Gowna where afterwards he set his poem 'An Impoverished Irish Peer', published in 1937 in a collection called *Continual Dew*. A longer poem, 'Sir John Piers', was inspired by a visit to the ruins of Tristernagh House near Lough Iron. In 1807, for a wager, Piers had set himself to seduce Lady Cloncurry. His attempt ended in the court of the King's Bench, and his ruination by John Philpot Curran, counsel for Lord Cloncurry. The poem was published in 1940 in Betjeman's collection *Old Lights For Old Chancels*.

The carefree frolics at Pakenham Hall in the summer of 1930 reached their peak with the arrival of Evelyn Waugh, 'still the same little faun as at Oxford,' Christine remembers. He was already famous because of *Decline and Fall* and *Vile Bodies*. Everybody laughed at these hilarious books, and even more at Waugh's true stories.

When the humour was right there was no better master of the revels than Edward. After dinner he would lead the party in lusty renderings of 'The Boys Of Wexford', 'The Bould Fenian Men' and 'Paddies Evermore'. His current eccentricity was a collection of recordings of Orange ballads, which he had memorised. So his solo contributions included 'The Ould Orange Flute', 'The Orange Lily-O', and 'The Protestant Boys' — 'Slitter, slaughter, holy water, scatter the Papishes every one!' Nobody will ever know what sense the Englishmen, Betjeman and Waugh, made of it all. Typically Irish, they might have ventured, but how wrong they would have been!

Attendance at the Gate Theatre hadn't been neglected. Edward and Christine had driven to Dublin for every new play since the opening of the theatre's third season in August 1930. In October they even made three visits in one week, to see Shaw's blockbuster, *Back to Methuselah*, which was staged in three cycles, on three consecutive nights. On fine summer evenings the theatre wasn't crowded. 'It was nice and cool,' Christine remembered, 'but we didn't know then what a horror that was for the actors.' The reality of persistently poor houses came in December, with the first annual general meeting of shareholders.

A dismal announcement was made: unless the shares which were still available were taken up immediately, the Gate Theatre would be forced to close forthwith. As explained in the prologue of this book, Edward, without hestitation, apart from the struggle to shed his overcoat, stood up and made his bid for all the shares still available. Pleasant consternation broke out amongst the shareholders. Somebody had reprieved the Gate Theatre, and hardly anybody knew who the young man was.

Huddling back into his overcoat, Edward glowed with a new sense of achievement. As always, Christine found an accommodating reason to agree with his move. 'It was no hardship to him,' she said. 'It was only a pleasure for him to buy some more shares in the Gate Theatre.'

Chapter 9

Town and Country

Despite an early introduction to fox-hunting, Edward had always disliked the sport. When he was a baby in his perambulator at Pakenham Hall, a fox was killed on the front lawn. Much to his mother's disgust, somebody had 'blooded' Edward by daubing his little pink face. If the uncouth gesture was intended to symbolise the making of another hunting man, it had failed abysmally. Not only did Edward dislike hunting, he didn't even admire horses. A fast car was more to his liking.

The search for a master for the Westmeath Hunt was a recurring problem. The Earls of Longford had traditionally held the appointment. Edward had been faced with the proposition several times, but had always diplomatically escaped. Confrontation came when he and Christine gave their first hunt ball at Pakenham Hall. They didn't know the traditions associated with such a function, but they needn't have worried. The indispensable Mr Andrews knew the routine like the back of his hand.

It was as a result of the eloquent speeches, and the references to 'the good relations that always existed ...' that Edward found himself once again in a dilemma. It was clear there was a local campaign to involve him in the question of the mastership of the Westmeath Hunt. He knew his duty to his neighbours; he knew the hunt was hard up and needed a little subsidising. Their appeal was to his social rather than his sporting instinct. His sister, Violet, saw the nub of the problem: 'He had never cared for riding and early in life had put on an amount of weight that would have made finding a mount difficult, even in a country famed for its production of weight-carrying hunters.' A face-saving compromise was reached: he paid his subscription, accepted a fictitious office and so identified with the hunt. 'It was comic,' said Christine. 'Edward became a non-practising joint master of hounds.'

Edward was more courageous as a businessman. As boldly as Mr Copithorne himself, he agreed to the expansion of the Leinster Hand-Weaving Company. They opened the Hand-Loom Shop, with a fashionable address in St Stephen's Green. Soon they transferred to a bigger shop in Dawson Street, where they sold only Irish goods. They displayed their tweeds on a stall at the Spring Show and the Horse Show,

Pakenham Hall. Christine's first impression likened it to 'a terrace of houses rather than a house, with improbable towers, and on the topmost a flag flying.'

and customers thought it a novelty to buy things from an earl and countess. But the venture wasn't economic — 'far from it,' Christine said.

For years Edward had been seeking an occupation that might give him some lasting satisfaction. In his various eccentricities, Christine had patiently walked behind him up every exploratory avenue to the inevitable dead end. And when he had tired of each new whim and turned elsewhere, she turned with him and somehow managed again to generate the required degree of sprightly enthusiasm for his newest notion, whatever it might be. Physically and mentally, she had had to become as clinging as his shadow.

After five years of marriage there were still no children. Naturally, this was a disappointment. It was a greater disappointment than Christine ever expressed, except perhaps to her doctors. But there was still every hope. Her dearest wish was to present Edward with an heir, and, unlike her alter ego, Martha Freke, she would never have found children a bore. In the meantime she indulged and mothered Edward. He was her 'dear child'. His freshly-washed, boyish bulk, accompanied by the diminutive Christine, often looking rather lost and famished, suggested rather a mother and her son on the way to the family lawyer, than a husband and wife on a cultural skite.

It was in her old age that she spoke most often of her regret at being childless. It was small comfort to be told that if she'd had ten they would hardly be still around, much less willing to care for her. One sensed it was because hers had been such a near miss at motherhood that her conscience was so troubled. Why had her one and only pregnancy miscarried? Was it her fault? Had she taken every precaution to ensure a live birth? And, most importantly, had she chosen the best obstetrician available? On the last point at least, one could reassure her that she could not have improved upon an outstanding master of the Rotunda Hospital, an admirable teacher, and an author with a particularly brilliant international reputation in his subject. In these discussions one sometimes noted a compensatory sense of pride in having once been pregnant: at least she had not been a barren woman, nor Edward an impotent man, as some unfeeling Dubliners would have it.

Sadly, at Christmas they exchanged not expensive presents but cuddly toys — teddy bears, in fact, until there was a collection at their bedsides in Pakenham Hall. After Edward's death, and when Christine no longer visited, they were packed and sent to Coole Children's Hospital nearby. But an unreliable messenger took the Dublin road instead, and there sold the lot. A pathetic epilogue to a pathetic story, reflecting the emptiness of substitution: the substitution of childishness for childlessness.

In the absence of a family, both Edward and Christine were in need of some other form of fulfilment. Country life had its compensations, but as a longterm prospect, and for people with a cosmopolitan outlook, its attractions soon palled. More and more they found themselves turning towards Dublin as an outlet. Sooner than could possibly be expected, an ideal occupation for Edward was to present itself.

In 1931 Gordon Glenavy retired from the board of the Dublin Gate Theatre. In its financially precarious situation it was up to the board to choose his successor carefully. But of course! The choice was obvious! There was that young Lord Longford who had already rescued the theatre from oblivion. With his title, his enthusiasm, his classical background, and — dare one say it — his money, there was no better man in all Ireland. He was invited. He accepted.

Christine was sure he would not be 'a sleeping director, but active and practising'. She was equally sure he was at last in the one place he had always wanted to work — an uncommercial arts theatre. She may well have discerned that the long search for an aesthetically rewarding occupation was at an end. She may even have recognised that this was, at last, the one occupation she could genuinely share without reservation. Her love of theatre notwithstanding, what she could not possibly have known at that stage was that from basement theatres to galvanised sheds,

The Georgian interior of the Gate Theatre. It was built as part of the Rotunda Assembly Rooms opened to support Dr Bartholomew Mosse's Rotunda Lying-in Hospital. Revenue fell away after the Act of Union in 1800.

even theatrically speaking, you can get too much of a good thing.

From the day Edward joined the board, he haunted the Gate Theatre, backstage as well as front. Night after night with Christine, he watched the current play from seats near the stage. In *All for Hecuba* Micheál Mac Liammóir caught them photographically: Edward 'with hands folded in dimpled content across his belly, motionless, watchful, absorbed', and Christine 'in hunched-up curves, her head a little on one side ... The head drooped a little farther towards the end of the run.'

When the show was over they went backstage and talked and talked: the construction of the play they'd just seen; that black-out at the end of Act II: the character who dies onstage — the actor had died too distressingly that night. There was so much to be discussed, so much to be learnt. Edward was like an eager schoolboy again, voracious for the technicalities of theatre.

'The best time to talk to Hilton Edwards and Micheál Mac Liammóir was late at night,' according to Christine. 'They would let us sit in their dressing-room while they took off their make-up, and then we went out to supper together; sheer pleasure for Edward and me, and also an extra meal, which must have put weight on us both.' Not on Christine, though these suppers were of the greasy kind, mixed grills and the like, in frowsy basement restaurants in and around O'Connell Street. But it was Bohemian, and for that, the tuck and the talk, Edward enjoyed every minute.

There was an occasion in February 1931, when Micheál found himself behindhand in painting the scenery for the next show. Frantic, he was taking every opportunity to catch up. The curtain had come down one night on *The Old Lady Says 'No'*, when, still in his Robert Emmet costume, he decided to put in half an hour's painting before going out to supper — that night it was to be The Savoy. He was at the top of a ladder in the scene-dock balancing a bucket of green water-paint when Hilton, washed, dressed and ready to go, shook the ladder saying: 'Come on, Micky. You can do that tomorrow.' Also hovering in the scene-dock were Edward and Christine, Edward becoming increasingly anxious about his supper. Full of concentration, Micheál went on with his work.

For half an hour Hilton continued to torment him. 'Come on, come on, hurry up, Micky,' he shouted, finally giving the ladder one rattling good shake. 'Take your hands off that ladder, you bloody drone,' Micheál shouted from the heights, a threatening menace in his voice. But it didn't stop Hilton, who resumed his tormenting. Suddenly exasperated, Micheál tipped the bucket of green paint over him. Violently furious, Hilton pulled the ladder from under him and a fight began. Edward and Christine looked on helplessly until, in falling to the floor, The Boys brought Christine with them — down on her bottom in the scene-dock. While Edward was prepared to watch a manly fight to its finish, knocking Christine over was another matter. Grabbing a shillelagh, a prop from *The Old Lady*, he waved it over the struggling actors crying out: 'The next man to move, I fell to the ground.' His choice of language presumably reflected the degree of his fury.

For The Boys — Hilton and Micheál never outlived their popular title — it was social uplift of a special kind to be seen supping in public with the aristocracy. Supper, in fact, entailed another performance, no less histrionic than the earlier one in the theatre. But this act would be directed specifically at the gawking groundlings at the other tables, who might thus be lured one day to patronise the Gate.

Indeed, the theatre's clientele had shown an upturn. Curiosity was growing. People agreed that after your first visit the Gate grew on you. And of course, the presence of Edward and Christine in and around the place brought to it an air of respectability, of which it stood in some need. Mac Liammóir's colourful flamboyance aroused a suspicious curiosity in Dublin's uptight ultra-conservative circles.

Indeed, the survival of the Gate Theatre in the stifling, inward-looking cultural atmosphere of the thirties was a miracle in itself, difficult to explain. In the peculiarly repressive form of Christianity prevalent in the Dublin of that period, rumour ran riot and knowing heads nodded: communism and the fleshpots were the true intent of the Gate Theatre; their plays were so way out that young people should be discouraged from frequenting the place; and as for backstage participation — well that of course made you a galloping fellow-traveller.

As an instance of how the place should be avoided, the 'Holy Joes' would cite the dutiful absence of priests and politicians from the theatre's clientele. True, the likelihood of politicians like de Valera ever attending a performance at the Gate Theatre, or indeed at any theatre, was as remote as a trip by the Pope to the Folies-Bergère. As for priests, their attendance at any theatre was banned by the Archbishop of Dublin. Mercifully, what the 'Holy Joes' didn't know was that, with the most welcome approval of Hilton and Micheál, priests in large numbers attended the dress rehearsals of any play that interested them. Thus was avoided that most heinous of Irish moral evils — that of "giving scandal".

It was the period when the higher echelons of the 'Holy Joes' loved to bandy the word censorship. Many a piece of literature and many a harmless film had meanings read into them that their creators never intended, but were sufficient to have them banned. Through an oversight somewhere there was no stage censorship in Ireland — officially, that is. But of course there was the unofficial censorship: the bottle-breaking and the pepper-throwing pickets; the shocked letters to the agony columns from the Catholic mothers-of-ten, and of course there were those of adolescent mental age who liked to hawk their schoolboy innuendo, like calling Mac Liammóir's performance in *The Marriage of Saint Francis* by Henri Gheon, the marriage of Saint Francis of a sissy. The mission of the Gate Theatre in helping to liberalise Ireland was to be long and arduous, but despite all that little minds could do to destroy the reputation of the Gate, the theatre survived with the moral support of a handful of intellectuals, people like Edward and Christine Longford.

In those days Christine's admiration for The Boys was great: 'On the stage Hilton would play the villain and Micheál the hero, but offstage both were heroes and saints. They were perfect partners. When they were planning a production, you couldn't guess which had an idea first, they both had so many. We had ideas too, though we were only outsiders; we remembered shows we had seen and plays we had read, bare scripts of plays we wanted to see in action; and we had ideas about writing.'

Never a dullard when the subject interested him, Edward was learning rapidly. One night he brought The Boys home to Leinster Road and fed them cold turkey. He told them he'd written his first play — first that is, if you exclude those he had turned out in his nursery and at Eton. It was called *The Melians*, and it was about an insurrection on the island of Melos against the tyranny of Athens. For those quick on the uptake, there was a parallel with the Irish situation.

Christine relates that: 'Edward enjoyed writing *The Melians* much more than political propaganda. He put politics into it, but not party politics, nothing to do with Cumann na nGaedheal or Fianna Fail. The subtitle was "A Drama of Patriotism and Imperialism".' The patriots were the Melians and the imperialists were the Athenians and the date 416 BC. Certain that the lord would provide against losses, The Boys agreed *The Melians* would go on later in the year. In the meantime Edward and Christine went on holidays, this time to Hungary and Yugoslavia.

Since her schooldays Christine had had a lot of friends who were Serbs, 'bright, handsome boys who were refugees of World War I, saved by the English and picked to be sent to Oxford. Osmond Esmonde was kind to them, my mother adored them and fed them on tea and cream buns; they sang strange and beautiful folk music and danced and played fiddles. Now they were all in Belgrade, and they were the party in power: top civil servants, professors, directors of banks, editors of newspapers, and one was an Orthodox bishop, with long mane and beard and cylinder hat. It seemed the only place where an Oxford degree led straight to success.'

This discovery was the making of that holiday. Edward and Christine were lionised. The entertainment was overpowering. The speeches were overwhelming. 'Edward and I were both thanked for my mother's kindness by more people than ever knew her or me. Edward loved it.'

On their return, they moved house, just a little further up Leinster Road, to a fine stucco villa standing in its own extensive grounds. 'It was called Grosvenor Park, which we thought was West British and snobbish; we called it 123 Leinster Road, but the name was deeply engraved on the gateposts.' It was the setting for many a fundraising Gate Theatre garden party. On her own admission, the happiest years of Christine's life were spent in this house. In time, it became a site much desired by property developers and the house disappeared. I have an illustrated advertisement for the site given me by Christine and kept by her for purely sentimental reasons. She had written on it 'I. Times 24/11/78.' It describes 'a unique development of 46 town houses, Grosvenor Park, Leinster Road, Rathmines.' *Sic transit* ...

At Pakenham Hall in the summer of 1931 friends and relations with the swallows came and with the swallows went. Henry Lamb was there, pursuing his painting of the series of family portraits. Christine began her second novel, *Country Places*. Using a well-observed family called Pybus of Castlepybus in Newtownpybus, it takes humorous sideswipes at the weaknesses of the landlord classes. It contains more than an element of biography. Lambert Pybus, for instance, is a merciless send-up of a young man with dark curly hair, just down from Cambridge, and who is an extreme Irish nationalist. He creates such a shindig at the International Jumping Competition at the Horse Show that he is arrested, and spends that night in the cells having the time of his life thinking about all the patriots who had been in gaol for Ireland, especially the Protestant ones. Which of course was going further than Edward had done, or ever meant to do.

That other humorous novelist, Evelyn Waugh, was back, and so was John Betjeman. Christine and Edward were showing their sympathy for the little faun, who was suffering the humiliation of having just been divorced. Such a social and mental battering had this very English Englishman taken in his own country that he had sought their advice about purchasing a home in Ireland. But the wind and the rain of County Westmeath soon changed his mind. 'We were all glad to make Evelyn laugh,' said Christine. 'He would come down to breakfast and enquire "Who's got any funny letters this morning?" That was the professional writer, keen on the scent, and we handed them over at once as a solemn duty. He read rapidly and handed them back. The material was stored for the future.'

Evelyn Waugh must have been still around in September for the first night of Edward's play, *The Melians*, at the Gate Theatre. It had an hilarious Melian ballet danced by some high-spirited young ladies. Sitting next to Christine, Waugh regarded the principal dancer, leaping about in her transparent, trailing draperies. Throughout the dance, in purposefully audible tones, he enquired of Christine: 'Is that Edward's mistress now? She looks like Edward's mistress. Go on, Christine, is she Edward's mistress?' Waugh's holiday was doing him good, banishing his sense of bereavement.

With *The Melians* safely launched Edward sought a subject for his next play. It was the Englishman, John Betjeman, who told him about the Irishman, Joseph Sheridan Le Fanu, the first-rank writer of nineteenth-century ghost stories. Having learned about dramatic

Betty Chancellor and Coralie Carmichael in *Carmilla* in May 1932. Adapted by
Edward from the story by Le Fanu, it was John Betjeman who
gave the idea to Edward.

construction, and knowing what Hilton and Micheál could do with
scenery, lighting and music, Edward chose to dramatise *Carmilla*, the
best vampire story ever written. To facilitate many quick changes, Hilton
Edwards kept the stage as clear as possible, using only significant objects,
perfectly lit, against a background of unlit blackness, the scenes being
linked with the music of Chopin.

Carmilla was such a success that Christine too instantly contracted
that chronic disease known as playwriting. For her first effort, *Queens
and Emperors*, she turned again to Roman history. 'It was mildly funny,'
she said, 'but better forgotten, except for the kindness of Hilton and
Micheál and all concerned. Micheál gave me a magnificent backcloth of
the Coliseum with a smart Roman audience in boxes. The theatre on the
cloth was more densely filled than the Gate during the run of that Roman
holiday; but like Edward, I did better later.'

Dismal attendances still dogged the Gate. But to the sum of The Boys'
optimism must now be added Edward's. He had been made chairman of

the board of directors. Being 'Daddy of them all' made him feel good. Ideas for new plays teemed in his head. Now and then, to keep things ticking over, he had to dig deeper into his cheque book. But then, having bought his way in to his most exciting eccentricity ever, it was up to him now to support the roof that covered his house of dreams.

A Dublin woman stirred things up with a notable first play called *Youths the Season?* Mary Manning's mirror of Dublin youth introduced a whole new dimension to the Gate. It proved that classics and importations weren't compulsory. A modern play set in Dublin could, and did, stimulate attendances. In March 1932 the same gifted woman started a Gate Theatre magazine called *Motley* — 'Invest me in my motley and give me leave to speak my mind.' Edward had to pay to keep it going. In a page called 'Processional' the young editor spoke her mind. When Fianna Fail came into office for the first time in 1932, she wrote: 'We notice none of the candidates in the recent election made any promise or formulated any scheme for the improvement of the cultural life of the country. We would like to put some of our TDs up on the stage of the Gate Theatre to tell us what they are going to do about the establishment of State Theatres and properly equipped town halls throughout the country.'

The change of government meant little to the Longfords, beyond the fruitless fear of the time: what would de Valera and his 'Irregulars' do, now they were in office? Some who used to snub Edward, could now afford to fraternise, reassured that their political party was at last in the ascendant. Jack Yeats, for instance, an ardent republican, now became a friend. But these people need not have worried. Edward's interest in politics, such as it was, had waned. While he remained faithful to Cumann na nGaedheal, as one might remain faithful to a football team, he had ceased to write their propaganda for them. Like a moth to a star, Edward's concentration was now attracted to a single focus of brilliant limelight, the Dublin Gate Theatre.

It was inevitable that one day Hilton Edwards would present Micheál Mac Liammóir as Hamlet. He had promised to do so, but to Micheál the waiting time seemed interminable. He was word-perfect, for he had played Laertes on tour to Anew McMaster's Hamlet. Edward too was interested. He had a mental list of the Hamlets he had seen. He knew Micheál was right for the part — and the sooner the better, he thought.

Hamlet burst upon Dublin in February 1932. The critics who were, in the main, general duty reporters, pretended pleasant surprise. Leaving Certificate classes crowded in, and your social standing for the moment stood or fell on whether or not you had yet seen the Gate *Hamlet*.

Mac Liammóir's Hamlet would be revived many times in many places.

Micheál Mac Liammóir as
he appeared in February
1932 in his first Gate
Theatre Hamlet.

It flopped only once — inevitably, in London, where the great James Agate called it 'a broth of a Hamlet'. Believing — and rightly — that it was coals to Newcastle, Hilton Edwards had been against taking it to London. Edward was of the opposite opinion, and, for better or worse, Edward's opinion was gaining strength in the affairs of the Gate Theatre.

For the growing success of the theatre, credit must be shared by its several powerful actresses. Coralie Carmichael never received due acknowledgement for her part in the foundation of the theatre. She had been in the McMaster company with Hilton and Micheál. In many a pub and commercial room up and down the country she had listened patiently to The Boys as they poured out their dream of their own theatre in Dublin. And from the curtain-up on *Peer Gynt* at the Peacock Theatre, she had been with them through thick and thin, sometimes working for buttons and more often for less. A tall, vivacious actress, with a beautiful voice, and a staggering emotional range, Coralie Carmichael was an indispensable strut in the artistic fabric of the Gate Theatre. Edward, however, had reservations.

Meriel Moore and Betty Chancellor came later. The talents of these women ranged from the poetry of Shakespeare to the slapstick comedy of Christmas shows. On the matter of casting Hilton was strict. He had retained the duty unto himself. Edward didn't always agree with his choice, particularly the casting of actresses. Edward was developing irritating likes and dislikes on technical matters of theatre that were, as yet, beyond his understanding. But he had never feared to express his opinions, however unwelcome, and he wasn't going to change now.

A good example of unfortunate miscasting was the invitation to Edward's adored Sara Allgood, who was then in Hollywood, to play Madame Ranevsky in *The Cherry Orchard*. The younger generation rushed to the Gate to see the great Allgood, rather than Chekov's great play — she had been the brightest star of the Abbey Theatre's greatest days, they had been told. It was unfair to everybody, but mostly to the actress, who knew she wasn't right. Yet, night after night, on her first entrance, the action of the play was stopped, while Dublin clapped its hands off, saying 'welcome home' to Sally Allgood. Even Christine agreed: 'she didn't look well or right for the part; but she made me cry when she said "I love that man, I love him."' Allgood had a voice of haunting vibrancy. This was one of her last appearances in her native Dublin.

Holidays in 1932 took Edward and Christine to Dalmatia and Bosnia. Because of Le Fanu and *Carmilla*, Edward insisted on seeing Styria. It seemed little changed since Carmilla's day. 'The Styrians were kind and smiling,' according to Christine, 'and piled our plates with whipped cream.' Then home to Pakenham Hall and more cream, whipped and otherwise. In the dairyland of Ireland, Mrs Cruickshanks, the housekeeper, liked to titillate his lordship's tastes. Routinely, she sent up éclairs, meringues and every kind of exotic cream-smothered pudding. Edward ate them with a schoolboy's relish. That was before Christine began to wonder about his increasing weight.

Chapter 10

Good News and Bad

Edward suddenly wanted to see Greece, to breathe the ancient air of Athens, for, as Christine relates, he had set himself a rather extraordinary task. Encouraged, she says, by Hilton and Micheál, 'he was translating Aeschylus into English verse for the good of the Gate. They were planning to do the whole Tale of Argos, *The Oresteian Trilogy* — three plays in one night.'

From this remove in time, it seems incredible that a theatre, financially flogged, should turn back 2,500 years to the father of tragedy for a trilogy that guaranteed empty houses before the exercise had even begun. The translation of the *Oresteia* was the kind of academic exercise beloved by Edward. Its production on the stage would complete his bliss. As for The Boys, why should they worry if the damn thing played to empty houses? They would go back to the Ice Age for a play that was pleasing to Edward, as long as it came packaged with his gold-labelled guarantee.

The mixture of the artistic talents of Edward Longford, of Hilton Edwards and of Micheál Mac Liammóir in the early 1930s combined to make an elixir of theatrical life never again likely to be seen in Ireland. Edward's academic genius for translation into verse, Hilton's imaginative use of movement, lighting and music (the theatre theatrical was his credo), Micheál's unabashed use of colour in sets and costumes and, above all, Edward's bottomless purse — here indeed were the makings of theatrical treasure trove, teeming with every dramatic delight. But Dublin, dilatory as usual, allowed these golden days to pass it by, unnoted until it was too late.

In presenting the *Oresteia* of Aeschylus, Edward's stated object was to give the public 'in an easily accessible form what is, beyond doubt, one of the greatest, as well as one of the earliest of dramatic works.' He translated and versified the first two plays of the trilogy, *Agamemnon* and the *Drink Offering*, while Christine translated the third, *The Furies*. 'It might be said that I copied Edward, or I caught his madness,' she said. Titled *Agamemnon*, the trilogy was presented in February 1933. Predictably, it played to empty houses. Predictably too, Edward nobly stood over the losses. He was having the time of his life — even if his bank balance was taking a battering.

Agamemnon had a cast of fifty, including the youthful Cyril Cusack. Through its chorus of handmaids, it introduced two young actresses, both one day to become identified with Longford Productions. Christine remembered them: 'Eve Watkinson, from Trinity College, who could fence and play boys, covered her Eton crop with a mourning veil, and Cathleen Delany in clustering curls was a figure from an Attic funeral urn.'

Within a month of the disastrous *Agamemnon*, another Longford play was on the Gate stage, this time Christine's *Mr Jiggins of Jigginstown*. This play was based on a real-life oddity, Adolphus Cooke of Cookesborough, County Westmeath, who disappointed the expectations of his pretentious relatives by leaving his fortune to found a non-denominational school for boys. Cooke believed he would be reincarnated as a fox, and, sure enough, on the day of his funeral a fox was seen in his kitchen.

In Christine's version Adolphus of Cookesborough became Horatio Jiggins of Jigginstown. Into Mr Jiggins she had injected a pep tonic, making him a figure of high comedy. 'It might almost be called a success,' she said. 'I was learning sense and writing about Westmeath.' Despite a general recession, Jiggins played happily for some weeks. Then the failure of the public to understand Denis Johnston's modern *Everyman*, *A Bride for the Unicorn*, plunged the Gate directors into another state of gloom.

In fact, the slump had also hit Pakenham Hall. For his reckless prodigality, or artistic philanthropy — depending upon your point of view — Edward had his knuckles discreetly rapped by the family land agent and banker. 'Mr Stewart's office sent us a polite warning about the state of the world, and advised us to cut down expenses. Mr George Stewart had been succeeded by his son Robert, equally wise and kind; he didn't speak with the same air of command as his father, but he made himself felt all the same. We economised without tears, and moved to a smaller dining-room nearer the kitchen; here the food was hotter, and we ate more rather than less.'

A cut in the domestic staff was another economy. The head housemaid went, and was followed by some loyal cronies. 'This marked an epoch in social history,' Christine wrote. 'Three Protestant housemaids gave place to two Catholics, girls whose fathers worked on the farm. Until now local girls had been banned as unsafe, because they might "talk in the town"; but we had no secrets, the Orange garrison was no more, and good riddance.'

Nor did Mr Stewart consider the Hand-Loom Shop viable. 'Nor was it!'

admitted Christine, 'but it was very pleasant and national. Mr Copithorne's ideas expanded more than the bank balance; he brought sample goods to the "Foire de Paris" and made many friends, so he told us, though quota restrictions and import duties stopped them from giving him orders. He studied the fashions and saw as much nightlife as was right for a Plymouth Brother.'

England was feeling the slump even more than Ireland. Suffering acutely from her rheumatism, Edward's mother had moved from Mayfair to Knightsbridge, which she called 'a new part of London'. Edward and Christine saw her on their way through London. As always, her manner was quiet, hesitant, but as Mary Clive describes it: 'She had such an odd mind that you never knew how she would react to anything, so there were no safe topics of conversation.' Everyone was in awe of her, even Edward, her white-headed boy.

Stringent economies and, at the same time, trips to Greece didn't seem to make much sense. But Christine was quite clear-headed: Greece for Edward was a widening of horizons, an important stimulus to his writing. Besides, 'he was thirty and I was thirty-two, and we knew what we were doing. We were going to Greece for two weeks, carefully planned. Only two weeks? Yes, we weren't ruined, but we had to be careful and Edward was worried about the Gate.' An uncharacteristic note of pique is discernible in those words. Did Christine fear the best had been, the worst was yet to come — theatrically speaking, that is?

A passionate lover of Greece, Anew McMaster wanted to do a Greek play, not in Dublin, but in the country, where he always enraptured audiences. He asked Edward to do a translation of *Oedipus* in blank verse. 'It doesn't matter how blank?' Edward asked. 'Blank as you like,' 'Mac' replied, 'blank as blank, with rhyme for the choruses.' Edward was flattered. Already he could see 'Mac' as Oedipus. But he didn't begin his translation immediately.

'That summer Edward did something even more strange than translating Greek,' Christine recalled. 'One July morning we were alone at Pakenham Hall. It was too bright for fishing, too hot for walking, so he sat in the library and wrote in an exercise book. I strolled around the house and we met for lunch, and he told me he was writing a play. We met again for tea and for supper, and at bedtime he told me I could read it next morning, as far as it went ... Next morning I expected to see an act of the play. Edward brought me two acts and half of the third and last. There were very few lines crossed out, and he must have written continuously as if from dictation. He said "I had it all in my head." It was about Dean Swift and it was called *Yahoo*.'

Hilton Edwards as Swift in
Yahoo when it was first
produced in September
1933.

The strides Edward had made in the technicalities of playwriting showed when *Yahoo* reached the stage. He handled his material with an inspired sense of selectivity, using only what was theatrically effective. The dialogue was flawless eighteenth-century style. But it was the use of expressionism in the third act to capture the deranged mental processes of an old man which pinned audiences to their seats. In responding to their calls for 'Author' on the first night, Edward said: 'I wrote this play as a tribute to the man I regard as the father of modern Irish nationalism.'

David Sears, himself a dramatist, wrote in next day's *Irish Independent*: '*Yahoo* opens magnificently — one of the best acts ever written by an Irish dramatist ... The splendid third act shows the collapse of Swift's great genius into, in Pope's savage words "a driveller and a show". Here expressionism is used with striking success, and the author seems inspired with some of the "*saevo indignatio*" of his hero, for some of the reminders of our forgetfulness and ingratitude to Swift came like a slap in the face. The final curtain leaves us ashamed of ourselves, which is probably how the author meant us to feel.'

Christine's verdict summarises the whole affair: 'Hilton was quite terrifying, he looked like the Dean, and his personal success was immense

... *Yahoo* was one of the best things that had ever happened to Edward, or it may be one of the best he had done.' There was no doubt — *Yahoo* was Edward's masterpiece.

From his triumph Edward was soon reduced to depression. There had been a message: his mother was dying of cancer in London. 'He burst into tears,' Christine recalled. 'It was the first time I saw him cry, and the last; and our journey by the mail-boat and train that night was the worst in our lives, as we stayed awake thinking of death and his mother.'

They found her very ill, but unchanged in appearance. Because she was now helpless, there was less of her spartan regime: she had flowers, a radio, a silk counterpane. They had been told to behave normally, so they talked about books and pictures. His mother was pleased to hear Edward had been put on the board of the National Gallery. In the evenings she insisted they go out to see plays, as if it were a usual visit to London.

Summoned from Oxford, Edward's brother, Frank, burst into the bedroom, talking excitedly about some article he had just published. He was gently, but firmly, squashed. Once, Mary attempted to kiss her mother. Pushing her away, Lady Longford reminded her that she had never been very good at kissing. The saddest thing for her remaining five children was that even on her deathbed, Edward was still the only one their mother wanted to see.

Once, Lady Longford sent Edward away on a message. Alone, she talked about him to Christine: 'She said he made her perfectly happy. She was glad he was married and glad he had found work he enjoyed. At one time she had feared he was misanthropic, it was a tendency in the Pakenham family and indeed she understood it herself; but that was all over now, and he met people and made plenty of friends, didn't he? I was able to tell her he did, and that he was happy writing plays for the Gate. She began to talk of *Yahoo* and of Swift who hated the yahoo breed, and she was discussing the play when Edward came back. And that evening, while we were at some play, she died.'

The funeral was to be at Middleton in Oxfordshire, their mother's old home. Edward and Violet drove there to make the arrangements. Violet remembered her feelings that day: 'So accustomed was I to thinking of Edward and Christine moving inseparably together, I found the drive alone with him among the strangest moments in a week wracked with strangeness.'

Christine too had recollections of strange things: 'It was the first time we had seen a dead body. We had read in books that the dead might look younger and calmer than when they lived, and in this case it was true. Their mother was like a sleeping girl, her hair in two golden plaits over her shroud. Edward and Violet fell on their knees in prayer and I followed. Julia stood straight and still, detached as ever. I think she was then as much a sceptic as I had been at her age; but the habit of churchgoing and Edward's good example had brought me back to the faith of my fathers.'

Some days after the funeral Edward's sisters found a note among their mother's papers, saying she wished to be buried in London as quickly as possible, and as near as possible to the house where she died. 'She was anxious to give no trouble,' said Christine, 'and Edward and I swore to make clear our intentions about our own funerals, that "in the place where the tree falleth, there it shall be".'

While these sad proceedings were taking place in London, the year was ending in Dublin with a revival of Edward's adaptation of *Carmilla*. This was the fourth play from the Longfords, husband and wife, seen on the Gate stage in the year 1933.

A brake of some kind having been put on Edward's reckless philanthropy, the new year opened with another financial crisis at the Gate. A campaign of fund-raising began. The conflict between art and commerce was perennial. The real trouble, of course, was that the circle of Dublin's intelligentsia was too small. It was touching, but bad for business, that the cheap seats were always the best filled.

Money troubles caused board meetings to become stormy occasions. 'I'm quite sure Edward wasn't tactful,' wrote Christine. 'That was not one of his many virtues or talents. One thing was clear, that times were bad, and they disagreed about nothing but ways and means. Edward had ready cash and the Gate had none, so he paid some bills. It was as simple as that, so it seemed, and he hoped for the best. But there he was wrong. Indeed, Hilton and Micheál were suffering more than we knew.'

Yes, Hilton and Micheál were suffering. Hilton was agonising. He felt trapped by a wealthy playboy who was bidding to take everything over, lock, stock and barrel. Edward was now dictating about casting, about salaries, about contracts, about employing English actors. He had even turned down an offer of a lucrative tour to Egypt, which would have helped towards the theatre's financial independence. Hilton and Edward were natural antagonists. Hilton, the single-minded professional, viewed Edward as an interfering, screaming amateur, a spoiled boy with a new toy. For his part, Edward couldn't forgive Hilton his British nationality.

Edward could hardly be blamed so greatly. Without his money the theatre would long ago have sunk without trace. Hilton knew that. But if only Edward would realise that writing out a cheque for this and for that didn't give him the right to use the theatre solely for his own amusement. Exasperated, Hilton finally accused Edward of knowing nothing — absolutely nothing — about theatre. Edward contended that at least he was an intelligent member of the audience. Hilton begged him to remain a member of the audience and to keep out of his work.

Another irritant was the enforced cancellation of Flecker's *Hassan*, intended as the theatre's most sumptuous super-production. Poor misguided Edward expressed his disappointment. Christine reported the reaction of The Boys: 'If Edward was disappointed, their disappointment was greater; they had worked on the plans and he hadn't, they were artists and he was a rank outsider. He got on their nerves. We went out to supper together less often.'

In a chilly atmosphere, which was growing cooler, the season ended with no lowering of standards and without the theatre's domestic difficulties becoming public. Hilton and Micheál went to America to play with Orson Welles, while Edward and Christine went on holidays to Italy. The break might allow tempers to cool and mutual trust to be re-established, for it was unthinkable that any misunderstanding should be allowed to interrupt this brilliant combination of four such diverse and theatrically talented people; three self-willed men and one enigmatical woman.

Two months later The Boys returned to Dublin. 'Edward and Christine Longford were waiting to meet us at Kingsbridge Station,' Micheál records. 'The pleasure we felt at seeing them again was marred by Edward's telling us that he had once more refused the Egyptian offer.' Edward wanted to see Egypt as much as anybody, but think how many people were needed for Shakespeare — and the Gate must do Shakespeare — and what would it cost them for board and lodging? Were the terms good enough, or was it a terrible risk? Edward called it the riddle of the Sphinx.

Besides, he had always believed the mission of the Gate Theatre was to employ Irish actors to entertain Irish audiences. Hilton and Micheál believed that foreign tours could subsidise the theatre until Irish audiences decided to support it. In any case, Hilton wanted to be rid of their financial obligation to Edward and his consequent hold over them. Clearly, there were bumpy times ahead.

There were bumpy times too in the Leinster Hand-Weaving Company and the Hand-Loom Shop. Mr Copithorne fought with the charming girl assistants about their ideas of window-dressing. No better than a west Cork drapery store, he said. Anyway, the shop got on his nerves. He wanted only to make material, not to sell it, and he wanted more space to do his own spinning, dyeing and finishing. So Edward set him up in a big empty mill in Celbridge, beside the home of Swift's Vanessa, and took over the Hand-Loom Shop himself, moving it to No 6 Dawson Street. Christine thought this was 'a better place with a splendid window and plenty of room for friends and coffee and tea. The third Hand-Loom Shop became an artistic and uncommercial success. Everyone was happy about it, except our financial advisers.'

Next, to please the bank, Edward dropped being a master of hounds, and he took a job for which he was actually paid — as a director of Irish Bovril. Jokes circulated — Bovril puts beef into you! And where was Edward's high-minded Irish nationalism? — Bovril was British. 'Ah! not at all,' countered Christine, 'Bovril Saorstát Eireann employed Irish people, good Irishmen were in charge of the business, he made friends and enjoyed it. Now he could call himself a "company director", of Bovril, Leinster Hand-Weaving and the Gate. But only Bovril paid dividends.'

While the theatre was closed for the summer of 1934, Edward and Christine gathered the material, photographs, biographies and articles, for the *Gate Theatre Book*. Edited by Bulmer Hobson, it was bound in boards, gold and black and red-lettered. It was a limited edition and is now a collector's item. In the preface Edward wrote:

> The Gate Theatre is convinced that it has a distinct part in the intellectual life of Ireland, an intellectual life which for centuries past has found one of its principal outlets in the drama. The Gate is an intellectual theatre in that it presents a selection of dramatic masterpieces of all nations and all periods, chosen for their intellectual and technical significance; it was created by an Englishman and an Irishman working together in complete harmony; it excludes nothing but the inferior ... We have never received a penny of public money. The theatre is in fact a grand example of united constructive effort, relying as it does entirely on its own resources.

In the light of its financial difficulties and the differences of artistic opinion then bedevilling the theatre, the truth of Edward's last line was a little over-stretched. It was his effort to keep a brave face on things.

100

Chapter 11

The Storm and the Calm

There was a marked falling-off in the number of Longford plays produced at the Gate in 1934. Was there something significant in this? In fact, there was only one Longford play, a one act called *The New Girl*, written by Christine to fill an evening's programme. Edward had been working on his *Ascendancy*, a melodrama about his grandfather. It dealt with the weakening of the Irish Protestant ascendancy after the Act of Union. Produced in January 1935, the play fared badly, the critics and the public missing its symbolism. It was remembered principally for the young James Mason's performance as a wicked, attractive Irish rake.

The invitation to Egypt boiled up again. Hilton and Micheál were adamant; they wanted to take the company to Cairo. The British Council had guaranteed them. Edward was equally adamant: a tour would be good for the actors, and Dublin would appreciate them all the more when they came home — but what of the risks? Egypt was a long way off. He could help the Gate in Dublin, but supposing it crashed in Cairo? That might mean the end of the Gate Theatre. Of the other directors, Norman Reddin supported Edward, while Denis Johnston remained neutral.

The tension was relieved when a letter came from Anmer Hall of the Westminster Theatre in London, inviting the Gate Theatre Company to do a three-week season there in June. Everybody was delighted, including Edward. London was so much nearer home than Cairo. *The Old Lady Says 'No'* and *Yahoo* were chosen without hesitation. Hilton had reservations about *Hamlet*. Coals to Newcastle, he repeated, but Edward talked him down. *Hamlet* was to be the third play, and preparations got under way.

Meanwhile, Edward's translation of *Oedipus* (which he called and spelled *Oidipus the Tyrant*) was given an amateur production by clerical students at All Hallows College in Dublin. On the same occasion they staged Christine's translation of *Antigone*. With their knowledge of the classics and their training in speech, these students were the best of all possible amateurs. Christine did not think her translation as good as Edward's. 'I wasn't a poet, only a versifier,' she said. 'I was copying him again, or, as I prefer to think, we were overcome by the same passion.'

Oedipus set Edward off on a self-appointed task that kept him happy for years. He translated Greek plays with no thought of publication, and only a slender hope of production. After *Oedipus* he moved to Euripides and his version of the *Bacchae*, which he called *The Baccanals*, and which Longford Productions would stage in 1944. Others, which exist only in typescript, include *Medea, Hippolytus, Ajax* and *Suppliants*.

In May 1935, Edward and Christine went to Cambridge to see a production of *Yahoo*. Although different from the Gate production, Edward was thrilled with the new interpretation, particularly as they had cast Betty Chancellor as Stella. The new Vanessa was 'a whirlwind of passion, a tall dark girl called Jean Anderson whom he couldn't forget.' Of Jean Anderson, more anon.

'Edward's heart was really extraordinarily soft,' according to Micheál Mac Liammóir. For weeks after they had decided on London, and he had already given 'the most whole-hearted and generous support', he kept pleading to include this and that enthusiastic amateur. As usual, Hilton fumed. But another fare, another small salary, meant nothing to Edward. 'I'll help you over it,' he told Hilton. 'And so it went on,' said Micheál, 'and the company swarmed into the Westminster Theatre like a plague of locusts, screaming with holiday excitement.' Christine remembered another holiday touch: 'Between rehearsals the boys and girls from Dublin enjoyed the sunshine and fed the ducks in St James's Park.'

She was happy that the men in her life were at peace. 'We stayed in a small hotel with Hilton and Micheál, and there wasn't a cross word. The Boys and Edward never quarrelled except about business, and for three weeks they were a closely united front.' That was important; no Irish splits must be noticeable, because already the London gossip writers were swarming around. 'Fair, fat, rosy Lord Longford,' said the *Daily Express*. 'Likes the theatre better than public life,' said another. 'Comfortably off but unassuming.' 'May be seen carrying a cabbage home under his arm' — which Christine denied, because they grew their own cabbages.

Anew McMaster, James Mason (already working in films), and good old John Betjeman rallied in support. John publicised Edward as a rare visitor and quoted:

> The Irish peerage
> Must travel steerage
> If it has the courage
> To travel far.

'I used to imagine those lines were pure Betjeman,' said Christine, 'but John kindly ascribed them to Edward. They may have been a collaboration.'

The opening night of *Yahoo* ended with the audience cheering its head off. London was learning what the Gate was doing in Dublin and found it a pleasant surprise. Harold Hobson in *The Observer* called *Yahoo* 'the best piece of expressionism I have yet seen in the theatre ... The surging up of realism into fantasy is thrilling.' But James Agate in *The Sunday Times* thought the piece 'woefully short of humour, and this is odd since there was more innocent fun in Swift than the casual spectator of this play would imagine.'

The next hurdle was *The Old Lady Says 'No'*. Would London grasp anything of its meaning? The Irish colony certainly did. 'Though parochial in substance, the play is seldom less than universal in spirit,' said Harold Hobson. 'I found the play, the production and the acting enthralling.' *The Sunday Times* admired 'some brilliant acting, which seems to come quite naturally to Irishmen.' *The Old Lady* packed the theatre every night.

So far, so good. The reputation of the Gate in London now hinged on Mac Liammóir's Hamlet. The reviews were a mixed bag, and were, on the whole, patronising and disappointing. Yet, to a man, the London critics were intrigued with this new-style Irish Hamlet. But Hilton's judgment had been correct. But for Edward's persistence, *Hamlet* would have been left at home. Still, the visit of the Gate Company to London had been a success. It had done much to enhance the reputation of the Irish theatre, and however temporarily, it had restored peace to the Gate.

Printed Cotton, Christine's third novel, was published by Methuen in 1935, and was acclaimed another success. With her malicious wit, her swift character drawing, her acute observation of human failings and the pressures they exert on relationships, this novel is written with a new authority, a certainty of touch. Opening in a Protestant 'big house' near the Border, it moves to Dublin where its heroine is taken by her friend, Florrie, to the Dublin Arts Theatre. Identification of the theatre isn't difficult, nor are the originals of the leading actors hard to find:

> When Martin Mauleverer came on I thought he was the handsomest man I had ever seen, and I had a thrill which I believe was almost entirely aesthetic ... It was a Russian play, and the scenery was beautifully painted in bright colours. Florrie whispered to me that Martin designed all the sets. She said 'People say he's partly Russian, but I know for a fact he's partly Spanish and partly Norman-Irish. He can speak practically every language.' Then Linton Evans came on. He was playing the part of a mad Czar and looked perfectly revolting. He was mad but pathetic, and made me

Lord Longford, W.B.Yeats and Poet Laureate John Masefield at the PEN dinner given on the seventieth birthday of Yeats, 13 June 1935.

cry in places, and in places made me shiver when he let his jaw drop or twitched the muscles of his face. Florrie said he was quite young really, and looked all right in private life. He was the producer, and trained the whole company and swore at them just like the great European producers ...

Eventually, the heroine finds herself walking-on in crowd scenes at the Arts Theatre. How Linton Evans got his crowd effects directly resembles the haranguing production techniques of Hilton Edwards:

'Put more life into it ... Remember you're Irish chieftains or Viking chieftains, or whatever it is. Hold your heads up! Think of the glory of the Gael! The walk of a queen! ...'
'Left, right, left, right. My God, hasn't anyone any sense of rhythm. Not one of you could hold a job in the Salvation Army for a day.'
'Left, right, left, right, one, two, three, four, tymp! ... Tymp! I said tymp!' said Linton and put his hand to his head. 'Will somebody be kind enough to ask Fionn what has happened to the bloody tymp? If he isn't there, send him a postcard.'

In view of her successes, it is something of a mystery why Christine should totally abandon novel writing in favour of playwriting. A delightfully amusing read, which hasn't dated, *Printed Cotton* is a deadly accurate picture of the arty Dublin of the 1930s, before a division sundered the phenomenally successful directorship of the Gate Theatre.

A garden party in aid of the Gate was scheduled for Grosvenor Park. The Pakenham Hall tents, used for the school treats and the Castlepollard Show, were brought to Rathmines. Mrs Reddin and the young Reddin wives organised anything and everything to raise an honest penny. 'The Gate orchestra played and housewives made tea; fortune-tellers and roulette operated under the trees. The boys and girls who had been with us in London wore their best clothes and sold autographs, ices and flowers, and Edward sold vegetables.' With her usual humility, Christine does not say what part she played in the fundraising effort.

The new Gate season opened in October 1935, with Henri Gheon's *The Marriage of St Francis* translated by Father C. C. Martindale SJ. Dublin liked it. There were large audiences, but the cast was large too. There was no profit, and the directors were reminded that as St Francis was married to poverty, so was the Gate Theatre. 'Never mind,' said Edward, and wrote more cheques.

But, as Christine said, Hilton and Micheál had their pride. This situation couldn't go on for ever. They didn't want to be always dependent on his cheques. Board meetings went from bad to worse. The climax came when the Egyptian invitation was renewed for the third time, with, on this occasion, a heavily augmented subsidy from the government in Cairo. Acceptance, The Boys assured Edward, would mean they could at last pay something of the debts they owed him.

The storm broke at last. Edward was adamant. The Gate Theatre would not be closed, however temporarily, to facilitate a tour to Egypt. Norman Reddin supported him. Hilton and Micheál saw Egypt as the one way out, and they could see no other. That left the casting vote with Denis Johnston, described by Christine as 'the universal observer who saw both points of view.' 'Cautious, wily Denis,' said Micheál Mac Liammóir, 'retained a maddening neutrality.' Like a Solomon come to judgment, Denis Johnston finally offered a compromise that had long-term repercussions: if The Boys felt so strongly, let them go to Egypt on their own. They looked to Edward for agreement. His generosity exhausted, he made an uncharacteristic reply: their venture must be their own financial responsibility.

For better or worse, the parting of the ways was near at hand. As the Dublin Gate Theatre Company, Hilton and Micheál would begin their tour in Cairo Opera House in March 1936, while Edward began to plan the foundation of his own Longford Productions.

The split was not a split in the usual Irish sense of jealous divisionism. Jealousy was not involved. Harmony in the arts is the exception rather than the rule, and very certainly, the theatre is no exception. The Gate protagonists had endured a period of total mutual dependence, while Edward learned his theatre and Hilton and Micheál had their bills paid without question. The lord will provide, somebody had remarked unkindly. But he who paid an increasingly demanding piper very naturally began to try to call the tune. The amateur nature of his tune was resented.

Then began the years of barely disguised mutual toleration. The sundering elements were deep-rooted and implacable: on the one side, a gifted but self-willed man with an intense love of the arts and the money to indulge his whims, and on the other, two men, poverty-stricken in all but their teeming artistic invention and imagination, the elements that cast spells and make the magic of the theatre.

The five-year partnership of these three men had given Ireland a new theatre movement, whose artistry had gradually captured public attention. Briefly, it had impressed London audiences, in itself no mean achievement. Its reputation had now gone much further afield, as witness the pressing invitations of the Egyptian government. The pity was that the partnership of these men could not have been sustained to bring the Irish theatre to even greater international heights.

Remembering the brilliance of their combined achievements at the Gate in the happy days of their first careless rapture, it is an even greater regret that their parting should have generated rancour. It has been denied, but unfortunately it is true. Even Christine, with her boundless charity (and though she worked with them after Edward's death), never again felt the same warmth for The Boys as in their struggling days in the early thirties.

On 23 February 1936, the curtain rose at the Gate Theatre on the first Longford Productions presentation, *Three-Cornered Moon*, an American comedy about the slump, produced by Shelah Richards. 'With a brilliant cast' — which included Eileen Ashe, Joe Linnane and May Carey — 'the comedy becomes a masterpiece', said the *Irish Press* next day. The show was a complete success and Longford Productions had been launched.

Eugene O'Neill's *Ah, Wilderness!*, given its first European presentation by Longford Productions was another huge success, helped greatly by the young Cyril Cusack — 'the performance of his life', the *Independent* called it.

Edward was emboldened by these successes, and his next production was a greater challenge. *Armlet of Jade* was his own version of a Chinese legend, known to every Chinese schoolboy: it tells the story of the emperor's love for the lady, Armlet of Jade, who takes a younger lover and brings destruction on China; when the young man deserts her, the people demand her death and, with a breaking heart, the emperor orders her execution.

There was a large cast and time did not allow for sufficient rehearsal. 'I suffered terrors for Edward as never before,' said Christine, 'and he suffered nightmares.' Lia Clarke, the drama critic for the *Irish Press* noted: 'It was to be regretted that in a performance whose whole atmosphere demanded perfection that many actors did not know their lines.'

Smarting under the lash of justified criticism, Edward vowed that standards must never again be lowered for want of proper rehearsal time. He was still licking his wounds when he was invited to take *Armlet of Jade* to the Westminster Theatre in London for a season. This was to coincide with the great Chinese Exhibition, then running at Burlington House. Needless to say, the answer was Yes.

Armlet of Jade did good business in London and collected respectable notices for the play, the acting and the production. Mr Anmer Hall of the Westminster Theatre was so impressed that he invited the company to do *Ah, Wilderness!* for two weeks. 'It succeeded beyond our hopes,' said Christine. 'Our notices ranged from the *Morning Post* to the *News of the World* and *Ah, Wilderness!* filled a whole page with pictures in *Punch*. Quick as lightning, when the two weeks were up, Sydney Carroll transferred it to the Ambassador's Theatre, and Longford Productions reached the West End.'

But remembering the 1935 season, the newspapers persistently referred to Longford Productions as the Dublin Gate Theatre Company. Confusion ensued. When a cutting reached the management of the Cairo Opera House, Edwards and Mac Liammóir were almost accused of being fakes. They cabled London telling Edward to call himself Longford Productions, as had been agreed. With boyish mischief, Edward cabled Cairo: 'Hear you are having a wonderful season, so are we. Longford.'

The *Irish Independent* then published a letter:

Sir,
Our attention has been drawn to paragraphs in the newspapers announcing the second visit of the Dublin Gate Theatre to the Westminster Theatre. The company of the Dublin Gate Theatre, including Hilton Edwards and Micheál Mac Liammóir, is at present on tour in Egypt at the invitation of the Egyptian government and

has no connection with any other company from Dublin which may intend to visit London.

We will be obliged if you will correct any statement which you may have made to the contrary.

pp Hilton Edwards and Micheál Mac Liammóir
Isa Hughes
Sec., Dublin Gate Theatre Co., Ltd.
Alexandria. April 3 1936

By the time Hilton and Micheál returned to Dublin, rumour was rife. Newspaper headlines ran: 'The Gate Theatre to Close Down'; 'Must the Gate Go?'; 'A Matter of National Importance'. Board meetings became even more acrimonious. Liquidation of the parent company seemed the only way out. Christine summarised: 'The Boys' Egyptian tour was a success, they looked forward to doing another next year, and they couldn't work with Edward again. They issued their declaration of independence. They were ready to run a company of their own in the Gate and on tour, and were confident they could make touring pay for their seasons in Dublin.'

A meeting of shareholders gave the title Gate Theatre Productions to The Boys, and Longford Productions to Edward. It was decided that the parent company (of which Edward was still chairman) would remain in existence, with the same four directors, Hilton Edwards, Micheál Mac Liammóir, Norman Reddin and Denis Johnston, merely as the lessees of the theatre premises at the Rotunda.

Christine summarised again: 'The Gate would be leased for six months of the year to Hilton and Micheál, and for six months to Edward. The separation was final. And Longford Productions was an accepted fact.'

Chapter 12

Enter Longford Productions

Edward's Uncle Eddie, Lord Dunsany, said of the theatrical split: 'The Gate is a heresy from the Abbey and Longford Productions is a heresy from the Gate.' Edward contended that the original Gate had had the pure gospel of the Irish National Theatre, and that Longford Productions was faithful to that. 'But,' added Christine, 'all heresies claim to be the primitive church, and it was no use arguing. Heretical or schismatic or whatever we were, we had another engagement in London.'

This was another invitation to the Westminster Theatre. This time Denis Johnston produced his *Bride for the Unicorn*, with new incidental music from Arthur Duff, new front cloths from Norah McGuinness, new costumes, wigs, even new jokes. It was a huge success, the newspapers using words like, 'brilliant', and 'genius' and occasionally, 'crazy', 'obscure', 'surrealistic', 'extravagant'. 'But,' as Christine said, 'the word "genius" counterbalanced the lot.'

Intent on touring in Ireland, Edward recruited some professional actors in London to replace the Dublin part-timers who could not abandon their day-time jobs to tour. He also appointed a producer, Peter Powell, husband of Jean Anderson, who had played Vanessa in Cambridge. Jean, with Hamlyn Benson, Ronald Ibbs and Noel Iliff were to become well-known to Irish audiences. After the first Egyptian tour, Betty Chancellor, Cathleen Delany and Blake Gifford transferred to Longford Productions. Artistically, the company was now well set up.

In consultation with his producer, Edward decided to tour *Yahoo, The Moon in the Yellow River, Three-Cornered Moon*, and the most portable Shakespeare, *Twelfth Night*.

Harry Fine, a young man from Trinity who had acted and managed publicity for the Gate, was appointed manager. Christine noted: 'As he was Jewish there was some hope he was good at finance.' With a company assembled and rehearsing in Dublin, Edward sat down with his new manager and a map of Ireland. They marked the towns that had halls to let, halls of any kind, even cinemas. The itinerary was fixed: Sligo, Galway, Tralee, Limerick, Clonmel, Waterford, Kilkenny, Thurles, Cork, Belfast and Dundalk.

Encouragement came from Anew McMaster and his wife, Marjorie, a sister of Micheál Mac Liammóir. 'They told us about halls and hotels and digs, and warned us of dangers,' says Christine. '"Rats in the old town hall," "Icy blasts in the box-office," "Look out for Miss Blank, check her tots or she'll diddle you," "Beware of the bill-poster when he's drinking." But they knew helpful managers too, good town clerks and generous landladies who gave you supper after the show.'

It remained to be seen whether Edward would show the same staying-power as Mc Master, that great actor-manager who had the world at his feet, yet preferred to tour 'the smalls' of Ireland. 'Mac', who always shunned metropolitan star-treatment, used to tell a story of having gone straight from Bagenalstown to play Hamlet as guest artist of the year in the Stratford-on-Avon Memorial Theatre. 'And do you, Mr McMaster, really play in those small Irish towns?' some gushing creature asked. 'Yes, Madam,' 'Mac' answered, 'and do you know, some of them are no bigger than Stratford-on-Avon.'

It was Sligo that saw Lord Longford's debut as a travelling showman. Longford Productions opened in the Town Hall on 5 October 1936 with *Three-Cornered Moon*. Christine remembers: 'It was easy to smile in Sligo: the mayor, the sheriff, the town clerk and local enthusiasts welcomed the company. The house was full, the audience lively and wide awake. Not a joke misfired and there was a sense of occasion. Edward made a speech. From now on he always made a speech at the end, to announce the next show, not in a dinner-jacket if he could help it, but as tidy as possible, revealed at the final curtain bowing and smiling and opening his arms to his friends on the stage and in front.'

Christine always carried a needle and thread, for it wasn't unknown for Edward to burst his trousers or lose a vital button at a critical moment, necessitating an emergency mending job. While she realised he was gaining weight disgracefully, she still shied away from insisting that he diet. Indeed, she seemed to condone his love of food. He had begun the process of killing himself with kindness, and those around him, in their well-meant ignorance, merely laughed.

Galway was more formidable than Sligo. Though he had ensured beforehand that the Taibhdhearc wasn't playing, he still felt guilty at bringing English plays to the capital of the Gaeltacht. There were no such inhibitions in Tralee, where the audience loved the whole repertoire.

Limerick had its own peculiar problems. 'This town is picture-mad' somebody told them, and it was true. The old parish hall they played in was remote and uncomfortable. Audiences were scant. It seemed they preferred the warm plush of the cinemas, or the sanctity of Limerick's famous sodalities.

Twelfth Night, November 1936, with Harold Alleyne, Coralie Carmichael, Micheál Mac Liammóir and John Cowell. The front cloth was designed and painted by Micheál.

It was either on this tour, or some other when a Shakespeare play was included, that a matinée was held for the children of Limerick, and Christine allowed herself to be goaded into one of her rashly defensive actions on behalf of dear Edward. A mob of impatient children was banging on a side door waiting for admittance to the cheap seats. Eventually, their patience exhausted, they took to shouting through the chinks: 'Fuck off, Lord Longford, you can fuck off, Lord Longford.' From inside Christine heard the insults and her blood boiled. Flinging the door wide open, she shouted as she pursued the fleeing youngsters, 'And you fuck off too.' At a safe distance they stopped, rooted to the ground, as they watched her retreat into the hall. Never had they heard *that word* spoken so beautifully.

While she didn't use the word habitually, she was often amused at the horror it evoked in some people, while others gloried in throwing it around. 'Wives are often inclined to speak a more sophisticated dialect than their husbands, don't you think?' she said. It was true in her case. Edward didn't smoke or swear. Christine did both. He was religious, she was not. His worst swear word was 'bloody', and even that required some provocation.

As the tour progressed, Edward studied local histories and guide-books. In his paternalistic way, he lectured those of the company prepared to listen and to trek round grassy mounds and ruined abbeys. Waterford was exceptional, both for sightseeing and for theatre. While there was much of historical interest, it was the Theatre Royal which took Edward's special fancy. 'This theatre, our home for a week, was historic,' Christine records. 'Opened in 1784, it was the only Georgian playhouse left in the country, and still the best kind of building for showing a play.'

Waterford wasn't cinema-mad, though the Theatre Royal was usually given over to movies. 'A movie tycoon from a rival house said to Edward "They used to like Shakespeare here, but we '*edjucated*' them out of that!" Edward never forgot. He quoted those words for years.'

The cinema-theatre in Kilkenny could give Longford Productions only four nights. 'They were booked far ahead for popular films that came out of tins. Actors and costumes and settings and lights took up a great deal of room, and what a nuisance it was to change all the prices around from the back to the front and call the parterre the stalls.' Thurles was three nights only. There was little room backstage, and just enough time to unpack and pack. But the company didn't complain.

The move into Cork's legitimate theatre was heaven. The old Opera House was vast and Victorian, tiers of red plush in front and acres of room behind — 'even a bar backstage,' Christine noted, 'a thing we had never heard of.' 'The Opera', as it was fondly called, was one of Cork's many treasures. Its young manager, John Daly, made things clear to 'these Dublin intellectuals': the Gate Theatre was pretty small compared to 'The Opera'; the cast would need to project. 'It takes a good show to get by in Cork,' he warned them.

They got by creditably. 'Edward gave talks on the drama all over Cork,' said Christine, 'to the University, the Rotarians, the city fathers and Little Theatre amateurs. Wherever he went I went too, and we both enjoyed excellent food.' Here Christine confirms two things, neither of which affected their lives for the better. Firstly, that her self-assigned role no longer amounted to as much as a speaking part and was merely a walk-on as Edward's shadow. Secondly, that she enjoyed food as much as Edward, but without the same ill-effects. Christine never added an ounce too much to her weight. Her incessant smoking helped in this. She could smoke between courses and yet admire the flavour of the food. Edward on the other hand ate with concentration and with reckless disregard for the consequences.

At a big mahogany table in their bedroom at Cork's old Imperial Hotel, Christine began work on her adaptation of *Pride and Prejudice* for Longford Productions. She wanted to write more plays, and this was an exercise in technique she could practise on tour. And on the same table

Edward designed a logo for Longford Productions: a symbolic Shakespearean stage, to be printed on programmes and posters and notepaper.

From the South to the North, from Cork to Belfast, was a terrible change. 'We went from an Opera House to a Grand Opera House,' says Christine, 'but nothing else was the same. Our equipment was held up by long delays in the customs; the Black North, the frozen North, was dead on a Sunday, the stage was barely ready on Monday night. Our stage-managers suffered torments of apprehension and Edward was near persecution-mania. *Yahoo* went down well, and the Irish-Ireland lines were warmly applauded; but still he was sure that all his supporters were nationalists and the Unionists were his enemies. At the end he had to endure 'God Save the King', played with the curtain up and the cast on the stage, and our English actors were just as surprised as the Irish. Why couldn't they bring the curtain down as they did in England? The Grand Opera House had its own tradition of showmanship and it wasn't Edward's. He wasn't needed, and Harry Fine (his manager) let him escape back over the Border.'

Dundalk was the last date on the first tour of Longford Productions. The crowds stayed away. The hall was bad, Christmas was near and cold winds blew from the mountains. But they were all cheery because they were on their way home. On the last night Edward threw a breaking-up party at the Queen's Hotel. He didn't drink much, but at a party he liked to get tiddly — usually on wine — and to sing his favourite songs, or more correctly, to bellow them as loudly as possible.

The Polish national anthem, in Polish, was always included, and 'Paddlewick for Ever' from *A Bride for the Unicorn*. Then he would announce he was going to sing an indecent song in modern Greek, and nobody could be shocked. Sometimes the English public schoolboy showed itself:

I stuck my finger in a woodpecker's hole,
The woodpecker said God bless my soul,
Take it out, take it out, take it out ...

or

Shut the door, they're coming through the window,
Shut the window, they're coming through the door ...

If he thought a song might give offence he'd diddley-dee the risqué bits:

When first I met Mabel
All dressed up in sable
I thought she was able
To satisfy me ... diddley-dee

There was a song he particularly loved, perhaps because it appealed to
the rebel in him. It came from Ernst Toller's *Draw the Fires*, a play about
mutiny in the German Navy:

We fight not for our country,
We fight not for our God.
We're fighting for the bloody toffs
Who kick us in the mud.

Toller was a brilliant German dramatist who, in the early years of
World War II, was found in the wardrobe of his bedroom in a Paris hotel
hanged with one of his own ties.

Almost every year for the next twenty-five years, Longford Productions
repeated the pattern of their first Irish tour. The company varied from
time to time, but Edward and Christine were always there. Despite the
cheerlessness, the homelessness, and the inevitable punishment of this
nomadic life, they never flinched from what Edward saw as his mission:
to bring live theatre to the people of Ireland. If Christine was ever bored,
she managed to conceal it.

The Hand-Loom Shop became their central office in Dublin. From there
they announced their new season at the Gate Theatre. It opened with
Christine's *Pride and Prejudice*. James Mason, now an acclaimed film
star, came from London to play Mr Darcy. How much credit was due to
Jane Austen or Christine Longford or James Mason couldn't be
apportioned, but the combined effort was a great success.

Edward had always wanted to do *The Duchess of Malfi*, John Webster's
classical tragedy, and now he had his opportunity. Well aware it could
not possibly pay its way, he was impelled by a passion to share the beauty
of English dramatic literature with his Gate audience. There would be
many more similarly strange and exotic dramas in the future, plays which
no commercial company would dare attempt. Ireland will never know the
debt owed to Edward Longford for his reckless generosity in risking such
plays.

It was said, laughingly, that he did it to please himself — he wanted
to see these plays. Of course it was all done to please himself. Longford
Productions was the toy theatre in the attic now come to life. He was the

medieval nobleman leading his troupe of mummers to edify the peasantry. But Edward's sense of mission was there too. One way or the other, Irish theatre-goers were his beneficiaries, and are for ever in his debt.

It was through *The Duchess of Malfi* that I first met Lord and Lady Longford and their company. As a first-year medical student, I had borrowed time from my studies to 'walk-on' during the previous Edwards-Mac Liammóir season at the Gate. I had become one of those Dublin amateurs on whom the Gate Theatre so greatly depended. With the departure of Hilton and Micheál to Egypt, I had returned to medical school determined to catch up on chemistry and physics, when a postcard arrived: I had been cast by Longford Productions as Roderigo in *The Duchess of Malfi*. It was a temptation I couldn't resist. With St Augustine I prayed: 'Give me chastity and continency, but do not give it yet'. But I never had regrets. In due course I became a doctor, but in the meantime what I learned at the Gate Theatre always stood me in good stead: public speaking, lecturing and of course the warmth of lifelong friendships peculiar to theatre people — 'the eternal brotherhood of mummery'. Hilton Edwards used to say, 'We taught him his bedside manner at the Gate Theatre.' If there is an element of acting in the 'bedside manner', then perhaps he was right.

Peter Powell's rehearsals were no less exhausting than Hilton's. Hard work and exactitude were expected — demanded. Two things were noticeable in Longford Productions: the absence of the vicious temperamental outbursts between Hilton and Micheál, and awareness of the ever-present Longfords, as, muffled against the freezing cold, they sat in the front stalls, nodding and whispering in critical intrigue.

There had been rumours that *The Duchess of Malfi*, full of murders, and with a wicked Cardinal who saw visions of hell, and his seductive mistress, would shock a Catholic public. The public did come but in small numbers — the old faithful of the Gate weren't so easily shocked.

Shortly afterwards, there were posters outside the theatre: 'Lord Longford presents *Lord Adrian* by Lord Dunsany.' Dunsany was Edward's Uncle Eddie. As a preliminary, the author, with the stage to himself, read his play to the cast — something that was unheard of. Bored but obedient, the cast spent a shivering afternoon sitting in the stalls listening, principally to Edward and Christine as they laughed obligingly on all the right cues. Dunsany had a lisp and as a character in his play was called Bessie Branson, the cast, of course, laughed on all the wrong cues. The afternoon was redeemed by a lavish tea-party arranged by

Our Cartoonist sees "Anything But the Truth" at the Gate.

Anything But The Truth by Christine received a poor press, but packed the theatre in April 1937. It was included in the repertoire for the Longford season at the Westminster Theatre, London, later that year. The cartoon includes the author of this book.

Christine — masses of sandwiches and cakes; and Edward danced attendance on his Uncle Eddie, like a small boy trying to impress his schoolmaster.

But we hadn't finished with Lord Dunsany. His play was in the second week of its run when the late Austin Meldon, who had no lines to speak, warned us one night that he was going to insert a funny line during a presentation of a christening mug to the young Lord Adrian. Meldon's line was brilliant and got an uproarious laugh. We had just reached the dressing rooms afterwards when Edward came by knocking on the doors: 'Everybody on stage,' he called, 'on stage — immediately.'

Expecting a pleasant surprise — such as a transfer of the play to the West End — we found Lord Dunsany on the stage, flanked by Edward and Christine. Nobody had known he was in the house. Speaking in tones that made clear it hurt him more than it hurt us, he said he had heard lines in the play that night that he had never written; that laughter from the audience didn't excuse the liberty. He would be obliged if, for the rest of the run, all actors would kindly keep to the script he had set down for them. Silent throughout, Edward then waved his hand, dismissing the company. We left the stage like schoolchildren in disgrace.

To make my break with the theatre more difficult, I had been put on the pay-roll. Ten shillings a week in the 1930s was *money* to a penniless medical student. So I continued, week after week and play after play. The Gate had a so-called Green Room. It was off the beaten track and, unlike the old Abbey Theatre Green Room, wasn't frequented. It was ideal for quietly reading up anatomy and physiology. Indeed, I convinced myself I did more study there than I would have done at home.

Jean Anderson, with her fascinating voice and medieval good looks, became a tower of strength in Longford Productions. Her name will be familiar to another generation for the part she played as the universally understanding mother of three ambitious sons in the long-running BBC TV serial, *The Brothers* in the 1970s. As Longford's first leading lady, she brought a new and fresh charm to every role. Her Rosalind in *As You Like It* caught the scent of the musk-rose in the hidden places of the Forest of Arden.

But that production is noteworthy for another reason. Throughout the rehearsals the producer read the part Shakespeare called 'A person representing Hymen.' The character appears briefly at the finale to tie up the amorous knots. When the dress rehearsal had reached the point of this character's entrance, there was a pause. Then a rostrum creaked as if about to crash. Shrouded in white, a massive figure appeared, grasping a long white wand. Waving its wand with childlike gestures, it declaimed:

Peace, ho! I bar confusion:
'Tis I must make conclusion
Of these most strange events ...

There were sniggers as recognition dawned. It was Edward himself, making his first appearance as an actor. 'George Bingoe' the programme said. Christine liked to believe that 'his triumph was that he was not recognised.' But that was wrong, of course. Edward's voice was too distinctive and nobody could have been fooled; besides, his girth alone gave him away. The occasion was another mark of his deep personal devotion to the theatre, particularly the classical theatre — for I can't believe Edward Longford would have gone on stage in anything less worthy than a Shakespearean role. He played Hymen throughout the next tour.

Near the end of the season — and that much nearer my examination

— I was cast as a stage-Irish butler in Christine's latest play, called *Anything but the Truth*. It was set in an Irish 'big house', and hinged on a weekend house-party. It was frightfully sophisticated, with sparkling Coward-like dialogue. Packed houses laughed happily, but the press was strangely indifferent. *TCD Miscellany* was typical: 'Hamlyn Benson and Robert Hennesssy are cast in ideal roles, and their acting, their very presence is a joy to watch. The latter does look like he *is* an Irish country gentleman; but apart from him, the passing mention of Killarney and John Cowell as the butler, there seems no reason why one should strain one's imagination to conjure up an Irish country house. The weekend, moreover, is quite an alien institution in such a place.'

Christine was, naturally, disappointed: 'At the time I thought it was amusing. The jokes hit their mark and I had an excellent cast. Still, what was the point? What was the idea, if any? I imagined I had one, but somehow it failed to emerge.'

The trouble lay with Edward. He never gave Christine sufficient time to work on her plays, especially time to revise them. As fast as she could type what should have been a first draft, he was whisking the pages away to get the play into rehearsal. Had her gift been nurtured, and not forced, Christine might have become a playwright of some stature. Yet, her self-abnegation included her work as a dramatist, as well as everything else. She always maintained that if her husband hadn't been a theatrical impressario, no play of her's would ever have seen the light of any stage.

Longford Productions finished its first regular season at the Gate with *Carmilla*, Edward's adaptation from J. Sheridan Le Fanu. Hilton and Micheál then took over the theatre. The Gate was now open all the year round, and the staff securely employed. There were two companies of professional actors operating, and the Dublin freelancers worked with both. Playgoers had accepted the Gate Theatre split as not a bad thing.

Chapter 13

'A Deep-laid Plan'

For most people becoming a theatrical proprietor would mean a greatly increased expenditure of nervous energy. For Edward and Christine it seemed only to make smoother the even tenor of their lives. Edward's humours of course had to be sensitively reflected, and acted upon, by Christine. When he was happy, so was she. It was, therefore, a matter of some importance that Edward's contentment should be sustained, and that nothing should ever be risked which might precipitate an outburst of his stupidly bold-baby tantrums. From a theatrical point of view, the greatest advantage he had over other managements was his personal wealth. He had bought his way to the summit of Irish theatre. On his way up he had learned how to avoid the pitfalls. Come what might, he intended to maintain his exalted position, despite the periodic nudgings from the family financial advisers.

Like theatrical seasons, summers at Pakenham Hall had assumed a pattern: Mrs Trew's annual visit, the school treats and of course the Castlepollard Show, when the Longford trophies had to be presented. Then the Pakenham Hall tents would be folded and despatched to Rathmines for the Gate Theatre Garden Party. Since the split, Mrs Reddin's charitable funds went to neither company, but to the Gate Theatre board for the maintenance of that part of the Rotunda building leased by them.

The Hand-Loom Shop also required attention. The Longfords' various duties were never delegated, or undertaken singly by one or the other. It seemed natural, indeed necessary, that every duty should be shared by Edward and Christine. They even shared the supervision of the Hand-Loom Shop stand at the Horse Show. Mr Copithorne, who was still hand-weaving in the ruined mill at Celbridge, kept the Hand-Loom Shop supplied with good stuff. He experimented with dyes. Killiney Blue, for instance, he copied from a pebble he had picked up on the beach one Sunday.

Their fashion expert was Noël Delany, one of two sisters who distinguished themselves in the lives of Edward and Christine. Noël was 'tall, pale, sinuous and exotic — elegant in a costume of any period'. Cathleen, the actress, a colleen with a head of clustering curls, was more

Above: Christine, in one of
the best photographs ever
done of her.
Right: Edward, in a typical
pose — before he became
grossly overweight.

famous. She was the *ingénue* of Longford Productions.

Long before the split, Edward had come home one day and said to Christine, 'We've got a new girl at the theatre.'

'What's she like?' Christine had asked.

'A cross between Helen of Troy and Paddy the Next Best Thing,' he said. That was Cathleen Delany's introduction to the Longfords and the Gate Theatre.

After the first Edwards-Mac Liammóir tour to Egypt, she joined Edward Longford's company at its inception, and became a part of Edward and Christine's 'family'. They even approved her marriage 'to an ideal husband', as Christine called him: 'John O'Dea didn't stop Cathleen from acting. He was an artist himself, a painter, an engineer by profession, a traveller of all Europe, a humorist, a philosopher.' Those who remember *Dublin Opinion*, will remember his distinctive cartoons, signed JOD. They are as relevant today as in the forties and fifties when he first published them.

From September to November 1937, Longford Productions did another London season at the Westminster Theatre. The repertoire included *Carmilla, Yahoo, The Moon in the Yellow River, Youth's the Season* and Christine's *Anything but the Truth*. Though it would have been exciting to go to London in the part I had created in Christine's play, I had made the painful break with the company three months earlier. Henceforth, it must be medicine only. And though I never acted on-stage in London, that bedside manner they had taught me at the Gate Theatre would soon come into use in comforting London's terrified sick and injured in the hell-fire of Hitler's bombs and rockets.

This was not a happy season at the Westminster Theatre. As Christine said: 'The curse of repertory was on us, we hadn't enough time. As a result the season was more rough than smooth.' Once again, her play got poor notices. 'I never tried to write a commercial play again,' she said, 'and I don't think I ever again involved Longford Productions in such a financial loss.' *Yahoo* was the last play of their season, and once again, it triumphed, 'and our season ended happily after all.'

The year 1938 marked a new departure in Longford Productions. Harry Fine, their manager, left. Edward took his place and managed the company from then on. Now there was no facet of theatre that he had neglected to study. 'I have always tried to keep up a high standard,' he said, 'and to avoid rubbishy plays and works of momentary interest, chosen for the publicity value of their titles. I have also refused to allow the Gate to become the theatre of a small coterie, and have always attempted to make our appeal as wide as possible, shunning both commercialism and artistic snobbery.'

Self-effacingly, he doesn't add that but for his generous subsidies, the seats should have cost four to six times more than they did. Until at least the late 1940s, seats at the Gate Theatre cost 4s., 3s., 2s.6d., and 1s. The 'shillingies', as we knew them, were at the back of the auditorium. While they weren't tip-up, they *did* have the best view of the stage.

Amongst his actors Edward was accepted as a theatrical impressario, but as a theatre manager they found him less well cast. True, he carried authority, but he lacked the forgiveness of even a stingy father-confessor. Indeed his mien discouraged confidences. In conversation he still looked at your tie instead of your face. You had to be careful what you said, even how you said it, or risk the wrath of the gods in the shape of one of Edward's celebrated tantrums. Oddly, Christine might have made a better manager. She was more astute in weighing the best intentions of business associates, but, of course, wilful as usual, Edward wouldn't take her advice. And when things went wrong, he'd wail his banshee wail: 'It's all a plot — a plot to ruin me.' Confused and embarrassed, Christine would try to defuse the situation. 'Edward is being difficult, isn't he?' she would throw out at anybody near at hand, without of course expecting them to agree. It was just her way of cooling things.

Edward had been in management for two years when Denis Johnston assessed the needs of a successful Dublin theatre: a company, a policy and authors. In a generalisation, he called the Abbey an author's theatre, the Gate an actor's theatre and Longford Productions a manager's theatre. For all that, like the British at war, Edward muddled through to his own satisfaction, but it would be impossible to compute the financial losses he suffered as a result of his unwillingness to accept professional advice, no matter how expert the adviser.

The 1938 season was launched adventurously with *King Henry IV*, Parts One and Two. Both parts had to be played in one evening, to show the whole shape and development of the plot. Peter Powell's judicious cutting and production avoided diminishing the character of the king. Music, lighting, settings and of course Edward's costumes, made *King Henry IV* a memorable event. Having praised it lavishly, Christine adds: 'But I'm not and never have been a dramatic critic. If I claimed to be impartial, who would believe me? I was an enthusiast for Longford Productions.'

Her own contribution to the 1938 season was her adaptation of Maria Edgeworth's classic, *The Absentee*, about a dim Irish peer and his wife, who, though social misfits, wasted their substance in London. The production was noteworthy because — to quote Christine — 'John

122

Betjeman painted some lovely designs for Lady Clonbrony's drawing-room, draped like a Turkish tent, and collaborated by post with Eric Adeney our artist. I copied fashion-plates of the year 1810.'

Edward did a translation of Molière's *Tartufe* which he had seen in Paris years before. It was in snappy rhyme, including slang like 'That shook you' and 'I'm no angel'. Anew Mc Master had a theory that rhyme didn't suit tragedy, but that for comedy it was first-rate. Part of Orgon's speech on Tartufe, the hypocrite in church, illustrates Edward's style:

> Oh! Had you seen how first I met the man,
> I know you'd love him as I only can.
> To church he came each day, with gentle air,
> And every day he knelt beside me there,
> And drew the attention of the congregation
> By the fierce ardour of his adoration.
> He sighed, he flung himself upon the ground
> And kissed it in humility profound,
> And when I left the church, he rushed before
> To offer holy water at the door.
> His man, full apt his zeal to imitate,
> Told me his virtues and his poor estate.
> I gave him alms, of which, through modesty,
> He always tried to give back part to me.
> 'It is too much by half,' he said, or 'No!
> I don't deserve the pity that you show.'
> I would not take it, so in front of me
> He flung the alms to poorer men than he,
> Till heaven bade me bring him here to dwell.
> And since that time have all things prospered well.
> For my good name he cares as for his life,
> *And even takes great interest in my wife,*
> Reports when eyes are made at her by fellows,
> And is of her six times than I more jealous.

It was decided, perhaps unwisely, to produce *Tartufe* in modern dress. *The Irish Times* thought that while Molière's masterpiece, like *Hamlet*, could stand modern dress 'it cannot be said to be improved by it. It [the play] could not be brought closer for our enjoyment than its own lines bring it.' For all that, *Tartufe* was a remarkable success for Edward, and for Longford Productions, and it was a personal triumph for Hamlyn Benson, the rotund actor who became an institution in the Irish theatre.

Hilton Edwards received so many mistaken congratulations on *Tartufe* that he gave up denying any responsibility for it.

Within the company, Longford Productions was known informally as 'Longford Prods'. Christine recalls that 'a regular member on contract was called a "Prod", a name that suggested the Protestant heresy; but in their theatrical faith they were strict and devout. They believed in the theatre ancient and modern. The Prod's programme took on a pattern: classical first, new plays next, but above all others Shakespeare, Molière, Ibsen, Wilde and Shaw.'

Longford Prods' second Irish tour was a great advance on the first. More plays and more actors were included, and more towns were booked. Their first night, in the County Hall, Mullingar, opened to 'Standing Room Only' and Edward was welcomed as a local boy. But the occasion was memorable for another reason: soon after the curtain rose on *Yahoo*, the lights failed.

'It wasn't our fault,' Christine pleads, 'the Shannon Scheme had an accident and the town was blacked out. The curtain came down and Edward appeared by lamplight. We had some candlesticks and the County Council provided more; backstage lamps flickered and candles guttered in bottles and cups and saucers. Presently, amid wild applause, *Yahoo* was resumed, looking perfectly Georgian, and Longford Prods played up to the top of their form.' This would not be the last unplanned blackout while on tour.

St Joseph's Temperance Hall in Longford was also packed every night. Not just once, but again and again, Edward was told 'You have a good name in Longford.' Two presentations provided special local interest: *Yahoo* by Lord Longford and *The Absentee* by Maria Edgeworth, who was a Longford woman.

Mc Master used to say about Irish country towns: 'You'll find a good hall and bad digs and vice versa.' Of nowhere was it more true than Athlone. St Mary's Hall 'was neat, clean and clerical', but the actors had to tramp the town for digs, and some had to double-up in beds in council houses. One landlady asked 'Are you from the circus?'.

Edward and Christine spared themselves such hardships: 'We stayed in hotels, and when we could, we secured a reduced rate for others, so some of the Prods stayed with us and some in digs.' In Waterford they favoured the Imperial Hotel, now demolished. 'Edward had fresh fish from the river for breakfast; every morning we heard good news at the box office, every night business leaped up and beat our earlier record, and we fell more deeply in love with the Theatre Royal.'

This season they stayed a fortnight in Cork, and 'we went back to Sligo,

Some of the Longford Productions' company outside Pakenham Hall while on tour. From left: Gladys Richards, Joan O'Rourke, Dan Treston, Maura O'Rourke, Milo O'Shea, Ann O'Connor and Edward.

Clonmel and Kilkenny and met old friends; we made new friends in the Town Hall, Nenagh, and O'Meara's Hotel; and in the Whitworth Hall, Drogheda, the City Fathers attended a gala performance of *As You Like It* in ceremonial robes. But we never crossed the Border again. It was too unpleasant, and the customs barrier gave us a good excuse.'

The climax of the 1938 tour was a three-night visit to the tiny town hall in Castlepollard, capable of seating one hundred people in comfort, or three times as many on occasions. 'Was Edward quite mad?' Christine asked herself. 'We consulted Mr Andrews and Mrs Cruickshanks, counted the beds in Pakenham Hall and provided digs. Not the best class of digs, I'm afraid, but old-fashioned, clean and cheerful. We had huge double beds and 'doubled-up' girls who would never share rooms in hotels, and they didn't complain.

'We knew what everyone liked to eat, and we gave them plenty of supper after the show. I believe Mrs Cruickshanks and Mr Andrews were on their feet for three nights. But only three nights, and in a good cause. Edward was mobilising all his resources in the cause of the theatre. His visit to Castlepollard was the most eccentric, uncommercial and characteristic event of the tour.

'Provincial touring was not economic, of course. *Nothing he did ever was*. Our prices, except in Cork, were 3s.6d. top, 2s.6d. and 1s. The tour didn't subsidise the Gate, nor the Gate the tour; *he subsidised both himself and to please himself*. We hoped and believed that Hilton and Micheál made money on tours abroad. The British Council took them to Greece and the Balkans, *while Edward brought Longford Productions to Castlepollard*.'

In the italicised lines, Christine, for the first time, weighs Edward's theatrical mission to the Irish people, and seems to find it wanting in common sense. What she hasn't allowed for is the satisfaction of Edward's sense of showmanship. In that tiny town hall in Castlepollard he revelled in the whoops of the yokels: 'Good man the landlord!' In Pakenham Hall he revelled equally in having his 'family' about him; like a dutiful father he ensured they did his bidding: early to bed and early to rise. Nor did his enthusiasm cause him to overlook his subtle feudalisms: digs in the town had been found for the stage-hands. Edward was dreaming his dream, and unlike Christine, his dream had no place for such considerations as cost-effectiveness.

Open house at Pakenham Hall for the members of his company, with all its lavish entertainment, was in stark contrast to Edward's newly acquired attitude towards his one-time contemporaries. Time was when they too were greeted heartily, but things had changed. It had begun with Frank's friends. Frank's set and Edward's didn't mix at Pakenham Hall. That was understandable. There is an inevitable divide between the friends of an elder and a younger brother. But as time passed Edward cut himself off from most of his older friends, particularly those in England. His relatives and John Betjeman were the exceptions to this. With so much talk of war perhaps he feared an influx of intellectual refugees with the outbreak of hostilities. For whatever reason, in 1938 he wrote to all his old friends telling them that he couldn't afford to have them at Pakenham Hall anymore. He even had the second floor cleared of furniture as a precaution. Mrs Trew was allowed to retain her place at the top of the house. This sudden and contradictory turn against his English friends was inexplicable, beyond being somehow connected in his mind with the advent of another British war.

The third year of Longford Productions opened in January 1939, at the

Edward spared nothing in providing costumes which were both colourfully attractive and historically correct. Here, Cathleen Delany and Vivien Dillon in *The Rivals* wear costumes of the 1780s of his design.

Gate, with *The Cherry Orchard*, with Jean Anderson playing Madame Ranevsky. She was young, but it was better than being too old. Unlike Sara Allgood, she took care of the comedy as well as the tragedy, for after all, isn't *The Cherry Orchard* called a comedy? It was Christine's favourite play and the lines: 'I love that man. I love him' still struck a strangely personal chord, evoking her feeling for Edward.

Then came their first Irish classic, Sheridan's *The Rivals*, for which Edward designed a Georgian playbill: 'The Rotunda Concert Room, Dublin, Mr Sheridan's Popular Comedy, The Rivals.' He dressed his cast lavishly, in the style of the 1780s, when the 'new rooms adjoining the Rotunda' had been built. The public responded, and once again, the crowded Ancient Concert Room became a place of eighteenth-century amusement.

'Edward was pursuing a deep-laid plan,' according to Christine. 'Having enticed the public with comedy, he proceeded to classical tragedy. He followed *The Rivals* with Marlowe's *Doctor Faustus*. Peter Powell's production conjured up heaven and hell, angels with wings and devils with horns and pitchforks and magnificent flames of hellfire.' The 'Deadly Sins' were in modern dress, 'Wrath' wearing a Nazi uniform as a sign of the times. *Faustus* was by far their most effective production to date.

Jean Anderson, John Stephenson and Simone Pakenham in Marlowe's
Doctor Faustus in March 1939.

Lord Dunsany gave them another of his weird plays, this time on the
Frankenstein theme. As before, he attended rehearsals of his play
Strange Lover. Denis Johnston produced his own play *The Golden Cuckoo*,
about a freelance obituarist who writes a notice about a scientist who is
later discovered to be alive. It contains plenty of good satirical fun and
some wisdom. For *King Lear*, Edward responded enthusiastically to
Shakespeare's stage-directions: 'Enter Lear fantastically dressed with
flowers.' He invented Pan-Celtic costumes, using a great deal of wool from
the Hand-Loom Shop. In fact, he could say in eighteenth-century style:
'All the characters new dressed in the materials of this country.' The
Longford wardrobe was growing rapidly and, for the want of storage
space, had spread into the Hand-Loom Shop.

Yeats had just died and Austin Clarke had replaced him as the best
living Irish poet. Clarke was bringing back verse to the theatre. Edward
was therefore delighted for the opportunity to present his *Sister
Eucharia*. Jean Anderson, Cathleen Delany and Nora O'Mahony played
nuns of conviction, while Blake Gifford, a devout Protestant, played a
Catholic priest who fails to deal with a difficult situation. Of course there
were critics ready to suspect Austin Clarke of attacking the clergy, but

A scene from Christine's play *Mr Supple*. The cast included Aiden Grennell, Iris Lawler and Charles Mitchel.

genuinely religious people thought *Sister Eucharia* a beautiful Catholic play.

With twelve plays produced in six months, Longford Productions completed their most successful season to date at the Gate Theatre. Despite talk of war, preparations were under way for their third tour, for wasn't there going to be peace in our time? Hadn't Mr Neville Chamberlain stymied that goose-stepping little German when he met him in the mountains at Berchtesgaden? And yet...was it for fun they had begun to dig air-raid shelters in Hyde Park? Even in Dublin they were already erecting concrete monstrosities meant to save the citizens from Nazi bombs. The stark realities materialised for Edward and Christine during that summer at Pakenham Hall.

Mrs Cruickshanks talked vaguely of the need for blackout curtains, and Christine suddenly thought that if blackout curtains were needed in the depths of County Westmeath, they would be all the more necessary in Rathmines — and at the theatre. But life must go on in the meantime.

Edward's sisters, Pansy (Lamb) and Violet (Powell), with John Betjeman and Cathleen Delany, poured tea for the annual school treats that year, organised as usual, on a strictly sectarian basis. Betjeman saw the funny side of these denominational junkets and was inspired to write a private verse on the subject, mentioning the local vicar Father Mauritz:

The Protestant tents are open to view,
The Protestant ass is tied to the tree,
The Protestant boys are loyal and true,
And Father Mauritz is coming to tea.
Slitter slaughter, holy water,
We'll bate the Papishes, every one,
We'll spit in their faces and make them run races,
The Protestant boys shall carry the gun.

Edward's Hereford bull, King Cole, won first prize at the Mullingar show, and, incidentally, got some useful photographic publicity for Longford Productions. Mrs Trew arrived, and her interest in the game of hurling grew with every visit. Then Edward's sister, Mary, arrived with a friend, Meysey Clive. They married in that winter of 1939 and 'the girls in the Hand-Loom Shop cut their photographs out of the picture papers.' Edward and Christine never saw Meysey Clive again: he was killed fighting in North Africa.

Those same picture papers, with their insistence on preparations for war, irritated some people, those who felt that if you banished all thoughts of war the damned thing would never happen. However, Longford Productions were committed to a tour. Producer Noel Iliff left, and was replaced by John Izon, who had worked at Oxford, Cambridge and the Old Vic. In the third week of August, four crowded cars, followed by a four-ton lorry and trailer laden with props and scenery, took the road to Killarney.

Sunday, 20 August 1939, was a gala occasion. Killarney's newly-furbished town hall opened to a packed house with Christine's *Mr Jiggins of Jigginstown*. But the audience was noticeably native. The English and Americans, in particular, were conspicuous by their absence. Life had suddenly become too serious to prolong holidays. Whatever lay ahead, people wanted to be at home.

Edward and Christine became unashamed tourists. 'Each day we drove as far as we dared around Kerry, and each night Edward, hastily washed and brushed up, welcomed his public with beaming smiles.' They saw Killarney's views, listened to mountain echoes, shot the rapids, and paid sixpence to see the Torc Waterfall. 'Sixpence for the prettiest waterfall ever seen,' said Thackeray, and the price hadn't gone up since. They did the grand tour of three lakes by land and water by way of the Gap of Dunloe. 'We all mounted Kerry ponies,' Christine recollects, 'sweet gentle creatures. A big one for Edward, "This pony reserved for his lordship," and mine was smaller. We were photographed with our ponies before we dismounted at Lord Brandon's cottage.'

By 2 September, when Longford Productions travelled from Killarney to Mullingar, the Germans had crossed the Polish frontier, and England and France were preparing for war. 'We saw evening papers and heard a man shouting "Up Dev". That', says Christine, 'meant Mr de Valera had forestalled the Great Powers. He had summoned the Dáil and declared our country neutral, and from that day the word "emergency" was the official name for the war which wasn't our war, but which we couldn't ignore.'

As they drove by Crooked Wood to Pakenham Hall, Edward said, 'Of course your mother must stay in Ireland.' 'You can't say must to my mother,' Christine replied.

Mrs Trew was waiting for them, and she had made up her mind. She wanted to see *Mr Jiggins of Jigginstown* in Mullingar, and then she would return to Oxford.

'I knew our emergency was her war, and we couldn't control her,' says Christine. 'Together and separately we begged her to stay. She was popular in the house, there was plenty of room and plenty of food from the farm.'

'There is more food in Ireland than in England,' said Edward. 'You don't eat much, but you'd be doing England a service by staying away.'

'You're very kind, Edward,' said Mrs Trew, 'but your argument doesn't appeal to me.'

'Can't you wait until Christmas at least?' he asked.

'I am English,' she replied, 'and I couldn't be neutral. Besides, there's my house. I must go back. The Germans didn't bomb Oxford in the last war, and they won't this time.'

Mr Andrews, the butler, tried. He told Mrs Trew the mailboat had ceased to sail, but she soon discovered that was a lie. The day after seeing *Mr Jiggins*, she took the mail-train from Mullingar. Christine never saw her mother again.

Chapter 14

Roly Poly and the War at the Gate

Britain's declaration of war caused Edward to reflect on his origins and beliefs. At Oxford he had supported the League of Nations Union. But the League had failed to stop the Italians in Abyssinia or the Japanese in Manchuria or the Germans in Austria and Czechoslovakia, and now it couldn't stop them in Poland. The League had failed in its intentions.

Edward loved Poland and France. And he didn't hate the English people, but only the old British Empire whose ghost still walked in the north-east of Ireland. In this war he would be a loyal neutral. A loyal neutral? One must sympathise with Mrs Trew's confusion when she had said: 'I can't understand Edward's attitude.'

Christine has recorded her assessment of Edward's outlook on England's war and Ireland's neutrality, and, needless to say, Edward's attitude was also Christine's: 'Above all Edward loved Ireland and hated war. From his schooldays he loved revolutions, rebellion, resistance, but hated aggression. He sang the 'Marseillaise' for the French Revolution and the 'Red Flag' for Red Russia, and wouldn't sing "God Save the King". And my sentiments were like his, as usual.

'Independently, spontaneously and before we met, we were on the same side. In the first war to end war, we were both observant children, though I was older. We both remembered how people told us it wouldn't happen again. When he was resisting the OTC at Eton, I was spreading peace propaganda at school. While he was learning Irish from Father O'Growney's handbooks, I was reading Bertrand Russell's *Justice in War-Time*. We were both militant in the cause of peace.

'Edward loved his English friends and relatives, it goes without saying. His sisters were married to Englishmen, living in England and loyal to that country, where they suffered extremely. Frank did a brave thing, he joined the British Army. Strange as it seemed and heroic, his action was more than brave, it was logical. His home and his life and career were in England; he lectured on economics at Oxford and was needed in English politics. As he wrote in *Born to Believe* and *Five Lives*, he was an Irish republican and an English socialist in one person; and with perfect consistency he could say "There was never a time when I have not been proud to call myself an Irishman." Edward's case was quite different. He owed no duty to England; he wasn't "Irish and proud of it," but Irish and thankful for it, Irish without reservation, he had no choice.'

From world events to local events — Longford Productions opened their season in Mullingar on Sunday 3 September 1939, the day England and France declared war on Germany. Mullingar had been a garrison town from the old days, and the season was well-supported by green-clad peace-keeping Irish soldiers in search of entertainment. It was the same in Athlone, where the boys in green were guarding the bridge over the Shannon. As their tour progressed, Edward and Christine took in all the places of local interest. They even climbed Croagh Patrick.

In Tuam they met trouble. Firstly, booking was bad. Commercial travellers warned them that Tuam was bad for everyone's business. They added: 'This town was rightly called Tomb.' A gloomy civil servant dealing with social welfare called it 'social ill-fare', and gave them a lecture on the economics of the West. The *béal bocht* was everywhere. Then they learned that the Archbishop was expected to die at any moment — which, of course, would mean cancelling the 'dramatics'.

'On Friday we heard the bell toll,' says Christine. 'Edward changed his coat and went hotfoot to the palace to pay his respects and to ask what we ought to do. Dr Walsh, the Archbishop's coadjutor, and soon to be his successor, was a friend of the theatre and Anew Mc Master and most sympathetic. He said there was no need to close till next day, and Saturday was always a bad night for shows in a country town. So early on Saturday we left Tuam in mourning and made our escape to the South.'

Edward loved O'Meara's Hotel in Nenagh where 'there was no shortage of butter or cream, omelettes were immense and a specialty of the house was milk-fed chicken'. Once when Edward and Christine were late for lunch, the cook reserved their chicken. Christine remembers: 'the voice of Statia, our favourite waitress in Ireland, rang out as she called down a lift "Chicken for two priests, chicken for Lord and Lady Longford", and then in a lower tone, "Mutton for two commercials". Her protocol placed us correctly between the church and commerce. Though our product was uncommercial we called it "business".'

It was at O'Meara's Hotel that Edward's bed collapsed with a loud crash, bringing excited actors and hysterical actresses from their rooms to the corridors in confusion — much to his annoyance and to Christine's embarrassment. It was not to be the last similar occurrence.

'Still the best of all dates was Waterford,' she contends. '*Urbs Intacta*, the maiden city remained untouched by emergencies. This year we had a Georgian play for their Theatre Royal. Edward glowed with pride as he presented *The Rivals*, first seen here in 1792, and our audience was more demonstrative than in Dublin. Alderman Tadhg (or Teddy) Lynch told us he wanted to see his city the social and cultural Mecca of Ireland, like Bath in Georgian England.'

In their room overlooking The Mall, Edward drew costume designs for *She Stoops to Conquer*, while Christine worked on another play. 'You could stay here a month and welcome,' said Paddy the boots. 'We said we were sorry we couldn't. The films were booked in the theatre and we had to travel. "You have a grand life," he said, and we couldn't deny it. We were stage-struck for life, and our stages were all over Ireland, south of the Border.'

Christine believed that but for Edward she would never have walked through a stage-door. Nor would she have written plays, much less had them produced. In spite of the façade of enjoyment, touring for her meant endurance and hard work, and the continual and diplomatic support, guidance and supervision of Edward. His public independence and private dependence — the latter total in its nature — were enervating. Her real interest in touring was in the incidentals, the countryside they traversed, the 'characters' in the commercial rooms of small-town hotels, from whom she took much of the material used in her later plays. Though she had respect for people's values, she had an immense curiosity about their lives. Her interest drew their confidences, satisfying the writer's need for copy. But for all that, there were times when even Christine couldn't hide her boredom. Indeed, once she confessed to Cathleen Delany that on the long tiresome journeys there were times when she prayed that Edward's car would crash and kill them both.

The onset of war did not immediately affect the plans of Longford Productions. Their tour continued through the autumn of 1939, winding up in Castlepollard before Christmas, with the company as guests at Pakenham Hall. The lasting impression of actors and actresses of that hospitable castle is not of its Great Hall, or its magnificent library or even its moat and dungeons, but of the amount of delectable food provided and consumed. Of all meals, the lavishness of breakfast — timed strictly for nine o'clock — seemed to capture their fancy. The sideboard groaned with silver dishes: bacon and eggs, sausages, pudding, tomatoes, scrambled, poached and boiled eggs, kippers, sardines and sometimes fresh trout. Edward would have a generous helping of everything and would strongly encourage his guests to do the same. At the other end of the table Christine would sit, folded in on herself, fondling a cup of black coffee between her cold palms, the inevitable cigarette dangling from her lips.

Jean Anderson remembers a discovery made on one of these visits to

Pakenham Hall: 'One night we were looking through a family album and came on a wedding photograph of Edward and Christine. I was struck dumb. There was this man looking like a Nordic god, slender and wonderfully handsome. Christine in contrast looking, as she so often did, as if she were trying not to be there. She never minded what she looked like.'

Though I was now immersed in medicine at the Royal College of Surgeons, I hadn't totally cast off the theatre. I was pressganged into taking an active interest in the College Dramatic Society, which meant acting. I didn't fancy the idea. I was then accused of being a theatrical snob: I would work in a professional theatre, but I wouldn't help my own college. I offered a compromise: I would write the Society a play and produce it. For my characters I drew heavily on my college friends and acquaintances to make what I called 'an inconsequential commentary on medical student life'. I called it *Birds in the Wilderness*.

Indeed, I had drawn so heavily on the characters of my friends — who were now my actors — that little acting was required of them. They had only to be themselves and all would be well. The reviews were surprisingly good, and somebody called me Ireland's only medical-student playwright. Heady stuff! But best of all: Edward and Christine turned up.

Although Edward had no time for amateurs, and believed one bad professional actor was worth ten good amateurs, he quite lost his head with excitement on this occasion. I had never seen him so outgoing. Needless to say, Christine mirrored his enthusiasm. This time Edward looked at my eyes and not at my tie, as he told me there had been nothing like this since *The Wind and the Rain*, a long-running West-End success about medical students. If I would rewrite the opening of the first act, he would transfer the production, exactly as it was, to the Gate Theatre for a week in January. My excitement was nothing to that of my cast. Those were the days when talent scouts picked up unknowns and whisked them off to fame and fortune in Pinewood or Hollywood. They were also the days before Equity existed, so there was no hindrance to Edward's extraordinary and unprofessional proposition.

In college the news had spread like wildfire. Our auditorium was packed for the remainder of the play's short pre-Christmas run. Then reality began to percolate through again. I was summoned to the office of the College Registrar, a cynical professor of chemistry of Scots origin. He asked if this was true? And was I aware the college authorities owed a responsibility to the parents of their students? And had I forgotten that some of the students concerned had examinations to face in January?

Hesitantly, I suggested the college should be proud. Was our proposition any different to a flattering invitation to the college soccer club to play Wolves at Dalymount Park? (Wolverhampton Wanderers was the team of the time.) Having first made a point of congratulating me on my play, the Registrar then firmly and finally slapped me down. He was aware that I had been play-acting at the Gate Theatre for some time. If I wished to dissipate my time foolishly that was my business, but I must understand that the college authorities could not stand by while I lured other students away from their studies. He made me feel unclean. Unless I gave in gracefully, I could become a marked man.

My dream shattered, I told the cast. There was consternation, particularly amongst the girls — indignation in fact. They were ready to challenge authority. But there was nothing for it. I went back to the Hand-Loom Shop and nearly wept into the coffee Christine gave me. Edward expressed genuine regret, while I tried, repeatedly, to express adequate gratitude. I hoped against hope that he might suggest his company doing the play, but he didn't. Nor, in reality, could I see his company playing these parts. But I was ever grateful to Edward and Christine for their generous gesture, which might have had some novelty value for Gate Theatre audiences. In college, and amongst my medical colleagues in the after years, my name was never remembered for academic distinction, but only as a 'play-actor' — that vile word peculiar to Ireland where it is used to denote some form of giddy reprobation.

The year 1940 saw some inevitable changes in the Irish theatre scene. The seasonal pattern at the Gate, for instance, was to be altered by war-time conditions. Edwards-Mac Liammóir Productions functioned more frequently at the Gaiety, leaving a vacuum at the Gate. Irish touring conditions had deteriorated so Edward gladly filled that vacuum. What the provinces lost, Dublin gladly gained, filling the theatre in appreciation of all Edward had to offer.

As usual, he purveyed the classics; Shakespeare, Sheridan and Shaw were high on his list. In the men's dressing-room this trio became bracketed vulgarly as the three shits, because in time they palled and actors yearned for the stimulus of new plays and the opportunity to create new characters. Nicknames, spoonerisms and syntactical contortions were part of life in the men's dressing-room. Edward's *Armlet of Jade* was known as *The Jaded Omelette*, while Christine's *The United Brothers* (about the tragic Sheares brothers) became *The United Buggers*. No disrespect was implied — just youthful exuberance, like the *patois* the actors derived from memorising so many eighteenth-century plays, wearing eighteenth-century costumes, and even being part of an eighteenth-century building.

While quietly making up, say, one actor would suddenly quote a line from Shakespeare, Sheridan or Marlowe. Another would 'ad lib' a reply: 'Eh gad, my lady was more grateful than a gentleman should reasonably expect.' A third would add another invented line:'T'were well she had no seamy side to her stockings.' This 'ad-libbing' could go on indefinitely. It had begun as an amusement, but it was a facility which sometimes came in useful, as when somebody 'dried' on-stage.

So much re-creation of the Elizabethan age in the eighteenth-century atmosphere of the Rotunda building cast an unreal spell over the Longford Players, whose work constrained them in a small closed world. They called it Longfordland — as they still do in reminiscence — a mythical geographical region first discovered, and so named, by Kay Casson. You 'entered' Longfordland and you made 'an exit'. Some laughed at the situation at the time, claiming that life in Longfordland was only a series of eighteenth-century romps. 'When we saw the sedan chair prop brought out', continues Kay Casson, 'we knew we were in for another trip to Longfordland' — Edward had scheduled another classic for production. Charles Mitchel (later chief news caster at RTE) says: 'The national anthem of Longfordland was "Over the Hills and Far Away".'

In retrospect, Longfordland now has something of the painful nostalgia of a child's well-remembered picture-book: sunshine and flowers, mountains of cumulus and a high sky of blue infinity. And that goes for the audience as well as for the actors. For us all, there is only a bitter-sweet remembrance of an era that can never be again.

In the public mind confusion still persisted regarding the two theatrical companies associated with the Gate Theatre. In their letter from Egypt in April 1936, to the *Irish Independent*, Hilton and Micheál had emphatically dissociated themselves from 'any other company' from the Dublin Gate Theatre. There was only one company to which their remarks could apply. Edward did not retaliate. If there was animosity, it continued to come from Hilton and Micheál, particularly Hilton, whose dislike of Edward had, if anything, grown with the split. The Boys never hid their feelings. 'That fat old fool,' they dubbed Edward, but they were still willing enough to cash in on his silent generosity. When their six-monthly leases of the theatre ended and they moved out, Edward on moving in invariably found their electricity and telephone bills unpaid. Invariably, and silently, he paid them.

When it was a matter of money, Edward was incapable of mean-mindedness. There were times when he tried to be assertive about salaries, but if the applicant had a hard-luck story, or pressed forcefully enough, Edward soon gave in. His lack of appreciation of the value of money came from his sheltered childhood, where the need for pocket-money, and the joy of spending it, were more of the experiences he had been denied.

In quietly paying those theatre bills, Edward would have taken the view he was doing it for the sake of the Gate Theatre, not because he feared to face Hilton and Micheál on the matter. Edward had no fear of actors. The only theatre people to whom he always deferred were stage-hands. In their presence his moral courage failed him. They could get drunk, they could womanise, they could even absent themselves, and Edward's reaction was, not a confrontation with the culprits, but a wily attempt to badger the already over-worked stage-management into even greater effort. It took the foundation of an actors' trade union to sort out the division of theatrical labour, but as far as salaries were concerned, Edward's rates were already generously in advance of those laid down by the newly-constituted Irish Equity.

The identities of Longford Productions and Edwards-Mac Liammóir Productions were at last clarified for the public when the 'emergency' came about in 1939. Up to that point only one company played in Dublin at any given time. Now it happened that often both were in Dublin, one occupying the Gaiety and the other the Gate. Neither suffered any diminution in support. But, sadly, the old rivalry persisted. Indeed, closer proximity may have fuelled the fire.

Periodic outbursts of bitchy rhetoric made theatre-goers aware that relationships weren't exactly cordial. One such outburst occurred in November 1940, resulting from the Edwards-Mac Liammóir presentation of Maupassant's *Boule de Suif*, adapted by Lennox Robinson as *Roly Poly*. Robinson had transferred the action from the Franco-Prussian War in 1870 to World War II in 1940, had substituted a bus for a postchaise, and had made the travellers evacuees, a word very much in use in the Europe of the time. Nobody suspected that Irish neutrality might be infringed as a result, much less that French and German moral susceptibilities might be injured. Because of the cataclysm wrought by *Roly Poly* on the Dublin theatrical scene, the story is worth recounting.

There had been titillating gossip leading up to the first night on 19 November 1940. It was an exciting occasion, appropriate to the combined talents of Maupassant and Robinson. The German and French ministers were present. (Ireland wasn't yet a republic, and diplomatically hadn't risen to the level of exchanging ambassadors.) The presence of the ministers of two nations already at war, might have indicated the possibility of offence being taken by one or the other — hardly both. During the performance the French minister, M de la Forcade, left the theatre in protest. Herr Eduard Hempel, the German minister, also protested. Such a sensation promised to make *Roly Poly* a whacking success for Edwards-Mac Liammóir, especially as the character Roly Poly (played by Shelah Richards) was a prostitute with principles and with no time for pietistical hypocrisy. But success it wasn't to be — only disaster.

The Government, always deeply concerned about the niceties of its neutrality, made a demand for the immediate withdrawal of the offensive play. On their arrival on the second night, members of the cast were shocked to find the theatre besieged by Civic Guards and a disgruntled public, all milling around in confusion. 'The Legion of Mary again,' somebody suggested, 'or Maria Duce.' Looking even more harrassed than usual, Seán Power, from behind his little box-office window, pointed frantically to a notice as he tried to explain: the play had been closed down by the Minister for Justice, but Mr Robinson had 'bought the house' so that ticket-holders could, if they wished, be admitted free of charge to judge the play for themselves. In a fury, Hilton Edwards made an impassioned speech from the stage to the newly-seated audience: he told them that on a show of hands they would give a private performance. With applause, the audience approved this proposal and the show began.

Backstage, confusion reigned for the whole of the evening. At the first interval the audience was informed that they were the guests of the author at a private performance of his play. Their money would be refunded at the box-office as they left the theatre. At the second interval it was announced that, as a gesture to the cast who would be thrown out of work, the audience had decided to make them a present of the cost of their seats. 'We were cock-a-hoop,' says Liam Gaffney, a member of the cast, 'although in those days money wasn't as important as it is today.'

At the final curtain Hilton Edwards made another speech, this time both serious and witty. He announced that as a gesture the cast had decided to present the audience's gift to charity. This was the first the dismayed cast had heard of this latest gesture, on what Liam Gaffney remembers as 'this night of gestures'. After their defiant performance of *Roly Poly* , the Gate Theatre closed until another play could be mounted.

Next day in the *Irish Press*, in a notice with reservations, Lia Clarke thought Guy de Maupassant and Lennox Robinson were at their best apart: 'During this play a potential play by Lennox Robinson alone reared its head in the scene between the German officer and Roly Poly and it reappeared in the second-last scene between the same two characters. It seemed a pity that what the author himself had to say here — what he touched upon fugitively and delicately — was not pursued and brought to its full expression. I cannot but think it was the best thing in the play because it was first-hand, spontaneous and sincere. I will still hope that a play will be evolved around these characters who for a moment last night became Lennox Robinson's own.'

Had Robinson, in his enthusiasm, gone too far? Perhaps he had — for a puritanical Irish audience, but what were the French and Germans objecting to?

On 23 November 1940, the *Irish Press* published a statement: 'Messrs Hilton Edwards and Micheál Mac Liammóir, directors of the Dublin Gate Theatre, informed the *Irish Press* last night that they have been authorised by the Department of Justice to publish a statement to the effect that the play, *Roly Poly*, by Lennox Robinson, has been withdrawn at the request of the Ministry of Justice. The request, it is understood, was made on moral grounds. The theme of the play, and the characters depicted, also made it objectionable to foreign residents who witnessed its performance. The action of *Roly Poly* is laid in France in 1940, and the characters are French and German. Members of both nationalities objected to having their countrymen associated with the subject of the play. On Wednesday night a member of the French Legation left the theatre as a protest. The French and German ministers in Dublin made representations to the Department of External Affairs.'

On 26 November a statement from Mr G. Norman Reddin, a director of the Dublin Gate Theatre, was published: 'A report appearing in the issue of your paper in regard to the production of a play written by Mr Lennox Robinson entitled *Roly Poly*, which is alleged to be a dramatisation of the famous French masterpiece, *Boule de Suif*, has come under my notice, unfortunately in a way that certainly does not please me. As a life member of the Dublin Gate Theatre, I wish absolutely to dissociate my name from the production of the play.'

The Dublin Gate Theatre, to which Mr Reddin refers, was the parent company, of which Lord Longford was Chairman, and which existed only to lease the Rotunda building as a theatre. The company, however, was not responsible for the presentation of plays. That responsibility lay with the two theatrical companies: Longford Productions and Edwards-Mac Liammóir Productions, which were two separate and distinct companies. It was the latter company which had staged Robinson's 'offensive' *Roly Poly*.

Edward and his Longford Productions were on tour. As usual in Ireland, a whiff of scandal and everybody became intensely occupied in a holier-than-thou sprint from the scene of the immorality — even literary immorality. On 6 December 1940, from Roscommon, Edward inadvisedly addressed a letter to the *Irish Press*:

Sir,
With reference to the recent production of *Roly Poly* at the Gate Theatre, and in view of the amount of public interest evoked by the withdrawal of the play, I would like to make it clear to readers of your newspaper that I am in no way responsible for the production of this play, or of any other play presented at the theatre, except those presented by Longford Productions. I would also like to make it clear that the Dublin Gate Theatre Co. Ltd., has not been responsible for any play presented at the theatre since 1936.
I am, Sir - Yours, etc.,
Longford.
Chairman, Dublin Gate Theatre Co., Ltd.
Manager, Longford Productions.'

With this denial, Edward, understandably, brought the wrath of the gods down upon his head. Had he expressed himself only as Chairman of the Dublin Gate Theatre Co, he might have got away with it. But it was in his capacity as Manager of Longford Productions that he roused The Boys' tempers and laid his neck upon the chopping block. To say the least, it was shortsighted of Edward. It was another of his enigmatical 'strokes'. His letter looked like nothing so much as taking the opportunity to rub in salt when the wounds suffered by Hilton and Micheál were still at their rawest.

On 7 December they published their reply:

Dear Sir,
We notice with pleasure that Lord Longford and Mr Norman Reddin have at last found a suitable moment to state the fact of their dissociation with our work on the stage, a fact which we ourselves have endeavoured to make quite clear to the public ever since 1936. It is also a fact, as Lord Longford points out, that the Dublin Gate Theatre Co., Ltd., of which Lord Longford, Mr Reddin, M Jammet, Mrs Bannard Cogley and ourselves are all directors, has not been responsible for any play presented at the Gate Theatre or elsewhere since that date. Had Lord Longford's publicity for his own productions been clear on this point, as ours has always been, there would be no need for the sudden avowal of what should be already obvious. We are happy that the combined work of Guy de

Maupassant and Mr Lennox Robinson should have had, among other excellencies, the result of this unexpectedly bringing to light a statement too long left unmade by any but ourselves. We started our work in Dublin in 1928, before we had ever heard of Lord Longford in connection with the world of theatre, and our mutual association during six years has already taken its place in past history.

Yours faithfully,
Micheál Mac Liammóir
Hilton Edwards
Dublin Gate Theatre Productions, Limited.'

The *Boule de Suif* affair was a sad reminder that all was far from well between the companies sharing the Gate Theatre. It showed the depth and intensity of the venom that still existed between men who, in other circumstances, might have contributed even more generously to the artistic life of their country. The lights had gone out over Europe as World War II was waged, while inside neutral Ireland the battle of the Gate continued to be waged with all the ferocity of a schoolyard fracas.

In time, peace was restored to Europe — to the world — but not to the Gate Theatre protagonists. As late as March 1960, Orson Welles, an erstwhile pupil at the Gate Theatre, appeared at Dublin's Gaiety in a medley of Falstaff scenes from Shakespeare, which he called *Chimes at Midnight*, and in which he was supported by Hilton and Micheál. Charles Mitchel, then a member of Longford Productions, was present at the first night. Welles' acting was excellent, but sadly, he made an unfortunate curtain speech in which he referred to 'the splinter group at the Gate' — the influence, no doubt, of Hilton and Micheál.

'I boohed', says Charles Mitchel, 'loud and long. I boohed in a theatre for the first time in my life.'

Chapter 15

The Rough and the Smooth

During the war years, with his company based principally in Dublin, Edward made a habit of visiting Pakenham Hall almost every weekend, because he feared the Government might consider the place for evacuees. The responsibility of his old home was becoming something of a burden. With his interests concentrated wholly on the Dublin Gate Theatre, and with, at last, the realisation that he was not to have an heir, Edward, on an impulse, offered Pakenham Hall to his younger brother, Frank, provided he paid for the furniture. Frank had heirs. Thus the continuity of the Pakenhams at Pakenham Hall would be ensured.

In *The Pebbled Shore* Elizabeth Longford tells of the confusion endured by Frank and herself in trying to adjust to the idea of living in Ireland. But eventually Edward's strange and impulsive proposition fizzled out as mysteriously as it had begun, and he continued his war-time weekly visits to Castlepollard. A willing victim as usual — or so it seemed — Christine accompanied him, despite the rigours of a tiresome train journey to Mullingar, with horse transport for the last twelve miles. Motor cars had been laid up for 'the duration' until petrol became available again.

There were times when Christine confessed she wasn't feeling up to it, but Edward, with his usual insistence, made the journey whatever the weather. She went, never openly questioning his thoughtlessness. His irritation tolerance level was so low it required only minimal frustration to precipitate tantrums on a grand scale.

Christine tried to prevent these tantrums, which had come to have a recognisable warning pattern, by indulging his every whim. When things boiled over, he would sulk, tramping heavily out of the room. Christine would quietly follow. Out of sight she would go through whatever maternal ministrations were necessary to restore his sense of equanimity. If not of pathological origins, then his flaring temper, like his lack of feeling for others, was the legacy of a spoiled boyhood. The absence of a father's discipline, and the indulgence of an adoring mother who had condoned his bad manners, had made Edward a problem man. Christine was now a surrogate mother, ready and willing to humour the big bold boy whenever his will was challenged.

At its most extreme, Edward's temper could be a frightening sight.

When somebody blundered grossly, he would first become sulkily silent. Then his tongue seemed to double up in his mouth, his face turned from red to purple, making him look like a Chinese war-god in a fit. His outburst would end with a cry: 'Christine, Christine, what'll I do now?' It resembled a typical childish tantrum carried into adult life. One may hazard a guess that perhaps the origins of Edward's tantrums wasn't wholly due to bloodymindedness. Whatever its source, the drama of the catharsis always spread gloom in the company.

When the tantrum was over, a sense of relief evidenced itself in unusually animated conversation, as if in their embarrassment people were trying to pretend that nothing strange had happened. As for Edward, he would be all sweetness and light again, as if he had just purged himself of some pesky devilry — provided that in the meantime he had intimidated his opponent into giving him his own way again. Always in dread of a resultant attack of apoplexy, Christine would sacrifice anything to prevent these frightening episodes.

One group who could cause Edward to blow his top regularly were the critics. He used to say: 'A critic won't kill a good show, but he'll throw it back three days.' Like Hilton Edwards, he was highly critical of critics, particularly those whose reviews he considered lacking in balance. Gabriel Fallon of the *Standard* was for a time Edward's particular *bête noir*. Fallon would make his presence felt at the Gate Theatre by sitting prominently in a front seat, a position Edward preferred to reserve for the more exalted. His reviews made a habit of exaggeratedly lauding young actors while on their way up. When they were established, he then invariably knocked them. Perhaps Fallon felt that young actors needed encouragement, whereas those who were established must be made sing for their suppers. At any rate, his style displeased Edward to the extent that he took the unprecedented step of banning Fallon from the Gate Theatre until he had purged his contempt, according to Edward's judicial code for erring critics. Years later, Fallon was proud to boast how warmly — how flatteringly — Edward had been pleased to welcome him back again. There is an old theatrical adage: Better to be noticed badly than not at all.

A story still extant among ex-Longford Prods concerns an incident in Galway in the 1940s. In his generosity, Edward was the first theatrical manager to give his actors contracts (which of course caused jealousy in other theatres). Margaret Lawlor's contract was principally as Secretary to Longford Productions (1940-1945), and 'to act as required' — on the stage, that is. Because of her administrative work, any parts she took were necessarily small. For one such part, the *Connaught Tribune* gave her a rave notice, ignoring the remainder of the cast — clearly what Edward considered an imbalanced review. He worked himself into one of his purple rages. Instant depression gripped the entire company. Fed up with his stupid hysterics, half of them resigned on the instant.

Edward paced the floor, wailing, disconsolately: 'The company's finished. What'll I do, Christine, the company's finished?' In the midst of the turmoil, Dan Treston, the producer of the time, slipped a gramophone record on the turntable. In a moment the public address system boomed out *The Dead March in Saul*. Edward's wail changed to a fighting challenge: 'Who the hell's put on that record?' No reply, only the strains of the funeral march. 'Who the hell's put on that record?' he yelled above the din. Nonchalantly, Kay Casson stepped up and popped a fruit drop in his mouth. He liked anything sweet. Immediately he was silenced and everyone laughed, and that was that — the end of another storm in a teaspoon.

'Edward and Christine had rather a different sense of humour,' Jean Anderson remembers. 'Christine had a very dry wit, her *bon mots* slipped in quietly and shyly but always spot on. Edward enjoyed and thrived on "disaster", or any dramatic happening.'

If a man's unreasonable rages can have any merit, then there *was* something worthy about Edward's outbursts. While they exploded in a white-hot screaming passion, they passed quickly, like a single clap of thunder and a blinding flash, and he never held any animosity towards anyone afterwards.

On the other hand, if one of his players crossed him, or caused a disagreement, that player might well find himself on the transfer list. Edward's was an iron will. He had the aristocrat's feeling for authority. He ruled one part of his kingdom like a despot, namely, that part of which actors made up the citizenry. Regarding the other part he was a moral coward. Stagehands, farmhands, domestics — their laxities, their insubordinations were ignored, were perhaps beneath his contempt. It was as if he considered his actors as his own, his children, who must be disciplined, who must be imbued with standards above the common herd.

Only one of his actors ever became a challenge to Edward's ring-master routine. Endowed with a glowing ego all his own, the unpredictable Maurice O'Brien managed to create the impression that by his presence in the company he was lending a rare professionalism to an otherwise drab outfit. Once, on a sunny Saturday afternoon when most sensible Dubliners had gone to the seaside, the Longford Players were reluctantly preparing for a matinée performance of Vanbrugh's *A Trip to Scarborough*. As Lord Foppington, O'Brien looked magnificent: cream and gold costume, powdered wig, quizzing glass — everything. Parading to and fro, like an impatient turkey-cock, an impish idea suddenly struck him. Throwing open a window overlooking Cavendish Row, he leant out loudly beseeching the passers-by: 'Give us bread, give us bread, for we're only the play-things of a mad earl.'

Edward used to tell a story about Maurice O'Brien as Volpone in Ben Jonson's play of the same name. Each day's rehearsal revealed that O'Brien was making no attempt to learn his lines. Eventually props came into use, including a large bed in which Volpone had a big scene. The producer complained that, in addition to his shaky lines, O'Brien's voice was muffled by the bedclothes. Another attempt was made to get things right. It was no more successful. And then the horrible discovery was made: O'Brien had taken the book into bed with him and was reading the lines under the bedclothes. On being stripped of his covers, he looked around, shamed innocence on his face. 'Well what do you expect for seven pounds a week?' he asked.

Not for the first time had Edward been thrown a cap intended to fit. He earned these tart rebukes by stubbornly sitting through rehearsals, nodding knowingly to Christine, and never seeming to realise that there are times when an actor and a producer must be left alone while they wrestle with the tortuous task of shaping a human character from an author's script.

There was another occasion when, due to somebody's sudden illness, Eve Watkinson had to take over three parts, in addition to her own. A period of intense rehearsing was necessary. One afternoon she was struggling to master a situation in Christine's play, *The Earl of Straw*. She was half-conscious that two people had come in and had sat down in the darkened auditorium. She struggled on with her formidable task: remembering lines, remembering moves, matching the one to the other. To help her, perhaps to urge her on, somebody erred by whispering at Eve: 'They're out there, Edward and Christine, they're out there.' In pent-up exasperation she shrieked back: 'Well they shouldn't damned well be out there.'

With the Edwards-Mac Liammóir Company at the Gaiety Theatre, Longford Productions occupied the Gate until 1943. Confinement to the Gate Theatre was irksome to Edward. His primary aim, after all, was to bring good theatre to the people of Ireland, not necessarily to Dublin alone. Besides, he loved touring. Some said it was because he got an Irish breakfast, whereas at home Christine had introduced Continental breakfast in the interest of his weight problem.

One of the compensations of having to stay in Dublin was their visits to the zoo. Both Edward and Christine loved animals, but because they were often away, ownership had to be confined to cats. Edward liked cats for themselves, Christine for their aesthetic and voluptuous qualities. There were several at Grosvenor Park. The Gate Theatre cat was Hedda, while the Hand-Loom Shop cat was Socks — each appropriately named, given their surroundings. Years later, in her old age, Christine had a fat marmalade cat called Orlando, which used to emerge from the shrubberies on Ailesbury Road to welcome her home at night. Christine spurned the comfort of an electric blanket, and allowed Orlando to sleep on her bed to supplement the warmth of her rubber bottle. Getting his Munchies in the supermarket was always more important than getting something for Christine to eat. When she died Orlando disappeared, never to be seen again.

At the zoo it was the bears which fascinated Edward and Christine. They fed them buns, to the indignation of critical onlookers: 'Wouldn't you be surprised at Lord and Lady Longford, an' a war on!' But Edward and Christine had a thing about bears. Pigeons too fascinated Edward. Studying their habits, he concluded they were cruel birds. From the gents' toilet in the Gate Theatre he used to watch their antics on the roof of the Rotunda buildings. He noted with horror how they threw their young out of the nest to launch them into flight.

There were changes in Longford Productions personnel during the war years. Producer Peter Powell left, to be replaced by Gerald Pringle with Carl Bonn as designer. John Izon arrived as an actor, later to become a distinguished producer. Christopher Casson, son of Sybil Thorndike and Sir Lewis Casson, who had begun with Edwards-Mac Liammóir on £5 a week in 1938, transferred to Longford Productions in 1942 and bettered himself by £2 a week, eventually attaining the princely salary of £10 a week. Those were the days when prettified shop-girls, without a day's training, could suddenly soar to salaries of thousands a week as actresses in the celluloid empires of London and California.

Longford's work at the Gate was improving by leaps and bounds. It now had continuity, undisturbed by the constant restlessness of touring. Writing of a production of James Bridie's *Tobias and the Angel* in February 1941, *The Irish Times* notes: 'Lord Longford's players improve with every season, and last night's production showed them at their best.' Christine said that 'the play, the acting and the production combined to make the final harmony which is called a show'. No show was allowed on-stage in which any element was neglected.

As well as memorable productions, there were individual performances of remarkable artistic merit. Martinez Sierra's *The Kingdom of God* in March 1942 so affected the emotions of audiences that it resulted in vocations to the church. Every notice was a rave notice in the manner which Edward could have considered unbalanced, but they raved in praise of one of his favourite actresses. Even his old *bête noir*, Gabriel Fallon, published a blinding panegyric: 'The play is Sister Gracia's play, and the part is Cathleen Delany's part. Her playing of it is an almost completely flawless triumph. The recently consistently fine work of this actress has reached an apex in her playing of Sister Gracia. And the apex of her Sister Gracia lies in her extremely sensitive and delicate playing of the difficult second act. I have never seen Cathleen Delany play better; I have seen few actresses play as well; and I have seen none to approach her Sister Gracia.'

Cathleen Delany believes that Sierra's Sister Gracia is one of the greatest parts ever written for a woman. She is certain it was her greatest triumph as an actress, and this despite the impact she made internationally in 1987 when she starred in John Huston's last film, *The Dead*, an adaptation of Joyce's famous short story from *Dubliners*.

Another milestone in the history of great Irish acting was Anew Mc Master in Sophocles' *Oedipus the Tyrant*, as translated by Edward. It was thirty years since Sir John Martin Harvey had done a stilted version by Professor Gilbert Murray in Dublin. Unlike Yeats, in his Abbey Theatre version, Edward had sacrificed great poetry for a great play. Christopher Casson, who played Teiresias the prophet, remembered his mother playing Iocasta in the Yeats' version. He also remembered his father's theory that Yeats had written the chorus first and the characters followed to fit in. Mc Master's moment as the blind man at the end of the play is to Christopher Casson 'one of those exquisite moments of theatre to be remembered all one's life: a vertical performance rather than a horizontal one'.

Even on a June night, in the stuffy confines of the Gate Theatre, the audience, silent and spellbound, heard McMaster use his voice as vibrantly as an organist strikes chords in a vast cathedral. It brought to mind something of what the Athenians must have seen and heard in the fifth century B.C., when 30,000 sat in the open air at a play which must have been more like a religious ceremony. Edward's translation, John Izon's conception and 'Mac's' interpretation of Oedipus was indeed a happy conjunction of talents.

Six Characters in Search of an Author, Luigi Pirandello's experimental drama, deals with a group of characters who invade a theatre during a rehearsal, when reality and illusion become inextricably mixed. Some of these 'characters' are in the audience and hold discourse with those supposedly on the stage. On occasions during the play's run at the Gate Theatre, the intellectual excitement becoming too much to bear, members of the real audience rushed from the auditorium and down the stairs to where Seán Power manned the box office. There they begged of him whether Lord Longford knew what was going on in the theatre. No greater compliment could have been paid to Pirandello, and to Longford Prods.

By the mid-forties Edward's inspiration as a dramatist was showing signs of fatigue. His plays were coming with less regularity. He had never tackled what might be called fictional plays — as Christine had. But it was generally agreed that his translations and adaptations, from outdated and potentially tiresome sources, possessed a surprising brilliance, largely due to his knack of giving them a contemporary idiomatic twist.

For Longford Productions, war-time torpor began to lift as early as 1944. First, they made two short appearances at the Gaiety Theatre, something which lifted Edward's morale, as had their pre-war appearances in London. Next, there were some significant recruitments to the company. Some years earlier a beautiful sixteen-year-old girl in the Vivienne Leigh tradition, had begged Edward to give her a chance on stage. He had sent her away to learn something about life and the theatre. She did. And in the meantime she had made some electrifying appearances in other Dublin theatres. Edward saw her at the Peacock in Patrick Hamilton's thriller, *Rope*. He sent for her. It happened to be Iris Lawler's twenty-first birthday. Her name was to become permanently linked with Longford Productions. Later on, through television, she was to become what Mc Master most dreaded, a household name. Eve Watkinson, probably Ireland's most dynamic actress of the time, also joined the company and became their leading lady until she left towards the end of the forties.

War or no war, with his own forces strengthened, Edward advanced in 1944 for an extended theatrical *blitzkrieg*: the Old Testament and translations from the Greek were, as yet, a little advanced for Tuam, or Tullamore. So a little light relief had to be included. When Elizabeth McFadden's *Double Door* was toured, even sophisticated Cork — always highly critical of Longford Productions — found it a welcome change. 'We're tired delvin' into history with ye,' Edward was bluntly told, while Christine's smile, for once, was bitter-sweet, the cap fitting too perfectly.

It was in Cork too that the news came of Mrs Trew's death. Christine had to cope with a crisis of conscience. For all their old differences, she was devoted to her mother. She owed her everything in life. She would have continued to see her, at least once a year, but for the war. She had written to her every day. Naturally, she dearly wanted to go to Oxford to see things through. And of course she wanted Edward to come too. But no, that wasn't to be. Edward was adamant. There was bombing in England: but Oxford had never been bombed. He was afraid of the Irish Sea: but the mailboat had never been torpedoed. You had to have travel permits: but in the case of death ... He would not have Christine go alone, nor would he agree to go with her — and that was positively that.

Influencing his decision, no doubt, was the fact that Mrs Trew had never quite endeared herself to him. Her criticisms had come too near the bone. He was untidy. He was too noisy. He was disgracefully over-weight. She had railed at Christine for not asserting herself about Edward's eating habits. Too late and too diffidently, Christine had tried. She had told him of her mother's disgust at his lack of self-control. Unabashed, Edward had snapped back, 'Mrs Trew would live on a lettuce leaf.' At one stage their relationship became so bad that she was banned from dining with himself and Christine and was confined instead to her room upstairs.

And so it was that Christine mourned her mother's death alone. That was part of the price of loving Edward. She could not leave him — that would be too unbearable for him. When she had had to go into Portobello Nursing Home he was devastated. People would call into the Hand-Loom Shop to enquire for her, and Edward would burst into uncontrollable tears. His dependence on her was as total as a toddler's. So Mrs Trew went to her grave in the absence of her only child. Christine wrapped up the situation by saying: 'I couldn't leave Edward. Who would fasten his shoes?'

Mrs Trew had been so right about Edward's eating habits, and despite advice, Christine, it seemed, had been so wrong. He has been variously described as having a gargantuan appetite, of eating prodigiously and indiscriminately, of demolishing oysters by the dozen, of indulging in baronial breakfasts. Yet it is said he wasn't greedy, merely juvenile in his approach to food — a sort of compulsive neurosis. At the drop of a hat he would gladly celebrate any actor's birthday, engagement, or any old anniversary by taking a party to the Bailey or the Unicorn. It was said to be a pretext, because Edward was himself feeling in need of his own idea of a square meal — which was an unkind, view, for whatever else he was Edward Longford was generous to a fault.

Once in a Galway café he was having a meal with several of his company. 'These chips are awful,' somebody said. 'Are they?' asked Edward, continuing to devour them. On another occasion, at Jammets, somebody didn't finish his lobster. 'If you're leaving that,' said Edward, reaching for the plate, 'then I'll have it.' The actor was embarrassed at a belted earl enjoying his leavings. Another story concerns the doctor who advised him to diet and to cut his weight by half. In that way he might beget an heir. 'Not a crumb,' was Edward's decisive reply.

Unaware that she was destroying his lordship's health, Mrs Cruickshanks, the housekeeper at Pakenham Hall, delighted in sending up lavishly mouthwatering delicacies, such as eel pie and stuffed pike. That was when Edward still liked to fish in Lough Derravaragh. His sister, Violet, particularly remembers such treats as Mrs Cruickshanks' meringues, 'pale, golden paragons of deliciousness'.

Sissy, their cook at Grosvenor Park, was first-class and used ingredients which came fresh from Pakenham Hall. The table groaned when they entertained, and Edward loved entertaining. Left to himself, Edward's appetite was suicidal, and if he didn't kill himself, Christine, blinded by love, was well on her way to killing him with kindness, or so it seemed. She stood by quietly watching his indiscrimate eating. Indeed, she appeared to indulge him, often selecting tasty bits from her plate and transferring them to his. To prevent the risk of tantrums, Christine condoned Edward's appetite in public. Only in private did she dare try to bring some common sense to bear, but seldom was she successful.

There was a summer holiday when Frank's children were staying at Pakenham Hall. *In loco parentis*, Edward and Christine presided at meal-times. Edward liked a pyramid of mashed potato on his plate. But a Mullingar doctor had just issued another dreadful warning, which had stirred Christine more than it had Edward. She was being unusually vigilant about his intake. At dinner one evening he picked up his knife and fork, and surveyed his plate with its strict potato ration. 'Where's my potato — I want more potato,' he said. 'Edward, dear, you know what the doctor said,' Christine began. 'I want more potato,' Edward's voice was up a few decibels. 'Now Edward, dear, don't be difficult,' she pleaded. There was a moment's pause. Then an animal shriek rent the room: 'I WANT POTATO.' In terror, the children fled. As usual, Christine succumbed. She called to the butler, 'More potato for his lordship.' The butler called down the hatch, 'More potato for his lordship,' and the cry echoed from minion to minion through the nether regions of Pakenham Hall. The emergency ended when his pyramid of potato had been restored to his lordship's plate.

Christine would never be able to help Edward with his problem. His addiction was food.

Chapter 16

Poetry, Politics and Prevarication

Edward compensated for his neglect of translations of plays from the Greek by his translations of poetry from the Gaelic. In the forties he published four books of poetry, the originals of three of which were written in the bardic metres, dating from between the thirteenth and the seventeenth centuries.

Poems from the Irish is a collection of thirty-six poems for which, mostly, the original authorship is unknown. Edward considered these poems to have enough originality and poetic merit to justify his attempt to render them into English. He took on the task 'for the sake of those who do not read Irish with any ease or any pleasure, and who are apt to assume that there is nothing worth reading in Irish.' In the course of this work he concluded that the English language was 'singularly unfitted to express some of the finest flights of Gaelic imagination.'

I cannot judge these poems in their original Gaelic, and one must allow for that language barrier in translating, but according to Edward's version, Irish poets of the Middle Ages wrote their love poetry with an almost pathological preoccupation with women's hair: long fair curls, clustering curls, raven brows, hair of yellow, hair of gold, and so on. There is hardly a poem in the collection where hair isn't dragged in — dare one say it — by the hair. The resultant rhyming becomes trite and repetitious.

Another collection of twenty Irish bardic poems, *More Poems from the Irish*, was published in 1945. In this collection Edward shows that facility for rhyming which he showed to such good effect in his play, *Tartufe*. There is nothing 'private' about these poems. They are refreshingly simple, straightforward, understandable and enjoyable. Continually, one's sense of surprise is aroused, that poetry of such feeling was being written in Ireland seven hundred years ago. In a note Edward regrets what might have come from the Gaelic poets had circumstances been different: 'If we remember that the systematic annihilation of Irish culture was in full swing before Shakespeare and Spenser began to write, there is no reason to believe that Ireland, had circumstances been favourable, might not have achieved as much in literature as the larger island. It is a fascinating speculation, if no more. Some small part of what Ireland actually achieved in poetry, before her ruin, will I hope be guessed from these translations.'

More Poems from the Irish has an apologetic introduction in verse by Edward:

To the Poets of Ireland
Pardon me, Bards, if I in this offend,
That I in alien clouts a Muse have dressed
Whose beauty showed in native mantle best.
Believe me still your follower and your friend,
Who lop your liberties your fame to extend,
That should amaze the world from east to west,
And for your glory have your gait compressed,
If loving homage can my fault amend.
Still in dark beds and close your bodies lie,
Whose narrow prison sets the spirit free;
O may your fame mount glorious to the sky,
Given by bonds a greater liberty!
I would not soar; content enough I sing,
If I can add one feather to your wing.

Some have questioned the sincerity of Edward Longford's nationalism. In his cultivation of the Irish language, they said, he was a poseur. For shame! To put his nationalism into perspective, one has only to recollect the circumstances in which he first taught himself Irish. A lone schoolboy, nursing O'Growney's grammar at Eton College, he made himself a very obvious minority of one — and that at a period when Ireland's popularity in England was even lower than usual. His persistent pursuit of ultimate perfection puts many native Irishmen to shame, those who grew up in Ireland, went to Irish schools, and yet see nothing wrong in almost boasting of their ignorance of their own language. The difference was that Edward's learning of Irish was voluntary whereas frequently tyrannical clerics, believing themselves professors of Irish, succeeded in generating only hatred for the language in their students.

Edward's industrious translating resulted in a third collection of poems, published in 1946. Called *The Dove in the Castle*, it is divided into three parts: the first, 'Love and Hate' (twenty-six poems); the second, 'Odes and Elegies', (thirty poems), and the third, 'Divine Poems', (thirteen poems). This collection ranges from the ridiculous to the sublime. Occasionally a poem reminds one of an entry in a schoolgirl's autograph book. The effort at rhyming in 'Marginal Note', for instance, is stretched to Gilbertian lengths:

Your poem-book's so short of space
My little verse can hardly barge in.
Your shadowing hair and radiant face
Receive my tribute in the margin!

As before, these poets show an extraordinary interest in hair.
Occasionally the heart is acknowledged to exist, as in a poem called 'Rain':

Things out of sight are out of mind,
And love untended droops and dies.
The heart its damps and droughts will find
Alternate as the changing skies.

The Dove in the Castle includes a poem which Edward calls 'To an
Anti-Poetical Priest.' Written in the thirteenth century by Giolla
Bhrighde Mac Namee it challenges a church decree preached by a bigoted
priest against the poets of Ireland:

Rome never made your silly rules.
What, banish all the bardic schools?

Patrick and Columcille came and went, but never did they

... ban from Ireland evermore
The arts that were her joy before.

The poem ends by visualising how barren life would be, were Rome to
get her way:

The glorious feats of men of worth
Will pass for ever from the earth.

The narrative in this poem reflects the exalted position of the bard in
the society of the time, and the awe with which his praise or his blame
was acclaimed. Edward's translation grips his reader by making real and
tangible the essence and the spirit of far-away mythological Ireland.

In the severest days of the country's shameful book-censorship, several
translators, with Gaelic in their repertoire, were attracted to Bryan
Merriman's *The Midnight Court*. It was fun to compare the results, or
more accurately, to measure the bawd which had survived. Strangely,

Gaelic bawd never plagued the Censorship Board with the same horrid nightmares as its English equivalent — perhaps because Gaelic was legally, and still is, the first official language. Eroticism, provided it was written through 'the medium', was as sanctified as the Gospels.

Inevitably, *The Midnight Court* attracted Edward. His version was published in *Poetry Ireland* in 1949, edited by David Marcus. In his introduction Padraic Colum noted that the narrative had a natural attraction for a dramatist. Edward had put the old woman and the young man 'on the witness-stand and made them speak as they would from there'.

Be that as it may, *The Midnight Court* was Edward's translatory *tour-de force*. It is highly entertaining, there is no bawdiness and it isn't even risqué. True, there is an editor's note concerning three deletions, denoted by asterisks, 'made solely at the printers' request.' The context suggests censorship where the asterisks appear — by the printers! Quite understandable in the intolerant and illiberal days of 1949.

Apart from its literary value, Edward's *Midnight Court* is remarkable for its use of amusing alliteration:

An uglier female than I saw before,
Broad-beamed, big-bellied, bearded, bony, slow...
Healthy and hearty, fleshy, fresh and fine,
A whopping whelp, this proper pup of mine!...
No leggy gander, no consumptive chap,
No shapeless slob, no cramped, contracted clod,
A bounding, bouncing, brawny boy, by God!

The corpus of translations from the Gaelic bards left by Edward Longford is considerable — greater than is generally realised.

Until they began to organise themselves, actors belonged to one of the most exploited professions in the world. Their moral welfare took precedent over their material needs. There were two Irish organisations, divided on the usual sectarian basis. The Catholic Stage Guild (of which Charles Mitchel was one-time President) had its club-house in Marlborough Street. Then there was the Actors' Church Union, of which Edward was patron, which had a hostel in Northumberland Road. These organisations had chaplains, held meetings, religious and otherwise, and talked a lot. Sometimes they were addressed by visiting stars. Once they had a Hollywood B actor who would never be a star. His name was Ronald Reagan.

Once considered *infra dig*, the idea of some form of trade unionism began to catch on in the post-war years. In Ireland an organisation known as WAAMA was set up. Its name became the butt of comedians and cartoonists. But the Writers', Actors', Artists' and Musicians' Association was soon taken more seriously. In particular, skin-flint theatre managements took notice. WAAMA was concerning itself with the salaries and conditions of service of its members. It laid the foundations for the coming of the Irish Actors' Equity Association in 1946.

Edward as a theatre manager was in advance of his time. Equity could find no faults. His salaries were already above the minimum laid down by the new body — a source of jealousy in other theatres. To outside actors, Longfordland was a land flowing with milk and honey. If you were in those Elysian fields, you were safe. Somebody once asked Maurice O'Brien, 'Are you working?' 'Yes, dear,' he replied, 'I'm safe in the bosom of the lord.'

With his natural generosity, Edward as a proprietor lacked the instincts of a businessman. His ingenuousness left him open to manipulation by people by whom he had been too easily impressed. Christine was more astute. She observed and judged people. She mixed with the company. She listened, and while she was always sympathetic, she did not suffer fools gladly.

Yet for all Edward's generosity with salaries, there were still the quirky contradictions of his character. He could pay without question the bills left behind by Hilton and Micheál, but he would *not* turn on the central heating until he absolutely had to. He would pay the Tillies and the Willies — the amateurs who helped out as required, who were at best apprentice actors — yet he would haggle with his star actors as if he were playing some amusing game of chance, the outcome of which didn't particularly interest him. As usual, it was as if his actors were his children: one didn't discuss politics with them, nor was money a suitable subject for conversation.

While he was the first theatre manager in Ireland to put his actors under contract, these were gentlemen's agreements never set down on paper, but always scrupulously adhered to. On its arrival, Equity did away with such honour-bright arrangements. Likewise, when stagehands turned up three sheets in the wind, or not at all, Edward expected a little give and take — that the stage-manager (who might also be playing in the show) should step into the breech and manhandle stage furniture between the acts. Equity tidied that one up too. In fact, Edward's lack of ordered professionalism, which had once so infuriated Hilton Edwards, was now being forcibly rectified by the rules of Equity. Edward was learning, for instance, that money alone was no longer the sole criterion for running a repertory theatre.

With the Abbey Theatre, Edward's was the only company paid on a fifty-two weeks per annum basis. But his company earned both their salaries and their security. They were committed people. Every year they toured in the severest months of the winter. In the dressing-rooms at the Gate they constantly talked theatre — unlike the Abbey where poker, a tip for the 3.30 and Guinness monopolised the conversation.

Edward tried to relate his salary increases to seniority — the greater the seniority, the greater the increase. But things didn't always work out that way. A move for a rise might be initiated by an actress who was not necessarily a senior. To ensure success she might dab on some wet-white to help her look wan. If she impressed him as a deserving case, Edward would give her an increase — perhaps even an ex gratia payment, if her sob story had been sad enough. The news would quickly spread. Somebody else would approach him. 'I was waiting for you to ask me about that,' Edward would say naively. He never moved until some member of the company did. But then he made no bones about increases all round. As one actor put it: 'Edward was the best employer in the world as long as he got his own way.'

When touring he had another way of distributing his money. He advanced his players a month's salary to enable them to pay their fares and digs. This was called 'subbing'. When the company played in Mullingar and Castlepollard, they became house guests at Pakenham Hall, and everybody quietly forgot about the advances. That money was never paid back to Longford Productions.

Despite 'subbing' the players found budgetting difficult on tour. One young actor, always short of money, had been paid his fare from Waterford to Kilkenny, the company's next stop. Trying to economise, he walked to the suburbs and began to hitch a lift. The first car he flagged down was Lord Longford's, heading for the same destination. Edward gave him a lift — and no questions asked! Such was the careless generosity with which Edward conducted his business affairs.

As a politician he performed little better. Any interest he might have in politics derived from his activities in the theatre: would the Government ever acknowledge the place of theatre in Irish society? He had long since ceased to work for Cumann na nGaedheal, now Fine Gael. Unlike Yeats, Edward could never see himself in a blue, black or brown shirt, and it took him many years to forgive de Valera for his part in the Civil War.

Unlike Frank's idolatry, Edward's admiration for 'Dev' grew slowly. It was clinched by the political dexterity shown by him in recovering the ports, in all but casting off the Commonwealth (it was his successor, John A. Costello who finally did so in a speech delivered in Ottawa in 1948), and in maintaining Ireland's neutrality through World War II. To Edward such services to his country made Dev a true nationalist, one worthy of his place in political history. And there was another thing which fanned their mutual admiration: Edward could converse with Dev in Irish, something which made both their hearts glow.

For all that, there was an element of surprise when Edward was nominated to the Senate. On 13 November 1946, the Chairman of the Upper House said: 'I have to announce that the Taoiseach has nominated Edward Arthur Henry Pakenham, sixth Earl of Longford, with his prior consent, to be a member of Seanad Eireann to fill the vacancy caused by the death of Professor William Magennis.'

And with that announcement, Senator the Earl of Longford was introduced and took his seat. Was this to be the beginning of another career for Edward? Definitely not. While it still had novelty value, he took Christine and a party of Longford Prods to lunch at the Bailey, and afterwards to a sitting of the Senate. They expected to hear him speak. He didn't. Instead, he happily fell asleep. That gesture hit the key-note, and the death-knell, of Edward's political career.

His contributions to the Senate debates — seven in all — were selective. The subject matter had to be of, at least, indirect interest. He contributed one line, for instance, on the Auctioneers' and House Agents' Bill 1946, and nothing at all on many other bills. However well delivered, a reading of his Senate speeches is disappointing. They suggest no rhetoric, they tend towards repetition, and there is no sense of humour. His passionate interests predominate; the theatre and the Irish language.

In March 1947, Erskine Childers, then Parliamentary Secretary to the Minister for Local Government, introduced the National Health Insurance Bill 1947. The bill proposed to increase the upper limit for this insurance from £250 to £500 a year. Edward's speech is of historic interest, as well as for its concern for the Gate Theatre and for its actors:

> I want to talk for the moment about a class of people of whom, I am sure, senators know very little — the members of the theatrical profession. The greater number of the actors in Dublin, with the exception of the beginners, get salaries of between £5 and £10 a week. It does arise in the case of my own company, the Gate Theatre, that there are a round dozen of them — practically all — who get salaries of this amount, and the bringing in of this measure will be

a very serious increase in the weekly bill of a concern which is carrying on under great difficulty and I think the same applies to most of the other concerns in Dublin. We might gladly pass this if we were quite convinced that it was going to be of any practical value. Actually, I am quite certain that the actors themselves would hotly deny that it was of any benefit at all.

Edward went on to explain how actors, because of the irregular nature of their employment, were tacitly — and probably illegally — exempted from national health insurance. He continued:

Then, suddenly, I think certain actors applied to be put under the scheme and the scheme was enforced. We, the managers of the Dublin theatres, tried to find out from the National Health Society whether or not actors were included under the scheme. For two years we were not given any answer at all. Then, suddenly, we were informed that we were liable for arrears.

He then dealt with the anomaly of small-part actors, some of whom received a guinea a week, not as a salary, but to cover their expenses. To include these actors in the national health scheme would mean increased expenditure for them, and many would not continue with acting as a career.

Edward's concern was for professional actors. His speech continues:

Many of the regular employees get benefits from the company far exceeding anything that will be paid under the scheme. Very often you will find that actors who are sick for weeks are paid their full salary, getting £6 or £7 a week. As Senator Douglas suggested, this sort of thing can hardly continue if they are brought under the new scheme. There are a number of anomalies which do arise and I can say why it tacitly but illegally happened that they were exempted from the national health scheme. I would like the Parliamentary Secretary to consider this matter. I am sure there are many other professions in which the scheme is a hardship rather than a benefit for the workers. I want to see the workers well-treated and getting every benefit which they possibly can get and I want to see everything being done for their good but I do not want to see hardship inflicted either on myself or on anybody else. I would like to be assured that the worker is going to benefit in all cases by the raising of this exemption figure from £250 to £500 ... The matter should be very carefully considered. So far as the workers who are to benefit are concerned, I do not want to stand in their way but let us be sure they are really going to benefit before anything rash is done.

In June 1947, *A Plan for Education* published by the Irish National Teachers' Organisation was discussed by the Senate. Having urged greater expenditure on education 'if this nation is going to amount to anything in the future', Edward then spoke about Irish, his favourite language:

I am strongly in favour of the teaching of Irish. Why not have compulsory Irish if you have compulsory mathematics? I myself had no particular love for mathematics when I was at school, and I am afraid that much of the time I spent studying that subject was wasted. I was not taught Irish when I was young. When I reached adult age I had to try to teach myself, and get others to teach me Irish. I cannot see, as I say, why there should be any more objection to compulsory Irish than there is to compulsory mathematics ...

Was this Edward's pay-off for his nomination to the Senate? No. It was the outlook for which Dev selected him in the first place.

On an Imposition of Duties Bill to protect Irish workers manufacturing radios, Edward had this to say:

We have been learning a great deal about the blessing that wireless is to the people of this country. I am not denying the great educational value of wireless, but I do not think, simply because the Danes have four times as many wireless sets in proportion to what we have that they are necessarily four times a more civilised people.

In November 1947, to subsidise increasing food costs, a supplementary budget was introduced. Income tax, beer, cars, tobacco — the old faithfuls all took their usual hammering. Duty on cinemas 'and other forms of entertainment' was increased by one hundred per cent. Rural senators moaned about the shoddy prices for cattle and pigs and the folly of buying Constellation aircraft for a prestige Irish air service across the North Atlantic. Edward's concern, of course, was for cinema 'and other forms of entertainment'.

It is regarded as a grievance, that in order to get food, our drink, or our cinemas must be taxed. I am, perhaps, not entirely impartial on the question of cinemas. I think the cinema is something which can very well afford to be taxed. It is an industry which is almost entirely in the hands of foreigners and which, to my mind, does very little good to this country. I am all for providing people with entertainment, and if the cinemas were Irish owned and provided Irish films, I would not object in the least, but, in the meantime, would it not be possible to provide some other form of entertainment which would not involve the expenditure of large quantities of dollars? Drink may be a necessity and cigarettes also be a necessity, although I am a non-smoker and, perhaps, do not drink as much as some people do, but I cannot see that we need all these cinemas. They are spreading around the country, and appearing in smaller and smaller places, one result of which is the complete destruction of the theatrical companies which used to tour the country and the throwing out of live actors and actresses.

I would much rather see a revival of the theatre all over the country — not necessarily highbrow. Let it be low-brow, if you like — variety, music hall, or any other type — but let it be some form of entertainment which is native-owned and employing live Irish actors and actresses and providing a form of entertainment which the people will enjoy just as much as these miserable films which, I cannot believe, from a national or any other point of view, are any good for the country. They may be a pleasant thing to have if we can afford them, but I am not sure we can ...

This was part of Edward's last contribution as a Senator. His frolic with politics ended on 6 April 1948, with the replacement of de Valera as Taoiseach by John A. Costello and the first Coalition Government.

The recruitment of Charles Mitchel and Aiden Grennell in the mid-forties added greatly to the strength of Longford Productions, by now already a formidable repertory company. With Eve Watkinson, Cathleen Delany, Iris Lawler, Maurice O'Brien, Blake Gifford and Christopher Casson as leading players, and with John Izon producing, Edward had assembled a company capable of all the classicism he could desire. But more than anything, Edward desired touring: 'We have always made a great point of showing our work to the provinces,' he said, 'for we feel that Dublin is not Ireland and that a purely Dublin theatre can never do all that an Irish theatre should do for the nation.'

Seasons at the Gate Theatre were all very well. Edward enjoyed them, and Christine too. Night after night they sat in the first two seats on the right-hand side, chuckling delightedly and leading the applause, for they were already fully familiar with the plays, having sat through the rehearsals. Their 'audience reaction' wasn't always to the liking of the players. Isolated laughter and applause can disconcert actors in action.

Edward's enjoyment of theatre proprietorship was surely linked with a naive desire to show off. At the Gate he would stand about in the vestibule, looking unhappily awkward, while trying to play the welcoming host. At the intervals, with Christine, he would mingle with the audience, but without an easy social grace. It was of course an added thrill for visiting Americans to rub shoulders with a real earl and countess who had left their castle to move informally, if somewhat stiffly, amongst the plain people of Ireland. And at the end of the show, Edward, at the top of the stairs, would shyly bow his patrons out, while at the bottom of the stairs stood the ever-patient, much put-upon Christine.

On tour in the country towns things were different. There is no doubt that, as he believed fervently in his religion, so Edward Longford believed in his self-appointed mission to bring good theatre to the Irish people. It was his act of faith, hope and generous charity. As well as pouring his family inheritance into his mission, he was also prepared to work actively in its interest. Nothing was too menial for him, nor for Christine. With an old scarf tied round her head, she would nightly run the box office. When the audience was seated, she would 'count the house' like Yeats long ago at the Abbey — not so much for its profits as for the extent of its losses. Edward's activities might be no more involved than selling programmes, but unwittingly, he could be good at that. Once an American soldier asked Christine if it was true the outfit was run by a lord. 'Yes,' she assured him. 'By a real lord — you know, an earl?' 'Yes,' she said again, 'there he is,' pointing to Edward, who was standing in the foyer with a bundle of unsold programmes in his hand. 'Wha!' exclaimed the GI, 'an earl selling theatre programmes?' 'Why not?' said Christine. Moved with filmstar adulation, the young man went up to Edward. 'Gee, Earl, I'll buy the lot,' he said, and he did.

There was another side to touring, a less attractive side for Edward and Christine: The local hoi-polloi tried to lionise them. There were invitations to dinner, to stay in cold, draughty mansions, to do a bit of hunting. Apologies were sent: dinner-time coincided with their show; they preferred to share hotels with their company; they didn't hunt, thank you very much. And when some tottering Lord Dashington threw a luncheon for the company and said he wanted to see this dashed play they were doing — the one by that bounder Wilde — easy chairs or sofas had to be hired and installed in the front row of the local hall to meet the situation.

They had learned of the local hoi-polloi from grim experience. Christine told a story of so-called entertainment in a certain Irish big house, whose invitation they had reluctantly accepted. She and Edward had returned after the show, about midnight. There was no supper — theatre people's most enjoyed meal of the day. The family had gone to bed. With a flickering candle they had had to negotiate several flights of black marble stairs, then a corridor of creaking floor-boards to a massive bedroom, its three high windows open to an Atlantic gale. No, Edward and Christine really preferred the company of their players, who were their friends, their children, their own.

Because Edward's mission was touring, he expected every player to accept it without question. When employing a new actor he would say: 'If you won't tour, you're out.' Indeed, once an actor failed Edward in any way, he was out — out and finished forever. In 1947, after years of touring, Cathleen Delany was unable to travel. She found herself out, finished and forever. Although a pillar of Longford Prods, and a lifelong friend of Christine, Edward never cast her again.

From his earliest association with Edwards and Mac Liammóir, Edward could not resist the temptation to cast plays, a function which Hilton rightly held to be sacred to the producer. Edward's enthusiasm went even further: given to favouritism, he wanted — always — to cast certain players in every play, and to hell with their suitability. Like a child with a favourite teddy bear, Edward usually had a favourite actress — oh, nothing emotional, nothing carnal, as somebody said — purely Platonic, purely spiritual. Anyway, Christine kept a kindly eye on things. No, it was just as if he needed some kind of doll to dress up splendidly for the top of the Christmas tree. Whoever she might be, he insisted on casting her in every play, on giving her the best available costumes, on publicising her talents widely. Always so innocently well-intentioned, he could never see that by miscasting and over-exposure he was destroying rather than making somebody's acting reputation.

Edward's attitude to Cathleen Delany reflects his unfortunate weakness for favouritism. Once the apple of his eye, time and again, like his later favourites, she found herself miscast. On one occasion she was forced to play a chain-smoking drunken harridan. She couldn't even light a cigarette with conviction on the stage, much less play a drunk. But once Edward had decided, there was no way out. A castigation of a player's performance by a critic made no allowance for silly miscasting. It reflected only on the unfortunate player, who had no right of reply. Nobody is more sensitive to miscasting than an experienced actor or actress.

Iris Lawler and Aiden Grennell, husband and wife, and for many years leading players in Longford Productions. Iris became a household name when she played in the long-running RTE serial *Tolka Row*.

Iris Lawler, another favourite, was later to share the same trials: the best the wardrobe could offer, first-class publicity, Edward's blessing, but as well, over-exposure and thoughtless miscasting. Edward was convinced that once a player gave one dynamic performance, he or she could reproduce that phenomenon at will, in any part from Lear to Charley's Aunt. Casting was one of his weakest points, yet it was an aspect of theatre he loved, but was never to learn.

Deirdre O'Meara, that actress of a thousand parts with RTE Repertory Company, whose voice was known far and wide throughout Ireland, was discovered by Edward in the Dublin Shakespearean Society. She attributed her subsequent successful career entirely to him, although she had a dramatically short innings with Longford Productions. He cast her as Sylvia in Farquhar's *The Recruiting Officer*, a 'breeches part', once played by Peg Woffington. Horrified at the idea, the young actress refused. Edward argued for a whole evening: 'But you've played in pantomime,' he kept saying. 'Yes, but as a principal girl,' she kept replying. She held out against him, but he never cast her again. Her conclusion: Lord Longford had a power complex — his will had to be done, or else your head rolled.

With Hilton and Micheál in the United States throughout 1948, Longford Productions did record business at the Gate Theatre. The season was marked by another of Edward's successful translations: *The Great Magician* by the Spanish dramatist, Pedro Calderon. He followed this in 1949 with his translation from Molière, *The Hypochondriac (Le Malade Imaginaire)*. Also in 1948, *Tankardstown*, Christine's most popular play, was first produced. In it she caught the Irish *nouveau riche*, well-fed throughout the war years, and now ready to feed the hungry English — at a price. Its delicious sense of humour arose from Anglo-Irish misunderstandings. The characters might have been speaking a different language. *Tankardstown* packed the Gate before moving to Cork.

While at the Opera House, Iris Lawler 'got a mood on,' as she describes it. At the time she had £7 a week, most of which went in digs, so she confronted Edward in his office. 'I'm going home,' she told him. 'What d'you mean, you're going home?' he asked. 'I'm fed up paying all my money for digs. Give me £10 a week and I won't go home.' 'But we haven't got that kind of money,' said Edward. He was having his usual fun, like playing a fish. There followed a pause, Christine looking on in silence. 'All right, darling.' said Edward. 'You can have £10 a week.' Iris Lawler suddenly found herself the most highly paid member of the company — but not for long. The information leaked, and the others had to be given similar rises.

Longford Prods ended their 1948 tour in Wexford. Christine anticipated home and hot baths and what she called proper coffee. But always saddened at the end of a tour, Edward made a sudden decision. With the assistance of an Arts Council grant, Longford Prods would travel to the Arts Theatre in Salisbury where they would do a two-week season playing *Tankardstown* and *The School for Wives*. Salisbury was chosen because Edward's sister, Pansy and her husband, Henry Lamb, lived near.

So in January 1949, Edward and Christine set out with Longford Productions on a night crossing from Rosslare to Fishguard. They all shared a few drinks before turning in. The cabin area had only partitions so from their bunks the players talked hilariously over the partitions far into the night. Eventually there was a bellow. It was Edward. 'If you lot don't bloody well shut up and get to sleep, you'll all be fired in the morning.' Instant silence followed, everybody squirming, trying desperately to remember what they'd been saying. Who could have guessed that Edward and Christine would be sharing the same partitioned area? But then Edward always had a sense of identification with his company.

There was still food rationing in England. Powdered egg was served for breakfast on the train. In disgust, Edward lifted it on his fork and dropped it back on the plate. Almost accusingly, he said, 'Christine, this egg is a fake — a bloody fake,' to which Christine answered mildly, 'There's nothing I can do about it, darling.'

Irish sausages were a great delicacy in post-war Britain. An enterprising young actor had brought a supply. To supplement his salary, he sold them to willing buyers on the train. Edward heard of it. 'I'm not going to have members of my company selling sausages to the British public,' he warned, like a schoolmaster conducting a party of obstreperous boys.

Apart from the local press confusing Lord Longford with a Lord Langford from the area, the Salisbury season went satisfactorily. Socially, however, it was tame. Typical was an invitation to a party in a glorious Tudor house built about a roof-tree. The company sat in a circle in a beautifully furnished Tudor room. Sandwiches were passed round, with tea for the actresses. Presently the hostess suggested: 'You men might like a little drink?' and she produced some bottles of beer. Edward acquired a few bottles, which he drank rather quickly, believing, like the others, the party was only beginning. But their hostess soon made it clear it was her bedtime.

Deflated, they were walking through cold, deserted streets to their digs when Edward decided he'd liven things up a bit. With a volume fit to lift the roofs of Salisbury he began *The Soldiers Song* in Irish. Surveying them with high suspicion, a Bobbie passed on the other side of the street going in the opposite direction. Presently somebody noticed he'd turned back and was approaching them. Edward stopped singing. He did so, he assured all and sundry, only on the grounds that he grudged the headlines his arrest might give the damned British press next day.

While in Salisbury Aiden Grennell and Iris Lawler became engaged. Edward and Christine were as pleased as if they were their own children. There was no celebration. That came five months later with their wedding in June 1949. Again, Edward and Christine glowed with a parental pride. Their wedding present was a Sean Keating picture. And when Mariana, the first-born Grennell, arrived, her godparents were Edward, Christine, Charles Mitchel and her aunt, Betty Brabazon.

Though the Longfords had no family of their own, they created one. It began with the members of their company. Jean Anderson remembers Edward as 'something of a father figure who took a great interest in all the problems of his players, both in their work and domestically.' Like

Robert Briscoe, Lord Mayor of Dublin 1956-57, with Edward and his brother
Frank. The occasion isn't known but the background suggests
the Gresham Hotel.

any family, they had their squabbles, but behind the endemic bitchiness
of theatre life, there was a respect, a mutual regard amounting to a
mutual love in Longfordland. Only in the after-years could the Longford
Players look back and truthfully say: 'We knew it was a happy time, how
much we never knew.'

Chapter 17

The Gate — a Fire Hazard

Recognition of the work done for his country by the sixth Earl of Longford first found public expression in the 1950s. His election in 1952 as a member of the Royal Irish Academy ranked him with the greatest Irish academics of his day. A jealously guarded privilege, membership of the Academy is accorded only to the most worthy. For Edward and Christine, both academics of England's purest strain, the honour of Irish recognition was something they warmly treasured, particularly as they had both long since dedicated themselves to the greater honour and glory of Ireland.

For Edward, more honours were to follow. In 1954, Trinity College conferred an honorary Litt.D., to be followed in 1958 by an honorary D.Litt. from the National University of Ireland. As for Christine, though her academic distinction wasn't given formal recognition at the time, Edward's honours pleased her more than if they had been given her. Praise of Edward was pleasure to Christine. In due time she would be honoured — too late, too late — less than three weeks before her death, but more of that anon.

In the 1950s Edward's love affair with the theatre reached the zenith of its rapture. He expended his heritage even more lavishly on his beloved with a reckless disregard for the realities of theatrical life. He made Hilton and Micheál still more jealous by flaunting his wealth in mounting rarely seen plays by such as Colley Cibber (1671-1757), George Colman the elder (1752-1794) and Charles Macklin (c.1697-1797), plays certain to empty any modern theatre. Equally, he mounted highly popular successes.

Perversely exuberant with his own sense of independence, he repeatedly broke a cardinal rule of the theatre: never break the run of a success. Edward did just that with William Saroyan's *The Time of Your Life*. His production introduced the play to Ireland and Ireland loved it and packed the Gate week after week. Also phenomenally successful were James Thurber's *The Male Animal* and Thornton Wilder's *Our Town*. Edward resented having to give up his seat to paying clients. 'Ah! cinema audiences!' he sneered irritably, and against the best advice he replaced such successes, and happily resumed his accustomed seat in the front row. As with casting, the choice of plays and the lengths of their runs were

A scene from Christine's play *The Paragons* (1950)

powers he reserved strictly to himself.

At prices current in the mid-1950s the maximum nightly takings at the Gate were £58. In January 1957, Christine's play *Stop the Clock* took £210 over a four-week period, less than the salary list for one week. Even in the early days, the cost of each play toured was approximately £4000. In time this figure rose to £6000 per play. When he launched his public appeal in 1956 for the refurbishment of the Gate, Edward's losses were said to be running at some £16,000 a year. At a minimum, the theatre cost him some hundreds of thousands of pounds. He was continually concerned with putting money into the theatre, while others were concerned only with taking it out.

Tours were intended to last six months, but they never did. Usually they took place from December to March, weatherwise the worst possible time of year. Nor, geographically, did they always proceed in the best interests of economy in transport. Their travels tended to zig-zag, rather than to take the shortest routes. Altogether, the costs of maintaining Longford Productions were immense, but the provincial Irish public responded with gratitude because they had never seen anything so lavish in costumes and scenery as Edward showed them.

Even if the theatre was his greatest and most expensive eccentricity, it was an eccentricity he delighted in sharing generously. Edward Longford gave to Ireland's culture something which only he could have given. To his touring policy the nation owes the immense amateur drama movement which erupted in the mid-fifties, resulting in the countrywide festivals of excellent productions which attract so much attention today.

In April 1954, Gervaise Mathews, one of Longford Prods' brightest stars of the time, died at the height of her powers. Edward is remembered at her funeral service for the emotional power with which he sang the hymns. Religion attracted him in a way it did not attract Christine. She was as cynical about the cosiness of the Church of Ireland as she was curious about the compulsions of the Roman Catholic Church. And clergymen who fawned — irrespective of the denomination — she found nauseating.

Edward had never forgiven his brother Frank for being so diametrically opposite in personality. As schoolboys, Frank didn't always fly to his defence when Edward found himself in a minority of one — a situation all too frequent. When Frank, a happy philistine with no interest in the theatre, became Chairman of the National Bank in 1955, Edward said: 'The best news for years! I'll break him with my overdraft!' The last straw came with Frank's conversion to Catholicism. A faithful Anglican, Edward was furious. And when Frank sent him a copy of his book, *Born to Believe*, Edward threw it across the room in disgust. Religion was not one of Edward's eccentricities, to be adopted with enthusiasm, and discarded at will. Religion was for ever, a source of comfort to which he adhered with a strong sense of duty.

But Frank was not the first Pakenham to become a Catholic. An enemy of Daniel O'Connell and of Catholic Emancipation, the second Earl's animosity was such that he strengthed the defences of Tullynally Castle by erecting four Gothic towers, a moat and six hundred feet of battlements. Yet his son, the Honourable Charles Reginald Pakenham, terminated a brilliant career in the Grenadier Guards to become a Catholic and a Passionist monk. When he was leaving, his uncle, the Duke of Wellington, said: 'You've been a good officer, Charles, now be a good monk.' As Father Paul Mary Pakenham he was amongst the founder members of the Passionist Order in Ireland. Appointed as the first Rector of Mount Argus, the Passionist monastery in Dublin, he died there nine months later.

Apart from religion and the theatre, to each of which he was constant, there were other ideas of passing fancy to which Edward gave an exclusive, if temporary, devotion. His cello and his harp whims are examples. The harp seed was sown as far back as 1938, when Christopher Casson first came to Ireland. Accompanying himself on a small Irish harp, Christopher sang ballads. His popularity in Dublin became tremendous.

Edward envied his facility. But it wasn't until 1944 that the seed germinated. In Christine's play, *The Earl of Straw*, a harp was played off-stage. Its strains haunted Edward, and he finally took the plunge. Never one for half measures, he bought a big orchestral harp, and took lessons. Because his stomach prevented him from getting close enough — as it also did with the cello — he had difficulty in manipulating the instrument. But he persevered, at first practising scales every morning in the theatre office, and woe betide the unfortunate who interrupted him.

During the rehearsal of a quiet, tense scene on the stage, painfully plangent sounds would float from the direction of the office: a long-drawn, tinging Doh, a silence, then an out-of-tune tinging Fah. This was Edward's effort at *The Minstrel Boy*. Horrified at this treatment of a beautiful instrument, Christopher Casson, the man responsible for the situation, was once heard to say: 'I wish he'd stop picking it, it'll go septic.' Then one day Aiden Grennell took a phone call. Eerily, it began with the plucking of harp strings. Through the sounds a voice said: 'This is an angel speaking.' It was Dan Treston calling from the Gate office, where Edward's harp stood beside the phone. As expected, Edward's latest whim soon died a natural death, but while it lasted, his devotion to the harp was bound up with his idea of a nationalist's devotion to the musical instrument that personified Ireland.

Surviving Longford Prods are agreed that their survival rate owes nothing to the skill of their late employer as a driver. The opinion is unanimous: Edward Longford was the world's worst driver. As with the harp and the cello, his stomach got in the way. But so did his temper. He expected people to give way — and they didn't. But like his cello, and his harp, he ensured the instrument at hand was always a good one. Exploits in his lavish Hudson Terraplane are most remembered.

When they played in Mullingar, the company stayed at Pakenham Hall. Like children for the seaside, Edward packed as many as possible into the Hudson for the twelve-mile journey. As they skirted Crooked Wood, past Derravaragh, Edward became apoplectic at straying donkeys, and poltroons who drove their cows against his fenders. Christine's admonishments were in vain. Curtain-down each night was a relief — the show was over — until Edward's passengers remembered the nightmare journey ahead.

At the Gate his parking place was opposite the theatre in Granby Row. He would drive straight out into the passing traffic — and the devil take the hindmost. When his engine stalled, there would be screaming panic, with busmen's insults flying like hailstones. But Edward never learned. As if of right, he would blandly repeat the performance an hour later.

Personally I was never driven by Edward, but on one occasion I drove with him so the speak. The occasion was Yeats' funeral. Sharing with me were Austin Clarke, Ernie O'Malley, Mary Andrews and my sister, Vera. Disgracefully, we played leap-frog with Edward and Christine, passing one another again and again, on the dash from Dublin to Sligo. I can testify that Edward proved himself no mean driver that day. Incidentally, because Yeats had been dead for ten years, nobody was in mourning. His body had been exhumed in France and was being reburied at Drumcliffe. Edward sported a red carnation. In a collection of photographs of the funeral on display in Sligo Museum, there is one of Edward and Christine, both looking radiant in Drumcliffe Churchyard.

In 1955 Edward had to face the thorny problem of whether matinées should be discontinued. The Longford Prods had no doubts. For years they had wanted matinées done away with. In his conservatism, Edward was thinking of his clientele of old ladies. Particularly important was a wealthy old Foxrock lady, a regular attender on Saturday afternoons. Backstage, they knew she had arrived when they heard 'Rug, James. Cushion, James,' which was her chauffeur's cue to make her comfortable before he left. Coming in, she would have enquired from Seán Power in the box office the time of curtain-down, so that her car could be ready. 'What time should my chauffeur return?' she asked one day, and Seán replied, 'About 5 p.m.' But he hadn't allowed for the impish humour that had descended on the cast that afternoon.

Edward was spending the weekend in Westmeath. The play was *The School for Wives*. The unpredictable Maurice O'Brien and the irrepressible Iris Lawler, aided and abetted by colleagues, decided to rush the play — the opposite of today's go-slow tactics. It was over in half the expected time, and the old lady had to wait for her car. On Tuesday morning Edward was back. He summoned the company to his office. A letter of complaint from Foxrock? Yes, they were certain. But no — Edward felt he should share his delight in conveying to them the congratulations of the lady for the wonderful acting she had seen on Saturday. Sometimes you can't win!

With Edward's weekends out of Dublin, an air of relaxation was noticeable at the Gate, especially towards matinées. Usually there was a Friday morning rehearsal, and a matinée and a night show on Saturday. But it was always the matinée that caused the players' resentment. When his translation of the Spanish play, *The Great Magician* by Pedro Calderón (1600-81) was produced (a play, incidentally, which Dublin otherwise would never have seen), a matinée drew an audience of five to see a play with a cast of twenty. 'Have they no homes?' an actor wondered. Edward was away, so in the name of common sense, the cast decided to cancel the performance. Instead, they all went off to the zoo. When this was reported to Edward by phone, he got into one of his towering rages, bellowing long-distance. When he returned to Dublin on Tuesday he never even mentioned the matter.

Then a rule was made. If an audience of ten or less turned up for a matinée, it could be cancelled, even in Edward's absence provided he was phoned. Inevitably, that led to a bit of statistical wizardry. When ten patrons were seated, Seán Power assisted the ruse by delaying newcomers in the hall until 2.30 p.m., the time at which an actor would go before the curtain and announce with regret ... Because Edward refused to have a phone in Pakenham Hall, a message would be phoned to the farmyard. And that was that.

Finally, Edward made his decision. The last matinée given by Longford Productions was in August 1955, during a revival of *Carmilla*, his adaptation from Joseph Sheridan le Fanu. The players wept no tears, nor could they be blamed. Entering a darkened theatre on a hot, sunny afternoon, to don make-up and costumes to play to half-a-dozen dodderers was too much like sacrificing everything for one's art.

Early in 1956 sinister rumours began to circulate: the Gate Theatre was a fire-risk. It was to be closed by Dublin Corporation. Perhaps that partly explained Edward's reluctance to turn on the theatre's heating plant. It was a cold spring and, as on tour, actors wore pyjamas under their clothes to keep warm. Tempers became frayed. Even Christine showed an unusual tendency to interfere during rehearsals of her translation of *La Dame aux Camelias* by Dumas the Younger.

Their players had long ago concluded that, like Yeats, what Edward and Christine lacked as playwrights was experience as actors, speaking lines to one another on a stage. Christine occasionally wrote uncertain cue lines, likely to throw an actor. And when that happened and a scene got mussed up, she would come round. 'Darlings,' she would croon, with charming devastation, 'you did it so much better than I could ever have written it.' As Charles Mitchel once said: 'Christine never used a rapier when a bodkin would suffice.'

Dublin liked a tear-jerker. It hadn't quite forgotten Garbo as La Dame. The play was a success. Iris Lawler gave it everything, taking a sadistic pleasure in nightly reducing strong men to slobbering emotionalism. Her personal concern was the ice-cold blast from the scene-dock everytime somebody opened the door to enter or leave the stage.

Christine, about the
mid-1950s, wearing a
creation from the
Hand-Loom shop.

Period plays were a challenge to Edward's inventiveness as a costume designer, an occupation he took very seriously, perhaps because he felt he owed it to his ancestor who had the duty of providing costumes for Shakespearean players at the Court of Queen Elizabeth. While his knowledge of the history of costume was vast, and his imagination virile, his success in transmuting his ideas into reality was limited. He was influenced by Mac Liammóir's genius for vivid, contrasting colours, using slits and gashes in the manner of Michelangelo's reds, yellows and blues for the Swiss Guard. Sometimes, when Edward's designs reached Burkinshaws in Liverpool for execution, the workers were perplexed by his slits and slashes in extraordinary places.

Opinions differ amongst the players — the people who had to wear his creations. Whatever the colour schemes, his historical detail was always accurate, down to the last stitch. Edward could tell you the significance of one or three buttons on your cuff, or the number of studs on the front

174

of an evening shirt. For Restoration Comedies he excelled himself with magnificent head-dresses for women. Nor did he hesitate to raid his family houses, and those of his friends, to bring genuine old costumes into the theatre wardrobe. Some of these were superb garments, but unfortunately, they were often unsuccessful on the stage because of their failure to reflect stage-lighting.

As a leading lady with some grim experience, Jean Anderson has nothing but admiration for Edward's designs: 'In classical rep. in England you hired costumes from London and it was a lucky dip when the hamper arrived whether they fitted, or whether the colour, or the period, were remotely right. The lasting memory is the "pong" of some of the clothes I had to look glamorous in! The one great bonus when I first joined Longford Prods was finding that because Edward loved designing costumes I had clothes actually designed for *me* for every leading role. Lovely costumes! I still remember a lot of them.'

For touring, scenery might sometimes be curtailed, but never costumes. Edward insisted on travelling with the costumes used at the Gate. He had no time for theatricality: the overall effect of combining music, lighting, tableaux and blackouts — the favourite armamentarium of Hilton Edwards. Edward's theatrical maxim was simplistic: wear a good costume and shout out your lines. Over the years a formidable wardrobe was assembled at the Gate. When Longford Productions was disbanded, it helped to form the nucleus of the new RTE wardrobe.

The Shaw centenary year occurred in 1956. Longford Productions did three Shaw plays: *Heartbreak House, Candida,* and *Mrs Warren's Profession,* the latter the official centenary production. Particular care was given to the manner of Shaw's billing. Time was when Edward insisted on the use of the full name, George Bernard Shaw, but meantime Shaw had written asking to be billed as Bernard Shaw, adding, 'Surely in Ireland the Hanoverian prefix is even more out of place.'

Edward's worries increased when the Dublin Corporation invoked legal action about the lack of fire safety at the Gate Theatre. Rumour had it again that the theatre was to be closed down. Admirers of the theatre felt that if it was once allowed to close, it would never re-open. It was all very bad publicity, and extremely depressing. The repairs, it was estimated, would cost £32,000, a staggering sum in 1956. This was the greatest challenge Edward ever had to face. A quarter of a century earlier, he had saved the Gate Theatre from certain extinction: could he be relied upon now to repeat that noble act of generosity to the people of Ireland, and to the generations that would follow them?

Of his six-year association with Hilton and Micheál, a period of perpetual financial embarrassment at the Gate, he said: 'During this time I continued to provide loans, or rather subsidies, as I never expected repayment.' Since he had launched Longford Productions in 1936 he had continued to maintain a loss-making theatre company, a tweed manufactory and the Hand-Loom Shop. His losses were becoming immense. Not for the first time, the family financial advisers frowned heavily on Lord Longford's expensive indulgences. Christine was long ago convinced that Edward was destined to lose money in everything he touched. By 1956 the financial situation could hardly be more serious.

The fact must be faced that if money was to be raised to repair the Gate, it must come from sources other than the Longford estate. Making clear that if the Gate Theatre collapsed, he would be found standing among its ruins, Edward launched a public appeal. No help could be expected from the State, and commercial sponsorship was yet unknown. Friends of the theatre resorted to the time-honoured methods of fund-raising, but of course, it was Edward's personal efforts that counted most. Few knew of the life insurance policy he realised, or of the antiques that he and Christine brought from Pakenham Hall to be auctioned.

Elizabeth Longford tells a story that may well be associated with Edward's reckless auctioneering, particularly of the family silver, in the interests of the Gate Theatre. As the eldest he was in line to inherit considerable wealth from his uncle, Edward Michael Pakenham, known as Uncle Bingo. Unfortunately for Edward, Uncle Bingo spied a silver bowl in the centre of a dining-table at his London club. 'Where did you get that bowl from?' he asked the club secretary. 'From Pakenham Hall. Lord Longford put it on the market,' was the reply. Without his nephew's appreciation of the earth-shattering importance of the survival of the Dublin Gate Theatre, Uncle Bingo, it was said, never forgave Edward. And so, that was the end of that financial expectation.

Many theatre-goers laughed at the pictures painted by Edward and displayed in the vestibule in an effort to raise money. He sold them for two pounds each, as well as his Christmas cards at one shilling each. The pictures are now collectors' pieces. But it is by his begging bowl that most Dubliners remember the portly Edward Longford, as nightly he stood in the Gate vestibule shyly shaking it at the departing patrons, or out in the streets rattling it at passers-by. Amongst them walked the ignorant begrudgers: 'Wouldn't you be surprised at Lord Longford, an' he wealthy enough to build a theatre, let alone repair one.'

Worried on the Gate Theatre's behalf, Edward was above such petty jibes. He wrote to his friends, past and present, all over Ireland and England, begging their help. As a result he turned up in the theatre office

The re-opening of the Gate Theatre in 1958 after its refurbishment by Edward and Christine. From left: Christine, President Seán T. O'Kelly, Mrs O'Kelly, Iris Lawler, Kay Casson and Edward with the President's Aide behind.

every morning with a handful of cheques. Their amounts were modest, but together they helped. He also appealed to Father Donal O'Sullivan SJ, then head of the Arts Council. He received a cheque for £1,000. Considering it derisory, Edward returned it. They doubled the figure, and that was the height of the Arts Council's contribution. Notably, Hilton and Micheál remained aloof from the situation, though in due course they would enjoy the benefits of 'the new Gate'.

The last play before the close-down for refurbishment was a special production of *The Old Lady Says 'No'*, to mark *An Tóstal*, Sean Lemass's former annual holiday celebration. An attempt was made to strike a happy note; it was a combined production, Hilton, Micheál and Edward apparently burying the hatchet for a special occasion. Micheál, of course, played Emmet, with Iris Lawler as Sarah Curran. But the camaraderie was strained. Some said it was like old times; the wiser knew it wasn't. As usual, Micheál was affable to everybody, with Hilton less so. At any rate an uneasy peace was maintained. In speeches after the last performance on 29 May 1957, the audience was assured the Gate would be re-opened in six months. There were some, not necessarily the pessimists, who went home that night, their minds full of doubts.

Chapter 18

A Broken World

When the Gate Theatre was closed, Edward kept his company together and thus aroused their loyalty and hard work. When they weren't touring, they did a Dublin season at the Bernadette Hall in Rathmines. Conditions weren't luxurious, but they far exceeded some of the so-called theatres they had to play on tour. Naturally, the players preferred Dublin any time. However, Cork never failed to appeal.

While playing 'The Opera' was always a backstage pleasure (it had that backstage bar!), capturing Cork audiences was always a difficulty. There was an undercurrent of artistic resentment against Dublin companies. 'Dublin has the technique, but Cork has the talent,' was as much as the Cork people would concede. A specially snide remark reserved for Longford Prods was: 'Yerra 'tis cold in de Opera even when 'tis full — an' sure ye're never full.' A similar insult came in Athlone: the company had arrived in pouring rain to find an empty hall. One local said: 'Not even the lord's company could fill that hall,' to which another added: 'Sure you wouldn't fill that hall if you were to bring the True Cross.'

As good as his word, Edward Longford reopened the Gate Theatre in January 1958 with a sparkling production of *The Tempest*. 'The new Gate' had now got concrete entrance stairs, a safety curtain, renovated dressing-rooms, and various innovations for the safety and convenience of the public and the players. Christine, in an interview in *The Word* in December 1969, summarised how all this was achieved: 'We'd had to knock down the place and build it up again for an enormous sum of money — about £30,000. To raise it we sold everything we could, and literally begged in the streets. We sold our clothes, our books. But we also had a lot of very kind friends. It was important and it is still very important that there should be another theatre in Dublin.'

There is no doubt but that it was Edward's initiative, imagination and drive — backed by the constant loving support of Christine — which, for the second time, saved the life of the Gate Theatre. It is a sad reflection that today there is no permanent memorial in that theatre to commemorate the man and the woman to whom the place owes its existence. All that remains is a photograph of Edward, appropriately with his begging bowl, and an unflattering portrait by Muriel Brandt of

Lord Moyne, Edward, Christine and Ria Mooney of the Abbey Theatre. The occasion isn't known, but the background suggests the Olympia Theatre.

Christine with Hilton and Micheál. (Hilton and Micheál are clearly recognisable, but Christine's features are hidden by a curtain of hair falling over her face. Of another Brandt portrait of Christine, Hilton once said, 'My God, she has spared her nothing!') Everything, it seems, that Edward Longford did for Ireland, Ireland sneeringly took for granted: 'Sure an' couldn't he well afford it!' The fact was that he couldn't afford it, and the worry of that debt helped to put him in an early grave.

Christine, in 1969, bears this out: 'We hadn't got the debt paid off when the theatre reopened in 1958. When my husband died in 1961, he thought he had paid it off. He had just written a fairly large cheque against it, but it didn't get paid because he died. And that wasn't even the end. There were a lot more bills coming in. But it's paid now.' By whom? Finally, by Christine Longford.

As a reopening show, *The Tempest* went well. Shakespeare could be

179

relied upon, if only for the school parties. Backstage, the actors had a rougher time. Shakespeare's stage directions call for a ship at sea and a storm with thunder and lightning. The effect of a rocking boat was obtained by mounting it on a barrel rolled to and fro by the stage-hands. But when the stage-hands got tight they took revenge on their favourite actors by promoting the tempest to a hurricane.

Peter Ustinov's *Romanoff and Juliet* ran for seven weeks to packed houses — and Edward didn't interfere by taking it off! Was he becoming wiser? Or was he tired? To his day-to-day managerial responsibilities were now added those of a massive debt. It was a worrisome burden, which in another man might have caused debility and loss of weight, even alcoholism. With Edward's temperament it caused further over-eating, the end-result, healthwise, being no different.

Edward feared illness as much as he feared doctors and dentists. He suffered from carious teeth, but he refused to go near a dentist. All his life he had wished illness away, and, of course, Christine had adopted the same idea, though neither went so far as to acknowledge Mary Baker Eddy, (1821-1910) the founder of the religious faith known as Christian Science. Edward could not understand illness or even injury afflicting himself, let alone another. When he was told an actor was ill, he would retort, 'Ill? I don't understand.'

Visiting Lissadell, when touring Sligo, the company were in that high gallery, made famous by Yeats with its 'great windows open to the south', when Edward asked the actors to recite lines to test the well-known accoustics. Suddenly he slipped, his great bulk falling heavily to the floor. Everybody rushed to his assistance, but he would have none of it. Visibly very shaken, he managed to get himself up. He had sprained his ankle, but he preferred to hobble around in pain, rather than see a doctor or visit a hospital.

Attendance fell away again through 1959 and 1960. Had the novelty of 'the new Gate' worn off? Ugo Betti's *Summertime* in October 1959 drew audiences as low as thirty-five. Edward had greatly exerted himself in fund-raising for the refurbishment, but he never despaired. 'It will pick up,' he would say. Yet he began to sub-let part of his six-month lease of the Gate to the Globe Theatre Company, where some of his actors found employment. Thus Edward's conscience was less troubled, for he had had to draw in his financial horns. Also, his theatrical keenness had become blunted. His few productions alternated with those of the Globe. There was no more writing, no more translation. Even Christine's inspiration had dried. Her last play came in 1960. Called *Stephen Storey*, it was about an elderly squireen botanist surrounded by plants. The name-part was played by Aiden Grennell.

Edward wasn't seen around for a day or two at the beginning of February 1961. Somebody enquired of Christine. He wasn't well, a bad cold. Next day they heard he was in Portobello Nursing Home. Aiden and Iris called, only to find him unconscious. Shocked, they told their colleagues at the Gate. Christine meant well. Faithful to Edward, she was trying to trivialise his illness, trying to pretend it wasn't there. That was how Edward would have wanted it.

What had happened soon emerged. A religious man, Edward never failed in his loyalty to the Church of Ireland. On Thursday 2 February, though not feeling well, he ate a hearty meal and set off to a church vestry meeting in County Kildare. On the return journey he felt distinctly worse, but managed to get through the gate at Grosvenor Park. Near the house the car slewed off the avenue on to the lawn. Christine happened to be sitting at the window. With Sissy, the cook, they managed to get him from the car and into the house. They called a doctor who admitted him to the nursing home. By Saturday morning he was dead from a massive stroke, secondary to high blood pressure. Not an unexpected end to a life-style such as Edward's.

That night I was at a dinner party in Stockholm with nine other doctors. I was in Sweden on a World Health Organisation travelling fellowship. The conversation turned to Ireland. A policeman, I was told, had been shot that day in Northern Ireland. Would he have been an Englishman? Unsuccessfully, I tried to explain that puzzle. A Lord Longford had died in Dublin — his photograph had been on Swedish television that evening. Did I know of him? Medical doctors to the exclusion of all else, I could not have explained to those studious Scandinavians how I knew Lord Longford, how I admired him, how as a student I had worked for him as a small-time actor. They would have thought that odd, flippant, even unprofessional. But for the rest of that evening my mind kept going back to Dublin, to Christine and to the Gate Theatre, for whose futures I now greatly feared.

The theatre had been leased that week to Gemini Productions. On the night of Edward's death the audience stood in tribute. Norman Rodway told them a message had come from Lady Longford that on no account were they to cancel the show, because Lord Longford would have preferred it that way. The show must go on — and it did.

Meanwhile, the tributes flowed. In Ireland death brings a respectability denied in life. The 'old fat fool' was suddenly half-canonised. 'With his passing,' said Hilton and Micheál, 'we salute with admiration

Christine at the Gate on 17 February 1961 with Frank and Elizabeth Pakenham. Frank had just succeeded as the seventh Earl of Longford following Edward's death on 5 February.

and respect Lord Longford's devotion to his country and to the theatre in Ireland for which we have all worked for so long.'

Anew Mc Master showed a fellow feeling: 'He was one of the very few Dublin managers who felt it was his duty to tour the provinces. His most outstanding contributions to present day cultural life were his gifts as a scholar, poet and a translator from the Irish, French and Greek. He never presented anything which he did not think was fine and worthy.'

Two Dublin theatre critics compressed their words into gem-like tributes: R. M. ('Dicky') Fox, Edward's contemporary at Oxford, said, 'In a way he belonged to Georgian Dublin, dignified, spacious, with a touch of grandeur'; and Seamus Kelly wrote: 'Perhaps the Nation might think fit to make the Gate its memorial to a good Irishman.'

The Longford Prods — men and women — wept unashamedly for, with their father figure, they had lost their future too. But Christine didn't weep. Often afterwards she wondered why she didn't weep. Controlling her feelings, she comforted those around her, because she saw it as her duty to do so. When her alter ego, Martha Freke, thought about the horror of widowhood she had asked herself would she commit suicide. 'No,' she told herself, 'she would be brave and live for her children.' The boys and girls of the company had always been Edward and Christine's children. Now they were Christine's orphans.

Among the crowds of Edward's genuine admirers, Dublin's intellectual periphery was also at the funeral, more to be seen at Mount Jerome than to pray for Edward's soul. Amongst those who 'paid their respects' was Brendan Behan. The story may be apocryphal, but he is alleged to have poured the contents of a stout bottle into the grave while he spoke his special tribute: 'Micheál Mac Liammóir may be the fucking queen of the Irish theatre, but Edward Longford was its fucking Pope.' If the story is true, no doubt his words were heartfelt and well meant.

And then they all went away, the moguls, the chancers, the entrepreneurs, all wondering if the Gate was up for grabs. Who held the controlling interest? Was the refurbishment debt paid off? Would it close permanently now? Or, most important of all — might there be a bit of money in the bloody place if a fella could do a deal?

Edward's sister, Mary, summarised his life with a sister's objectivity: 'It was bad luck that he succeeded to the title and property so young, and being favouritised obviously was harmful, but I think he was really born the way he was. However, he had a very happy life, doing the thing he liked best doing, and he solved the problem of being an Englishman with property in Ireland by turning himself into an Irishman.' She was struck by the wave of sympathy shown by the Irish people, a young man's gesture making a special impression: 'When Elizabeth Longford and I were coming back from Edward's funeral, the young Aer Lingus pilot came all the way down the aisle to the back of the plane where we were sitting to express a few elegant condolences. There's fame for you!' Doubtless, like so many others, he owed the deceased a deep debt of cultural gratitude.

Amongst the wreaths left at the grave was one marked 'With affection and gratitude'. It was from Eve Watkinson, a one-time leading lady. Some people asked her what she meant by 'gratitude'. She meant just that. Edward may have been awkward, uneasy, and socially you would never have sought his company — in fact she never felt he was real — but he had the heart of a lion, his generosity was boundless, and she would always be grateful for the parts he had given her. 'I was a Longford actress, and proud of it.' In this, no doubt, Eve Watkinson expressed the feelings of all those Longford Prods who, over the years, had toured the length and breadth of Ireland, in fair weather and foul, the faithful children of Edward and Christine Longford.

On the Monday night after Edward's funeral, Mc Master opened a season at the Gate Theatre with Ibsen's *When We Dead Awaken*, an unintentional but oddly significant occurrence.

Lovers of the Gate Theatre were relieved when, one month later, after a meeting of the directors, newspaper headlines read: 'Gate Theatre To Remain Open — 25-Year-Old Split Healed.' At his death Edward had held the controlling interest in the theatre, and this he had left to Christine. Her concern was now to hand it over to whoever was best suited for the responsibility. She gave it to Hilton and Micheál, as those with the first right. By doing so she believed she was placing them in an ideal position to benefit from the State subsidy which was then, it was rumoured, to be granted. As a *quid pro quo* they made her chairman of the reconstituted board, a recognition of her pivotal position. Thus she became the rallying point of yet another movement to keep the Gate Theatre in existence.

A statement was issued: 'Lady Longford and Messrs Edwards and Mac Liammóir have agreed to join together, thus closing the split between Longford Productions and Edwards-Mac Liammóir, and restoring the original enterprise which led to the founding of the Gate Theatre. They hope in the future to be able to have seasons under their management in the Gate.'

Technically, Longford Productions died with Edward. The players had already dispersed, except for six whom he had kept under contract. Christine retained this group on the pay-roll for eighteen months after his death. Every Friday in the office she would first apologise for Edward's dying, and then pay each member — a sort of symbolic pat on the head: Off you go now, you're provided for for another week. While some were left out, it was embarrassing for those who were paid. Somebody called them 'the Chelsea pensioners'. Eventually, of course, it had to stop. The executors objected, Christine explained.

Evelyn Waugh's appreciation of Edward, published in the *Observer*, gave Christine great comfort: 'I have been asked by the new head of the family to record some memories of my contemporary, the late Earl of Longford. I accede gladly for he and his siblings are bound to me by long friendship ...' Ah, how nice! Their little faun of long ago had not forgotten. After a nostalgic re-run of Oxford, and of riotous holidays at Pakenham Hall, Waugh concluded: 'The Dublin literary world has been described by Mr Cyril Connolly as "warm and friendly as an alligator pool". Over this dangerous enclosure Edward and Christine floated serenely indifferent to the snapping jaws below. It is not difficult to become a public figure in Dublin. It is rare to be regarded with real esteem and affection. That, with Christine's support, was Edward's achievement.'

A few days later, Waugh wrote to Ann Fleming, then the wife of Ian Fleming, the creator of James Bond: 'Our best news is Edward Longford's

Thomas Pakenham, his cousin Lord Dunsany and his father Lord Longford outside Pakenham Hall (now renamed Tullynally Castle) on 21 June 1968 when the castle was first opened to the public.

death. Before the body was cold Frank was telephoning all over the United Kingdom trying to promote publicity. He persuaded me to write a panegyric in the *Observer*. It was a model of how such a thing should be done so as not to offend the family and at the same time to reveal the essential absurdity of the deceased ...'

Their little faun! 'Real esteem and affection'. The depths of deceit are unfathomable. Because she so admired everything written by Waugh, I am glad Christine was dead by the time that letter was published. It would have hurt her beyond measure.

Edward may have had shortcomings, but the ambitions he held, and the actions he took throughout his life for the restoration of the arts and of nationhood to Ireland, were factors which Waugh and his likes could not possibly have understood.

Chapter 19

A Woman of Great Importance

Friends, they say in Ireland, desert a widow. If the widow is in need perhaps they do. Christine wasn't deserted, but that had nothing to do with wealth or poverty. Indeed, she considered herself no more than comfortably off — her marriage settlement had seen to that. Far from deserting her, old friends rallied, and new friends sought acceptance.

Christine became a born-again personality, once more an individual in her own right, a being free to converse, to express her own opinions, to live her own life. She had walked so long in Edward's broadsome shadow that her adjustment to taking her own place in the sun required a little time. First things first: she had to check her over-use of the word 'we'.

The disposal of Pakenham Hall presented her with no problem. Together with the title, it had automatically passed from Edward to his younger brother, Frank. He wasn't interested and, in turn, passed it on to Thomas Pakenham, his eldest son. The contents, however, became Christine's property, which Thomas suggested he should purchase from her. In 1961 this could have meant £15,000-£20,000 to Christine. But instead, and as Mary Clive relates, 'Christine behaved with admirable generosity, waiving her legal rights to the furniture.'

Having disposed of what was left of the antique treasures she and Edward had so lovingly collected on the Dublin quays, she moved from Grosvenor Park to a flat in the precincts of the Merrion Nursing Home in Herbert Street. To reach her first-floor rooms you had to pass through the home. Christine worried about the noise her visitors might make. To dull it she covered her landing with Chinese mats.

At some later date structural alterations were in progress. The architect, recognising genuine Chinese craftmanship, instructed his workmen most carefully: Lady Longford's mats must be kept covered. He returned to find the air thick with dust, and plaster all over the mats. Unexpectedly the wall had collapsed. He stormed at the workmen. Their defence was impregnable: Lady Longford had passed in in the meantime and hadn't said a word. Feeling she was due an apology he knocked on her door.

'Who are you and what do you want?' she asked. 'I'm the architect. About this mess, I love you for being so indulgent, but ...'

Opening the door wider, Christine said, 'In that case, come in. I like to stand my suitors a drink.'

The architect was Brendan Ellis. It was the beginning of a lasting friendship. With his wife, Sheila, they were still around in Christine's sickly old age when many of her fair-weather friends had flown.

Once she had recovered from the demands made on her by Edward, Christine became an unrecognisably different person. Like a flower brought from the shadows to the light, she blossomed to become an outgoing socialite, a woman so greatly in demand she had no difficulty in filling her widowed days. Intellectualism was still her criterion for acceptance. Religion, politics, state-in-life — none mattered as long as you weren't a bore, and nobody was quicker with a spot diagnosis of a pseudo-intellectual than Christine.

Another group always sure of her attention were those she called the downtrodden. The oppressed could do no wrong. She was always on their side against the tyrants. In her quiet, sensitive way, she could do a thousand acts of kindness, often not even the recipients noticing. How many dispirited young actors did she mother when the world was against them? A cup of coffee, a word of encouragement and a pound note pressed into an empty palm. And the young poets and the would-be novelists? Occupied as she was with her own work, Christine heard them out sympathetically, and wisely advised them. Her years in the theatre had alerted her to latent talent. It was everywhere in Ireland. It needed only encouragement and direction.

No more than Edward, Christine Longford had no malice in her. Although there wasn't an immoral liaison in Dublin and its hinterland of which she hadn't heard, she never passed judgment. Their morals were their own business. Once only I saw her fiercely indignant, when an elderly gentleman of her acquaintance, a grandfather in fact, taking his possessions, walked out on his wife, a woman for whom she had affection. She loved to hear the current social misbehaviour. She would retell it with gusto. Having done so, she would laugh a little guiltily, saying that if there was a hell she would go right there for giving scandal. It was all amusingly innocent, and quite without guile.

She admired beautiful people, by which she meant handsome men and women of grace and charm. She admired beauty in its every manifestation: literature, painting, gardens, the movements of a horse, a bird in flight. Unless music had an association with a play — like Grieg's with Ibsen's *Peer Gynt* — she wasn't interested. She had one musical love — The Dubliners. She was a fan of Ronnie Drew's. Opera was to her a ridiculous expression of theatre and the only ballet she admired was the

Irish ballet directed by Joan Denise Moriarty.

Christine was sadly conscious that she was not a beautiful woman. Once at a Gate Theatre party, when everybody had had a few fortifying drinks, an emboldened young actor said to her, 'Christine, I would love to give you a kiss.' 'Go away,' she told him, 'that's your love of the grotesque.'

Unfortunately, for her own sake, she had little sense of dress. It was as if she deliberately made herself drab. Because Edward ran a tweed business she had little option but to wear his products. Irish tweeds became a *sine qua non*, part of her new Irishry. Besides, it was important that his contribution to the Irish economy should be seen to be done — and so, faithfully, she wore them, and they did not flatter her. After his death, and the disappearance of Mr Copithorne and the Hand-Loom Shop, Christine, perhaps now through force of habit, continued too often to dress in her colourless tweeds. Though she made a routine of using a powder-compact, this was the limit of her make-up. She was hesitant about lipstick. In fact she took no pride in her appearance. It was the only thing in which she lacked judgment. As if in compensation, her personality overflowed, touching you like convector waves of warmth from hidden sources.

Jean Anderson recalls a story Christine used to tell against herself. She was shopping in Clery's for material for costumes for the theatre. 'I'll have it on my account,' she told the salesgirl. 'What name?' the girl asked. 'Lady Longford,' replied Christine. Sneeringly doubtful of her customer, the girl exclaimed, 'Lady Longford how are ye!' 'I'm very well, thank you,' Christine assured her, 'and please deliver it to the Gate Theatre.'

Jean has another recollection: after the war she came on a nostalgic visit to Dublin and the Gate. 'I was told Christine was upstairs in the theatre, but I couldn't find her anywhere. I eventually tracked her down in the ladies' loo with a screwdriver in her hand dealing with an errant ballcock.' If there was anything useful she was capable of doing, silly pride never stopped Christine from getting on with the job.

Edward had been something of a Jekyll and Hyde, a bundle of contradictions. He was shy, yet authoritative; dictatorial, yet paternalistic. Christine's few contradictions were less marked. To describe her as a modest woman would be very much to understate the case. She was afflicted with a form of nihilism, a self-abnegation that became embarrassing. Like a lesser Royal she walked a foot or so behind Edward; if there was a cold cup of tea or smaller piece of cake, that would do for Christine; at home her fridge was usually empty and her flat cold; you could not pay her a compliment, even on her writing. She would denigrate it, as if she were an illiterate. An example: she gave me a copy of *Making Conversation*, her brilliant first novel. In it she wrote: 'For John Cowell with apologies, Christine'. I treasure it because this book calls forth praise and pride, but certainly not apologies. Christine would have made a wonderfully loving, obedient and self-sacrificing nun, with the capacity to administer just enough flavouring of lemon juice to keep her community salivating.

For three years (1961-1964) after Edward's death, Christine managed the Gate Theatre. That sense of business acumen she had never been allowed to exploit now came into its own. Her handling of lettings to visiting companies was on a strictly competitive business basis — and no nonsense. And if something went wrong she faced the crisis squarely — as when an ambitious young actor leased the theatre and got only empty houses. It was quickly evident that he couldn't meet his debts. His show was withdrawn, and he blamed Christine, threatening her with court proceedings. Instead of allowing things to drift, she stepped in and paid off all the debts. It wasn't a move that could have been repeated too often, but the young man happened to win her sympathy: he was an ambitious actor, and just then he was among the downtrodden.

During the period of her management of the Gate, her social life was inconvenienced. Not that she ever complained, but, again, like the dutiful mother superior, whatever function she was at, she insisted on leaving and returning to the theatre to ensure the evening had passed without incident. Taking leave of her friends she would laugh, saying she had to go back to the theatre in case the mice had got into the biscuits. Her term as manager ended when she had another illness requiring operative surgery.

Complete freedom eventually provided time for other activities. Written in her characteristically beguiling style, her regular book reviews in *The Irish Times* became that newspaper's favourite feature for many readers on a Saturday. But for Christine they were a tiresome chore she wished to give up long before she finally did so. Their transience, she felt, was as fleeting as yesterday's news. She wanted to do something of a more permanent nature. She wanted more than anything to do a biography of Edward, in which she would tell the whole truth about their original relationship with the Gate Theatre. It was a subject on which she felt resentful, sometimes even bitter.

But when she sat down to write, the truth would not come out. Perhaps, more correctly, she could not bring herself to allow it to come out. Her sense of integrity came into conflict with her desire not to hurt any living being. So her effort to vindicate all Edward had done, all the hurts he had suffered, for the Gate Theatre, became an exercise so reined-in, so self-controlled, that it resulted in a vitiated manuscript. Christine knew this. Though she continued to struggle with herself, she still failed in her effort.

It was a kind of failure not new in her writing. In her plays, for instance, she sometimes evaded putting the real drama on stage, before the eyes of her audience. Instead she would have characters discuss an off-stage incident rather than show the incident to her audience. *The United Brothers*, her play on the brothers Sheares, is an example. In Act III she used Marie Steele, John Sheares' love, and her mother, Lady Steele, to comment on the arrest of Henry Sheares taking place on the steps of 128 Lower Baggot Street, while they are watching from a back window of their house at 11 Merrion Square South. Dramatically that arrest should have been witnessed on-stage by the audience, but Christine funked it. As Christopher Casson said: 'There were times when she wouldn't let the drama come out.'

Was this literary evasion her sub-consciuos effort to spare people's feelings? As far as Edward's biography was concerned, she grew irritated with her own lack of courage. She wanted to tell all, yet she couldn't bring herself to do so. As a result, Edward's biography became an unmentionable subject. Time was when you asked how it was coming along. Eventually that enquiry only evoked annoyance. Her friends learned to steer clear of the matter.

Gifted in so many ways, and now that she had the opportunity a brilliant raconteur in her own right, another aspect of Christine was discovered rather late in life: she was a natural broadcaster. It was Patrick Maguire, later head of drama, RTE Radio, who persuaded her to become a panellist on a weekly programme called 'Survey', which ran for some years in the mid-sixties. It was devoted to criticism of the arts: books, plays, films and so forth. Participants included poets, critics, novelists, journalists, teachers, even one medic — myself. Panellists appeared in rotation to allow time for preparation.

One night I stepped from the lift in the old Henry Street studios. Always punctual, Christine had already arrived for her first programme. Sitting alone, she looked like one about to be led to the electric chair. 'Are you in this "Survey" programme?' she asked eagerly. 'Yes,' I said. 'Oh! I'm so glad,' she said, 'I wouldn't go through this agony for anybody but Paddy Maguire.' She was as nervous as a kitten.

'May I sit opposite, and talk to you? I hate talking *at* a microphone.' We agreed this little arrangement, for of course, it worked both ways. A familiar face to talk to is preferable any time to an inverted tea-strainer.

Years later, when I listened to a recording, I felt flattered that through me, as it were, Christine had told listening Ireland what she thought of mad Czechoslovakian novelists, pretentious exhibitions, Antonioni films in wide-screen panavision, and endless adaptations for the Irish stage. It was a fallow period when original plays were few and far between.

An encouraging chairman, Patrick Maguire brought out the best each had to offer. As we became familiar with one another, and with our medium, hectically heated discussions broke out — the essence of what such a programme is all about. The feedback included requests for a transfer from radio to television. There was a curiosity to see the faces behind the voices. That never took place. The senior service — as radio considered itself — would not yield. But the programme *did* bring the distinctive voice, and the warmth of personality, of Christine Longford to thousands who, hitherto, had known her only as a silent writer, and the self-effacing wife of the late Lord Longford.

In January 1967, we reviewed a re-issue of Rose Macaulay's *The Towers of Trebizond*. Christine glowed with enthusiasm. She found the zany humour of Father Chantry-Pigg and Aunt Dot irresistible. Their High Anglican caperings on their mission to Turkey struck a chord. The straight-faced humour was echoed in Christine's treatment of dotty Irish characters in her own novels. Indeed, if there was ever a writer who influenced Christine Longford, I suggest it was Rose Macaulay. There was a long-time heroic admiration going back to Oxford days when as a timorous undergraduate Christine was privileged to pour tea for the great novelist.

It was in March 1967 that Christine was given an award which brought her deeply genuine pleasure. For long and devoted service to the Irish theatre she was conferred with life membership of the Irish Actors' Equity Association. For any little thing she always greatly exaggerated her thanks and gratitude. For life membership of Equity, words failed her, because, with her habitual self-effacement, she did not believe she had earned such an honour. What she *did* believe — and what she would have others believe — was that, through her, they were really honouring Edward. She never failed in maintaining her adoration of Edward. Her ambition was to keep his memory green.

No wonder then she was horrified when ghoulish vandals desecrated his tombstone in Mount Jerome Cemetery. The work of the distinguished sculptor, Seamus Murphy, RHA, the tombstone bears the family crest, and the masks of Comedy and Tragedy. At first she worried that this attack might have been inspired by sectarianism or public ill-will, until she learned to understand that some of Dublin's vandals are incapable of controlling their indiscriminately destructive impulses.

A year later, in 1968, another honour came. Christine was elected a member of the Irish Academy of Letters. This time there was no doubt the honour was hers, and hers alone, for in his time, Edward had not alone been a member, but he had held the office of President.

Micheál Mac Liammóir was honoured by the Academy on the same occasion, a coincidence she could have done without. In spite of opinions to the opposite, I believe that Christine Longford disliked Micheál Mac Liammóir. The reasons are not difficult to find. Micheál couldn't resist making jokes, often at the expense of the saviour of the Gate Theatre. Edward's corpulence was an easy target; his Eton Irish was another; his ideas on professionalism in the theatre was a third, and there were more.

In his *All For Hecuba* he is too wickedly penetrating in his pen-pictures of Edward and Christine. We all have foibles; they mostly pass unnoticed. Put them under the microscope of an observant writer and they can become hilariously funny, or worse, ridiculously absurd. Micheál's reproduction of Christine's manner of speaking, was, alone, a source of offence. His treatment of Edward was even more so — something Christine could not abide from anybody, least of all from that sensitive and gifted man whom she had once so greatly admired, and to whom her husband had repeatedly thrown a lifeline when he and his theatre had all but disappeared beneath the waves of debt.

However thwarted, Christine was never a bitter woman. A wry observer, hers could be a mordant wit. Her simplest remarks often held a deeper meaning. For instance, she could quickly douse a conversational show-off. 'That was so clever of you,' she would interject, glancing apologetically round at the guests he had been boring. If she had nothing good to say of a person, she usually kept quiet. Of Micheál Mac Liammóir she was frankly critical. His penny-pinching when eventually he had amassed money. His reckless profligacy in the days when Edward's money was being spent: if an alpaca suit was wanted, it wasn't hired, it was made and it never went into the costume room afterwards — a tiny instance among many when Micheál's generosity became Edward's overdraft. Though she didn't often talk about it, she had not forgotten.

There was an apparent contradiction in the fact that Micheál's attitude to Edward was much more rational than Hilton's. There was a reason. The soulful Mac Liammóir of the Gate, like the soulful Yeats of the Abbey, was in fact the wakeful partner where money was concerned. Hilton Edwards' mind was occupied with anything but money. Whenever the matter arose, his retort was usually, 'Talk to Micheál.' Not even for unlimited subsidisation could Hilton curb his dislike of Edward. It was, therefore, important that Micheál be rational if the lord was to continue to provide. After the split, of course, finer feelings mattered no longer.

Another contradiction: I am equally convinced that Christine liked Hilton. She admired his professionalism. She even admired him as a man. Perhaps she allowed for Edward's lack of professionalism, when in the old days he so often put in his oar, enraging Hilton. These were the occasions when she had invented her well-worn excuse: 'Edward is being difficult again, isn't he?' Her liking for Hilton grew in their old age. She would come back from board meetings full of admiration for his handling of awkward situations, such as Micheál leaving the table in a tantrum and shouting sulky remarks from another room for the rest of the meeting.

There was one aspect of Hilton she did not condone: his repeated assertion that he was an Englishman in a foreign country. That was not Christine's idea of integration with the ould sod — for that was how she interpreted the position in both their cases. Her grandmother came from Youghal, County Cork, and her mother was an O'Sullivan, while Hilton's mother was an Emily Murphy, the daughter of an Irish emigrant father. Emily Murphy never saw Ireland, but never mind, as Christine would say. In part they had both derived from Irish emigrants, and that to Christine mattered at least as much as her religion.

Once she sent me a postcard with a bronze elephant of the Chou Dynasty. On it she wrote: 'Please forgive a pre-war postcard. The elephant never forgets.' Nor did Christine. While she forgave The Boys, she never loved them as in those shrewd days and nights of the theatre theatrical at the Gate and the fish-and-chip suppers in greasy basement cafés in O'Connell Street. She didn't have them at her parties, nor did she otherwise socialise with them. The relationship had become coolly formal and business-like, and was principally concerned with their agenda for board meetings at 4 Harcourt Terrace.

He who once slighted Edward, or his memory, slighted Christine for all time. Her self-effacement notwithstanding, an insult to Edward was the single insult she would not tolerate.

Chapter 20

Memoirs and 'Duties'

In November 1968, in the *Times Literary Supplement*, Pamela Hansford Johnson published a long article on Christine Longford's first novel, *Making Conversation*. It was a detailed analysis of a book which she claimed should be regarded as an English comic classic, like *Cold Comfort Farm*. First published in 1931, and reprinted in the same year, Ms Johnson's copy had cost her one shilling and sixpence.

One may wonder what motivated this adulatory article some thirty-seven years after the publication of the book. Not even acquaintance — much less nepotism — was involved. The two women had never even met, but Ms Johnson understood that Lady Longford was a delightfully funny person with a humour 'kind, but deadly'.

The motivation was simply the memory of a book she had greatly enjoyed. As when she had first read it, she was still intrigued as to how Lady Longford had caught so accurately the *feel* of genteel poverty, for in young Pamela Hansford Johnson's imagination Lady Longford 'must have been someone living permanently in satin and pearls'. Little did she know! But on her later reading she suspected something. 'There had to be truth here,' she concluded, 'the whole of this first novel rang with it.'

As a result of that *Times Lit.* article, Faber took another look at the thirty-seven year old novel and decided on republication. A new edition appeared in 1970 — a great boost for the morale of a lonely widow, still trying hard to hide the depth of her loss. At the time, Christine was re-living her life with Edward. She was working on the memoirs from which I have so copiously quoted.

Her visits to Pakenham Hall became more and more infrequent. Research there for her work wasn't necessary. Any theatre records that existed were in Dublin. As for letters, they were few enough, and they referred only to the earliest days of her relationship with Edward. Afterwards, there had been no need for letters. They had shared everything together. Whatever else she required was stored in her fabulous memory, which to the day of her death, never failed her in the smallest detail. Indeed, in many things, she became a geriatric phenomenon: she never even required spectacles, and her neat and legible handwriting never showed the least evidence of deterioration.

From the outset Pakenham Hall had overwhelmed her. Its size alone was intimidating. She never loved it in the way Edward did. To him it was home. There he would throw off his chalk-stripes, and in an old sports jacket, he would relax in a way that never seemed possible in Dublin. Christine, as in most other things, endured P. Hall, as she called it, because she knew how much Edward loved the place. It might have been different had she had children. But sadly, all there was to nurse there was the collection of teddy bears. Once, when Longford Prods were in residence, Charles Mitchel, indicating their palatial surroundings, asked Christine, 'D'you like all this?' 'I have to,' was her reply.

Nor did her title mean much to her. Infinitely more, she would have preferred that of 'doctor' — in its academic sense, that is. She never basked in the reflected glory of being the Countess of Longford. Far more important was her writing name, Christine Longford, and even more her simple 'Christine', the title that carried with it the unmistakeable sense of acceptance, of being wanted, of being loved, of being an essential part of the cultural life of the Dublin of her time.

Edward was different. He liked his title. It boosted the authority he somehow lacked in his mental make-up. It commanded attention. Nor did he see any contradiction in his ardent Irish nationalism and holding a title which, though granted by the Irish Parliament in College Green, was still part of the hated occupation of Ireland. Holding his title was for him simply a part of Irish history, something contributed to Ireland by the British for preservation, like Dun Laoghaire Pier or Georgian Dublin. It was also part of the feudal attitude; the noble baron with duties to his tenants, to his strolling players, to his audiences, in contrast to those absentee landlords to whom Ireland meant no more than an easy source of revenue. Not unlike Lord Byron (also, incidentally, a sixth baron, and also having a deep knowledge of the scriptures), Edward was a noble revolutionary who only wanted to serve his country well.

In writing his biography, Christine had been too lovingly adulatory. She had shunned the smallest suggestion of criticism. Edward was always right. If there was wrong-doing others were responsible. Yet unconsciously, and between the lines, she re-affirmed much of the Edward known to his players and to the public. Over-eating permeates the script, as well as her own well-meant indulgence of this deadly addiction. His capacity for swift decision-making shines through, though these were often rash decisions which flew in the face of common sense, and the facts and figures before him. His decisions on the choice of plays, and the lengths of their runs, sometimes amazed those around him. It was all part of that wilful rebelliousness which had characterised Edward

Christine with Jack Farrer at the opening of the RHA Exhibition, 10 June 1969.

from his childhood. Christine's memoirs were indeed a loving tribute to an adored husband with whom, she was proud to say, she had spent thirty-five blissful years. But, as in life so in death, her over-generous, tender, loving care dulled her judgment, making her final work unattractive to publishers.

Always a devotée of the National Library, she spent even more time there while working on her memoirs. It is as regrettable as it is extraordinary that the archives of Longford Productions went missing during the second refurbishment of the Gate Theatre in 1970. Nobody can throw light on their whereabouts, or even whether they may still exist in some forgotten attic. While it is sad that the Edwards-Mac Liammóir archives were allowed to leave this country for a foreign library, it is even sadder that the Longford archives should go missing apparently within the country. Usually very conscious of what should go into the family archives at Pakenham Hall, Christine displayed a peculiar indifference to the fate of her husband's theatre archives. The result is that, unlike the Abbey Theatre, despite its destructive fire of 1951, the Gate Theatre has lost all the archives accumulated over the first fifty years of its existence.

In her widowhood, there was no more independent woman than Christine Longford. She had learned the hard way. Shortly after Edward's death she was asked about her loneliness. She had no illusions about the matter. 'I think I see more people now than when I had a husband,' she replied. 'If one has a husband one doesn't need to have so many other friends. And then I had thirty-five years of happiness. It's pretty good to have thirty-five years of happiness, don't you think?' And how did she spend her time? 'I haunt the Gate Theatre. I do occasional odd jobs. I talk to people. I read books. I don't mind being on my own.'

Christine's stubborn independence was never more embarrassing than when we met on the No. 10 bus, as we did, frequently, in the early sixties. At the time I was Executive Secretary at the Royal Irish Academy, an appointment, incidentally, which she thought elevated me to the top echelons of intellectualism. The facts were otherwise, but that's another story! The Academy, squeezed between the Mansion House and St Ann's Church, didn't have a parking place, hence my dependence on the bus. On her way to the National Library, Christine would often board at Herbert Street, greet me brightly, adding loudly as she foraged in her handbag: 'No, you are not to pay my fare. I will not be a sponger' — a favourite word of hers. That command in an Oxford accent on the upper deck of the No. 10 never failed to attract attention. While she never objected to unlimited driving in my car, it was a matter of high principle never to have her fare paid by me, or indeed anybody else.

Hers was an old-fashioned sense of independence: decent people didn't sponge, and certainly a decent woman didn't. It was an independence unrelated to the women's liberation movement, for which Christine Longford had no time. Their stridency, particularly on sex, didn't appeal. Rather, it nauseated. Christine always saw things from the point of view of the theatre, and in the theatre male domination didn't exist. From the ancient Greeks onwards, there had been both actors and actresses in the theatre, their parts equally important, and that was how it would always be. Likewise with intellectualism: if she put her mind to it, a woman could always equal a man. So women's liberation didn't arise for Christine, but that gentle sense of womanly independence would always be something important in her life.

Part of her motive in writing her Memoirs or, more correctly, her 'Memoirs of Edward', was to try to keep his memory fresh. It was remarkable, and most hurtful to her, that people had so soon forgotten the thirty years he had straddled the stages of Ireland. There was a new generation of theatre-goers who didn't seem to know that but for a man called Lord Longford, there would be no Gate Theatre in Dublin, much less a wildly exuberant amateur theatre movement that had gripped the countryside as fiercely as had the GAA in earlier times.

She revised her Memoirs in 1971, when her writing capacity still flourished, but they remained incomplete at her death in 1980. She had grown impatient with the task — which was a pity, for as Mary Clive points out: 'Christine was such an amusing letter-writer — acid and terse — right up to the last.' Her impatience, as she admitted, was because she couldn't come to grips with the book.

Dissatisfied with her Memoirs, she said the book would not be published in her lifetime — from which it was assumed she had in fact told the whole truth. Time showed otherwise. In nineteen words she had skated over the 'split'. 'In fact the Gate split wasn't a shipwreck,' she wrote. 'Calm followed storm, and the Gate was safe for the present.' The 'Memoirs', although containing some 90,000 words, covered only seventeen years, from 1922 to 1939. It was as if she had lost the heart to go on. Yet, more than ever, Edward's name needed to be rescued from fast-approaching oblivion.

In the mid-seventies RTE televised a remarkable programme, with Hilton and Micheál at their most voluble. It was a post-prandial theatre discussion conducted by the late Jack White. Over the remnants of what looked like a good meal at 4 Harcourt Terrace, Hilton, a spent match in one hand, a still unlit pipe in the other, puffed and blew as theatrical wisdom poured forth in a spate of undiminished zeal. Micheál reminisced on a wider scale, for by then he was an international figure, having toured the world with his *Importance of Being Oscar*. The most remarkable thing about that remarkable programme was the lack of mention of the Longfords, much less of what they had done for the Gate Theatre. It was a sad display of thoughtlessness and ingratitude. Sensitive as ever to any slight to Edward, Christine was deeply hurt. She tried to laugh it off to anybody stupid enough to mention the omission.

Somebody somewhere very soon got the message. Amends were made. Christine was invited to do a similar programme. All alone, she was a diminutive and lonely figure on the screen, until her china blue eyes lit up, and her conversation flowed agreeably. Her generous tributes to The Boys exposed the niggardly attitude of the earlier programme. It was generally agreed that with effortless charm and grace she had quietly stolen the show. Egomania wasn't in her make-up. Christine was always a good friend, even to those who had ceased to be good friends to her.

In trying to keep Edward's memory alive, Christine's best allies were the ex-Longford Prods, those troupers who had shared the rough and the smooth with her, when together they had traipsed the rain-swept roads of Ireland for the pleasure of the populace. Once a Longford Prod actor and designer of many Gate Theatre productions, Alpho O'Reilly had later become head of design for RTE television. Writing about a radio production of Christine's play *The Hill of Quirke*, he referred to the neglect of Lord and Lady Longford's work for the Irish theatre:

> It saddens me to note how easily his and her work at the Gate Theatre and elsewhere is either forgotten, or set aside with a brief mention, when the Irish theatre scene is being discussed or written about. Yet they both sacrificed all their time and a vast fortune on maintaining the only permanent professional theatrical company — outside the Abbey Theatre — Ireland has ever had.

Longford Prods' one-time leading lady, Eve Watkinson, in 1978 pointed out to readers of *The Irish Times* that in newspaper articles on the travelling theatre in Ireland, the name of the late Anew Mc Master is usually honoured, while there is never any mention of Longford Productions: 'During two decades, this company regularly toured the provinces with a classical repertory of plays by Shakespeare, Chekov, Sheridan, Goldsmith, Wilde, Shaw *et al*, as well as works by modern writers. There must be many people living in the country who can remember the great pleasure that these tours gave. In Dublin, there seems to be a conspiracy to expunge the name of the late Lord Longford from Irish theatrical history: one wonders why.'

Why indeed! One is forced to conclude that shyness, modesty, decency, even an endless liberality with money — all is forgotten, unless in life one has had that peculiar capacity to stamp for ever the imprint of one's ego on the public consciousness. I like to think in a modest way I might count myself an ex-Longford Prod. If so, then the making of this book is my labour of love and admiration for two of God's gifted people in whose debt mine and future generations of theatre-lovers will always remain.

To me Christine's friendship was something very special. We had our arguments. We even had rows, mostly when she wanted to take on challenges of which she was no longer physically capable. She had her own GP and consultants, but being a long-time friend, who happened to be a doctor, there were times when I felt it necessary to emphasise a sensible routine in the course of everyday living.

One had, for instance, to contend with Christine's sense of

independence, while she in turn contended with the repugnant idea of advancing age, and how it might obstruct her habit of seeing every play in Dublin — her 'duty' as she called it. Walking alone in Dublin at night presented new and graver risks. Having frequented the city streets by night for nearly fifty years, she found the new situation difficult to accept, until she had her handbag snatched on O'Connell Bridge in broad daylight. That was more sobering than all the warnings one could offer. We compromised: retired and free at last of the daily grind at the Irish Medical Association, I drove her as often as possible.

Medicine had long ago curtailed my theatre-going. I was out of touch. Christine delighted in introducing me to a whole new generation of playwrights, producers, actors and actresses. I saw some glowing productions, staged with a sophistication new to Irish theatre. I also sat through tortuous evenings. I began to understand why Christine considered her play-going a duty.

As well as new people, I met some of the old. In April 1977 we saw an Edwards-Mac Liammóir *Merchant of Venice*, produced by Hilton at the Gate. Afterwards we went round to a dressing-room once filled with praise and people. Christine said to Micheál, 'You remember John Cowell?' Looking vacantly into space, he took my hand between his. 'John Cowell,' he repeated, slowly remembering, 'You left us to become a doctor.' I was stunned at the degree of his blindness, but greatly flattered that the now-famous Mac Liammóir should remember a small-time would-be actor of short duration at the Gate — and that so many, many years ago. That was to be our last meeting.

While it was a great honour to go to the Gate Theatre with Christine Longford, our visits there caused me a little embarrassment. She insisted on the two front seats on the right. Sitting alongside her in the seat which had been Edward's for three decades made me feel like some sort of wretched interloper. Besides, these particular seats were uncomfortable. The view was principally of the actors' feet, and there was a perpetual draught from the scene-dock. As well, Christine would laugh loudly at the least laugh-line. She led the applause, and sometimes even applauded an actor's exit. It was her way, she said, of encouraging the players. Sometimes she would nudge me. 'You're not laughing,' she would say, 'are you bored?' I assured her I didn't have to laugh out loud, I just laughed uproariously inside. Of course I was enjoying myself and I was anything but bored. And at the end of the evening, when we went round as we invariably did, the actors would take me on one side: 'For God's sake, next time take Christine to a back seat. In the front row, she distracts the hell out of us.' It never worked of course, because at the Gate Theatre I never led Christine anywhere. It was Christine who did the leading.

In the summer of 1977 I was researching for a book to be called *Where They Lived in Dublin*. Nothing pleased Christine more than to join me in foraging for old houses in the nooks and crannies of Georgian Dublin. Sometimes we were rewarded, and sometimes there was only disappointment — when the millionaire developers had got there first. Occasionally we drove outside Dublin, as for instance, to what James Gandon fondly called his Tivoli, a solid house named Cannonbrook, still lived in, on the heights above Lucan. Then there was Lord Northcliffe's birthplace at Chapelizod, and nearby was Sheridan Le Fanu's house by the churchyard. She loved Le Fanu, Edward having adapted him for the stage.

Christine adored driving — or, more correctly, being driven. It was remarkable that so few of her friends realised how much it meant to her to be driven, say, round the Poulaphouca Lakes. We would admire the lambs, stop somewhere to eat, and buy choc ices here, there and everywhere. She talked happily, reciting reams of poetry learned in her youth, and told the most convoluted and extraordinary stories. Too often her best stories came when I was trying to negotiate a centre-city traffic jam. My loathing of the other fellow left me incapable of remembering the wit and humour of all she said.

I think it was that summer I had planned with my sister and brother-in-law to drive to Gloucestershire where I had once laboured as a doctor. One day, quite suddenly, and with childlike appeal, Christine asked could she join us. She would so like to see the West Country again, and her birthplace at Cheddar. 'It'll be the last time,' she added whimsically. Of course she could join us — and welcome! Nothing better! She would make our trip complete. But alas! We hadn't allowed for that contemporary curse, that paralyser of society, the god-like picket. British Rail threw a strike, and within hours of our scheduled sailing time I was in a queue recovering our prepaid fares. Christine never again saw Cheddar or the West Country.

When the Merrion Nursing Home became a Cheshire Home she left Herbert Street for Ailesbury Road where she took a flat in a house owned by Dr Moira Woods. One day I found her in a fury. An unctious padre had called to welcome her to Donnybrook. She strongly resented the idea that the church should monitor her movements like that. Christine was not religious in Edward's organised-church sense of religion. Hers was a kind less immediately apparent. She was a Christian in the sincerest sense of that over-worked word. Simple, straightforward honesty was the talisman by which she measured her own religion and that of others.

Excepting those with some intellectual stature, she had no time for unctious or chatty hand-washers. She had no such reservations about Father Daniel Shields, a Jesuit wise in the ways of the world, a World War I chaplain, a classical scholar, and, most important, a one-time chaplain to the Irish Stage Guild. The admiration was mutual. After her death he said: 'At Mass I put her in my chalice every morning.' It might have mystified her a little, but she would still have recognised the tribute being paid her.

The year 1977 ended badly. In December Christine became gravely ill. Moira Woods arranged her admission to Sir Patrick Dun's Hospital. She refused an ambulance — she would go in my car or not at all. As happened so often in her declining years, one waived one's better judgment to please her. We arrived at the hospital in a downpour. I parked as near the main door as possible. Immediately a porter emerged, waving me off: 'You can't park there, that's the senior surgeon's place.' With an acutely ill woman in the car, I lost my patience, reminding the unfortunate porter that hospitals were for the sick, not for the convenience of surgeons, senior or otherwise.

Throughout that Christmas, Christine was as near death as any patient I have ever known. Every time one left her bedside one felt she could not survive another hour. She had lost all sense of time and place. She had receded into a state of semi-consciousness, into a remote and deathly silence, broken only by her own distressed respiration. Masses of flowers from her friends only added to the mortuary-like air of her room. Then quite suddenly one noted the antibiotic breakthrough. There was a tall flower arrangement on the window-sill. It resembled a light-house.

'That's nice,' I said — for something better to say.

Opening her eyes, she glanced at the flower-tower and said: 'A phallic symbol,' and implying a fullstop, closed her eyes again.

A week later she wanted a cigarette — confirmation that she was on the way back. Cigarettes, of course, were banned. A month later I was taking her to convalesce at Talbot Lodge, Blackrock. Nearing the gate she asked me to stop the car. It was the last depressing day of January, with frozen snow everywhere. She was as fretful as a small child about to be left at a boarding school. She begged a cigarette, her first smoke in two months. Again one's better judgment went by the board. Her recovery, however, was uneventful and complete. Soon she was back lunching daily in Mrs Gaj's restaurant in Merrion Row, and we had resumed our duties to the playhouses of Dublin.

On the night of 6 March 1978, my telephone rang just as the 10 p.m. radio news was beginning. It was Christine to say Micheál Mac Liammóir was dead. I held a portable radio to the phone while we listened to the details. She expressed no regret, only sympathy for Hilton in his loneliness. Later she was telephoned by the newspapers. She spoke the expected platitudes.

We had tickets for the Abbey Theatre for the following night. I asked would she prefer not to go — indeed would the theatre be open at all? Of course it would be open and of course we would go. So next night in the Abbey audience we stood for one minute's silent tribute to Micheál Mac Liammóir. It was all he was to get from Christine Longford.

Going home I enquired whether she would like to go to the funeral next day. Certainly not, but she would be grateful if I'd drop her at the top of Grafton Street at 11 a.m., she had a date with her dressmaker. Driving down Leeson Street next morning I enquired again if she wouldn't care to go to University Church. 'You may be sorry afterwards,' I suggested. Again the answer was an emphatic 'No'. As we passed the church people were already going into the service.

Leaving me at Grafton Street she said, 'You go to Micheál's funeral and tell me all about it tonight.' I did, and that night she absorbed all I had to tell. 'He had a good show then,' was her summing up.

Clearly, sometime, somewhere, Micheál Mac Liammóir had erred unforgivably. Christine was never so adamant, so absolutely decided about anything. To Cathleen Delany she said, 'Thank God, he won't be writing my obituary.' It was all so out of character. It was sad, so very sad.

Chapter 21

'Twilight and Evening Bell'

Plans for the celebration of the golden jubilee of the Gate Theatre were well advanced when Micheál died in March 1978. True to theatrical tradition that the show must go on, Hilton decided that there should be no interruption in the celebration scheduled for the following October. Part of the celebration was the publication of a *festschrift* called *Enter Certain Players*, a bouquet of tributes written by distinguished people on the work of Hilton and Micheál. Christine, still a member of the board of directors of the theatre, was invited to write a contribution on the work of Longford Productions.

Never, it seemed, had she been faced with a more trying task. For weeks she agonised. Paragraph after paragraph was drafted, amended, erased and discarded. For her peace of mind, it would have been preferable to have declined this invitation, but that solution might have been wrongly interpreted. The fact of the matter was that frequent illness had left her frail and debilitated, added to which she was undergoing continuous drug therapy for a cardiac condition. Nevertheless, and for all it cost her in angst and effort, she managed to produce a creditable contribution.

Opening with her congratulations to Hilton, and her assurance to him, and to all the world, that her admiration of him was undiminished, she then concentrated on the influence which had made Edward a man of the theatre. From the outset of his Longford Productions he had remained faithful to the Edwards-Mac Liammóir traditions. Characteristically, her contribution ends: 'In Edward's name and my own I send my congratulations to Hilton.' Sadly, that is the height of Christine's association with the Gate Theatre jubilee celebrations. Once again, illness intervened. She never even saw the memorial exhibition mounted at the Hugh Lane Gallery.

In expressing her admiration of Hilton Edwards, she did not exaggerate. It was a genuine — even emotional — thing she never tried to hide. Long ago, girls' dressing-room gossip saw it as an old-fashioned 'crush'. Others, narrowmindedly nationalistic, would nod and wink and smirk: 'Aren't the two of them English — isn't that enough?' But these were silly notions, far from the truth. To Christine Longford, Hilton Edwards was a manly man who knew his own mind, who commanded theatrical respect and, above all, who had the genius to bring a playwright's sprawling script to living, breathing life upon a lighted stage. For that alone she always gave him more than a sneaking loyalty — in spite of his studied disparagement of Edward. After Micheál's death, her sympathy for Hilton was really heartfelt. She knew from experience the loneliness he had to face.

For his part, Hilton gave her a respect he gave, probably, to no other woman — and I don't mean his operatic kissing of her hand. He bowed to her superior intellect, to her scholarship — even to what he called 'her needle-sharp wit that would lay a dragon low'. He recognised hers as a talent neglected, undisciplined, capable of infinitely greater heights in the theatre than she had ever attained. His notes to her in hospital were small literary masterpieces in their expression of concerned warmth and feeling. And when she died, Hilton stood out, the loneliest figure in that funeral throng, for now he was the last of the 'big four' who had given the Dublin Gate Theatre to Dublin.

In May 1978, my novel *The Begrudgers*, was launched at the Listowel Writers' Week. Christine was more excited about the event than if it had been hers. Michael O'Brien, my publisher, invited her along. My relationship with her in her later years was fraught with tensions, arising from what to me is that most awkward of situations: the friend who happens to be a doctor. While I would love to have had her support and company in Listowel (the friend!), my better judgment hoped she wouldn't undertake the journey (the doctor!). Just then, her condition was such that expertise at consultant level could become necessary at short notice. As I had hoped, she reluctantly declined the invitation.

In an understatement somebody called *The Begrudgers* a racy novel. Spattered with the four-letter word so prevalent amongst the Irish, it is a flagellation of the murdering, materialistic Ireland of the seventies. Christine liked it immensely, gave it to her friends, and in the ensuing weeks became the greatest public relations officer any man could have. She sought out people she thought I should meet; she lionised me quite undeservedly, and she, above all people, lectured me on diffidence and where it doesn't get you in this world. Her excitement grew with every passing week, for the book remained a No. 1 bestseller for three months. It was all part of Christine's policy: the encouragement of the smallest of small talents.

During the next eighteen months she was hospitalised on no less than four occasions. Understandably, she came to hate the very suggestion of admission to hospital. It wasn't that her intimates didn't rally round to keep her at home as much as possible. They did. But there were times when nervous depression intervened, and a terrifying bleakness took over. We would discover — Moira Woods or myself — that wilfully, or through forgetfulness, she would have ceased to take her medication. Things would be *in extremis*, and one or other of her doctor friends would have to call her GP or consultant, and that usually resulted in readmission to hospital. No wonder she disliked doctors (one she dubbed 'a non-conformist twit') and hated hospitals, though she always reassured Moira and myself that we were 'different'.

As soon as she had reached the earliest stage of convalescence she would phone: for God's sake come and take her home. This presented another doctor's dilemma. Christine could never grasp my predicament and no amount of explanation made things clearer for her. A patient is always free to leave hospital against medical advice, but usually nobody, and least of all a doctor, should take a patient out of hospital until he has been formally discharged by his consultant. Medical ethics created tensions that could strain a friendship. These phone calls usually ended in a row, but our rows were always blameless rows — I hope.

Between these illnesses, she continued to enjoy life, despite an obviously increasing frailty. We resumed our duties to every theatre company in Dublin, and daily I drove her to Gaj's restaurant. In foul weather I would strongly encourage her to stay indoors, but she would have none of that. Night or day, homely fireside comfort and warmth were alien to Christine's nature, the result of her years lived in cheerless theatres. Hers was a spartan existence: a piece of cheese in the fridge, hopefully; the central heating turned off, and all sources of warmth confined to a rubber hotwater bottle. No amount of advice would induce her to have an electric blanket. Orlando, the cat, slept warmly on her feet while she cheerfully cuddled the rubber bottle. She really required the services of a nurse-companion, but, typically, the idea was utterly repugnant.

Still, her greatest enjoyment was a dinner-party, hers or somebody else's. Entertaining four or six friends at the University Club saw her at her brilliant best. Afterwards she liked to do a *post mortem*: who was who, and what was what. Edward's spirit was never too far from these social evenings. After one occasion Christine said,'You had your nice suit on last night.' She was referring to a chalk-stripe flannel I wore in cold weather. 'That suit is old,' I told her, 'so old, the trousers have turn-ups.' 'Edward had one like it,' she said wistfully. It was at these moments one's heart went out to her in her long-lived loneliness. For her, Edward was still everywhere, through every hour of every day, and that was how it would always be for whatever time was left to her.

In 1979 a move was made to revive Longford Productions. Ronnie Walsh, Aiden Grennell and David Kelly had got together. The proposition was put, and Christine approved. She failed, however, to show the enthusiasm one might have expected. True, by then she was old and frail and ill, and anyway, any group calling itself Longford Productions couldn't be quite the same for her without Edward in command. Nevertheless, she went along with the idea, and hoped for their success.

Several plays were produced by the group at the Gate Theatre, including a Harold Pinter. The most notably successful was *The Three Sisters*. But the idea of a new Longford Productions didn't catch on with the public. Had it come ten years earlier when Christine was still energetic, it is possible, just possible, that she might have tried to blaze a new trail. Personally I doubt it. Edward's Longford Productions had, for

Christine with John Cowell at the launch of his book *Where They Lived in Dublin*, 11 December 1979. This was one of her last social occasions.

Christine, already taken its place in Dublin's theatrical history. 'Bliss was it in that dawn to be alive,' she had said of the Oxford Playhouse of the 1920s. For her, that same bliss flowed from the early Gate Theatre, and from Edward's Longford Productions. Ailing, alone, and in her late seventies, bliss for Christine was, regrettably, a thing of the past.

She came to the launch of my book, *Where They Lived in Dublin*, in December 1979. She had several interests: Edward was in it; she had helped me to hunt up some of the historic houses; she had herself written *A Biography of Dublin*. This time she was even more excited than before, announcing that the book solved her Christmas present problem. Later that night she joined a few friends at my place. Still happily smoking one cigarette after another, she accidentally knocked an ashtray to the floor. The merest chip was the height of the damage, but Christine would die or make amends. I received a far more luxurious ashtray for Christmas!

That winter we had our usual tussles about weather conditions. She complained of dizziness — what she called the 'staggers'. Yet she didn't fear icy footpaths, and refused absolutely to use a walking stick. But she would not stay indoors. Unless there was to be an accident, it was clear she must be driven. Fortunately, I was free, so I rang her every morning,

Christine receiving an honorary D. Litt. from the Chancellor of the National University of Ireland, Dr T.K. Whitaker, on 25 April 1980. She died less than three weeks later.

fixing a time to pick her up for her luncheon date at Mrs Gaj's. Sometimes I might be delayed a few minutes — a phone call or something. I would arrive at Ailesbury Road to find a freezing Christine waiting under the big tree by Moira Woods' gate. Unassisted, she might by then have negotiated thirty-eight slippery steps.

'Do you do it to thwart me?' I asked her one morning.

'No, dear, to save you time,' she replied with the mischievous defiance of a priggish little schoolgirl.

You could only try to save Christine from herself, but you could never be cross with her. Her charming naiveté was disarming. But neither could you laugh, at least not at the time. Only afterwards did the funny side of such peccadillos occur to you.

As she had done for many years, she spent Christmas 1979 with her long-time friends, Cathleen Delany and John O'Dea. She had set her heart on attending the Abbey Theatre's 75th anniversary celebrations on 27 December. I was priviledged to be her guest, but I had my fingers crossed again that all would be well, for her condition wasn't improving. However, she rose to the occasion and seemed to enjoy meeting old friends.

At the interval Hilton told us of his helplessness as a cook, and of how he missed Micheál. Christine told him how I lived out of a tin, and I told him how Christine couldn't even open a tin. (Long ago I had given her an old-fashioned tin-opener for iron rations on stormbound days, but she couldn't manage it — or that was her story!) Still the hypochondriac he had always been, Hilton related the details of his latest operation, and how my profession hadn't over-exerted themselves. 'Often, old boy, I had to ring my GP at two in the morning.' I tried to imagine his popularity with my profession!

Far from being intellectual, the conversation wasn't even elevating, and it never got round to *Juno and the Paycock* and Siobhán McKenna. Both it seemed were being taken for granted. Christine and Hilton had both grown old enough to be more immediately concerned with the grim business of just getting by. When it affects our friends, old age is particularly sad and disillusioning, even terrifying, because all its afflictions lie ahead for each one of us.

By telephone she booked seats for a new production of Hugh Leonard's *Da* with Godfrey Quigley, opening at the Gate on 2 January 1980. It was a bitterly cold, wet night. Driving to Ailesbury Road I decided whatever her disappointment, I was not taking her out. When I saw her I was even more certain that home was her place that night. She pleaded: no matter how she looked, she felt perfectly well — no 'staggers', no complaints, no nothing. Besides, I knew, didn't I, how much she'd wanted to see *Da*?

Most reluctantly I gave in. One usually did with Christine. At the Gate I saw her into the vestibule and left to park the car. When I returned she was standing furtively facing the wall opposite the box office. She appeared to be searching in her handbag. 'I'm back,' I said, 'shall we go and find our seats?' She didn't reply. I repeated myself, touching her arm. She shrugged me off violently. Suddenly I realised the awfulness of our situation. It was an attack of that feared and hated depression again. I ought to have known better than to bring her here. Instinctively I switched roles, from friend to doctor. I was no longer dealing with Christine, but with a patient, somebody well known who must be removed immediately from the curious eyes of a first-night audience, already crowding into the theatre.

With the help of the staff we got her to an empty dressing- room. I rang her own doctor, Tony Rutledge. When he arrived backstage he went the

Lord Longford leaving
St Patrick's Cathedral
with the Dean, Dr
Griffin, after Christine's
funeral service on 20
May 1980. Following
are her nephews
Valentine Lamb and
Thomas Pakenham.

wrong way and found himself opening a door leading on to the set of *Da*! That was a shred of light relief in the midst of thumping gloom. The nightmarish evening ended with poor Christine back in hospital.

Her prognosis was dismal. The next four months were testing for her and for her friends. Visiting could be an ordeal. She was silent and sad and withdrawn, and there was suffering in her face. But there was one question she always asked: Had I been back to see *Da* yet? Without much inner conviction, I told her I was waiting until she was better when we'd go together.

Rather late in the day, the National University of Ireland decided to give her an honorary D.Litt. The problem was whether she would be able to attend the conferring ceremony at Iveagh House on 24 April. I talked with her consultants. We could only wait and see. At best, it would be a matter of whisking her there and straight back to bed. At worst, she would have to be conferred *in absentia*. She begged me not to let her down, because this honour was for Edward too. I promised — if it were humanly possible. I promised, because to me this was a good woman's dying wish.

As if she had summoned back every vestige of her failing strength, she

210

was considered just about fit enough on the day to be taken out for the shortest possible time. Again, I had my fingers tightly crossed. Supported by Cathleen Delany, we got her to Iveagh House. During the ceremony Cathleen was allowed to sit beside her on a hassock, like a lady-in-waiting.

Christine's citation was written by Monsignor Michael Olden, president of Maynooth College. It was read by Monsignor E. F. O'Doherty. Ireland, wrote Monsignor Olden, should look back with gratitude on the day when Christine Trew, then a brilliant student of classics at Oxford, met Edward Pakenham, sixth Earl of Longford. 'Their intensely shared interest in classical language and above all, in the theatre, began a lifelong union which was to have a profound effect on the cultural life of Ireland.' When the new Countess of Longford had first come to Ireland in 1927, he went on, she was energetically challenged by the cultural needs of her adopted country, and within a year, her first book, *Vespasian and Some of His Contemporaries*, was published. Monsignor Olden recalled that *Vespasian* had been hailed as 'one of the liveliest volumes to spring from a dead language'. As a truly literary person, the Countess of Longford well deserved high honour from the nation and the university. Monsignor Olden then recalled that 'in 1957 when the Gate Theatre had to be reconstructed, she and her husband raised practically every penny that was needed. For the Irish people and particularly for the people of Dublin, the Gate Theatre will for ever be the monument to the selfless zeal and dedication of Lady Longford and her late husband.'

There was no exaggeration. Listening to the applause under the sparkling chandeliers at Iveagh House, its ornate ballroom crammed with the *crème de la crème* of academic Ireland, one's apprehension for Christine's immediate welfare was tempered with a modest sense of pride in having faced professional risks to make this moment possible for her.

When we got back to the hospital her room was like a flower shop. Her friends hadn't forgotten. Without even looking at it, she passed her parchment, still tied in its ribbon, to Cathleen Delany for safe-keeping — it must go into the archives at Pakenham Hall. Then, sighing tiredly, she sat on her bed. 'Darlings, I'm so grateful,' she said, 'I had to be there, for Edward's sake.'

Three weeks later Christine was dead. Aged seventy-nine, she suffered a fatal brain haemorrhage on 14 May 1980. Diffident, unpretentious, self-sacrificing — John Broderick called her 'a reluctant genius' — her only indulgences in life were hot baths, cups of coffee and endless cigarettes. In death it was different. She was honoured with the pomp and circumstance of a St Patrick's Cathedral funeral service — the Irish equivalent of Westminster Abbey. In the presence of the highest in the land, and with Handel's *Anthem* reverberating majestically, one could only try to imagine Christine's embarrassment could she but know of the unexpected greatness now thrust upon her. After years in the shadows she went forth in the sun.

Epilogue

The influences exerted by the Gate Theatre in the first sixty years of its existence are immeasurable. Despite great obstacles, Irish theatre is flourishing today as never before. Standards of production have reached levels of proficiency undreamt of in the twenties. Gone for ever are the pre- and post-London third-rate touring productions of flimsy West End concoctions — the theatrical pap once thought good enough for Irish audiences. Even the Abbey Theatre, whose actors were once capable only of kitchen comedy, now looks to a new horizon, perhaps not always with the sophisticated success expected of a heavily-subsidised national theatre. Irish actors have, however, learned to overcome their local accents when the need arises — something English actors haven't yet achieved. All this represents a theatrical transformation, its beginnings clearly linked with the foundation of the Gate Theatre in 1928.

From the beginning the Edwards-Mac Liammóir policy was international in character. Irish audiences were introduced to foreign playwrights of whom few had ever heard. With his arrival, Edward Longford threw open new and even wider casements, their vistas extending back in time to the earliest Greek dramatists and the beginnings of the theatre. But more important than all that, Lord Longford's vision, his idealism, his latest eccentricity — call it what you will — moved him to finance the Gate Theatre in the days of its extremity. Edward Longford, and no other, was the paediatrician who resuscitated that muling and puking infant in the appropriate purlieu of the Rotunda Hospital.

Nor did his influence end there. By nature he was a missionary. His gospel was the drama, and his self-appointed mission was to spread that gospel at its most colourful, enlivening the drabness of Irish rural life in the forties and fifties. Paying him the sincerest form of flattery the people imitated. Drama groups and drama festivals sprang up nationwide. The competitive instinct ensured rising standards. Today, despite the mesmerism of television piped into every living-room, the amateur drama movement exerts an immense counteracting power for good in a troublous land.

It is difficult to imagine that the Gate Theatre could ever have been born and bred without the individual contributions of the 'big four'. Their coming together was the tide in the affairs of men; their collaborations were the flood that led on to fortune. First, Hilton and Micheál: unknowns to whom the germ of the idea came with their chance meeting as touring actors in Enniscorthy. Theirs became the permanent loving relationship, always blessed with God-given genius. Then, Edward and Christine, liberal English-orientated academics in search of an identity in an illiberal Ireland. At the time, the likelihood must have seemed remote that four such people, so diverse in background and education, could make an impact great enough to influence a nation, ultimately earning for themselves the highest honours that nation could bestow.

The Dublin Gate Theatre of today is seen by some as the permanent memorial of its founders, Hilton Edwards and Micheál Mac Liammóir. Others like to think it commemorates Edward and Christine Longford, but for whose benevolence it would not now exist. Assuming there are no splits in heaven, it surely follows that the playhouse, made and maintained by the 'big four', is now their shared memorial in the city of their adoption. Their influence was great, but sadly, like Yeats and Gregory, much of their tradition died with them. The magic of Hilton's lighting and movement, the endless inspiration of Micheál's design, these have never been surpassed. Nor has another Edward Longford arisen, prepared to dissipate a private fortune in bringing theatrical splendour to the backwoods of Ireland.

What would its creators think of the Gate Theatre of today? As little, probably, as Yeats and Gregory would think of their creation. In each case, however, it is a real, a tangible miracle, that the thing created on a shoestring lasted long enough to be rescued by State subsidies. But, like religion, theatre thrives in adversity. Had there been such handouts in 1930, it is unlikely there would have been a Gate Theatre, for its conception was inspired only by the ready-made drama of bare Franciscan poverty, relieved by the coming of the fairy godfather. Together, those responsible for its birth and breeding were a phenomenon never to be repeated.

Christine Longford lived into the age of theatre subsidies. Indeed, she helped to negotiate them. With reservations, she believed in their efficacy in keeping theatre alive in times of inflation, not to mention the competition of television. But as one who had lived through the lean times, she would not have condoned the abuse of theatre subsidies. A cast of ten on a stage, with over one hundred backstage supporting staff represents rank over-growth resembling the public service. It is a recipe for decadence. It is Parkinson's Law battening on the public purse without commensurate merit in the end-product staged before a paying public. Subsidisation of the arts must be confined to the spirit of the original idea: a sum of money given by way of *assistance with essential expenditure*.

Without a defined policy, and after some wasted years of floundering uncertainty, when the Gate Theatre's future was threatened once again, the coming of Michael Colgan has heralded a new dawn. Like Edward Longford's deep-laid plan, Colgan lures his audience by alternating the popular with the erudite. He has a flair for style: a good play, well cast and well dressed-out with costumes, lighting and settings. Audiences aren't fools. They respond to quality, like discerning shoppers anywhere. And once you make them addicts, they become captive audiences.

The most hopeful sign of the success of the Colgan policy is the current attraction of the Gate Theatre for young people. In these hard-bitten times, it is refreshing to watch sensitive young faces as they react: eager, starry-eyed, absorbing the living theatre, all disbelief suspended. It is Gate Theatre history repeating itself.

The recession of the thirties saw a hard-core of penniless Dublin youth whose fortnightly treat was the current play at the Gate. These were the faithful occupants of the 'shillingy' seats, for whose small support the Gate directors were grateful. Edward Longford regarded these clients in a special way. None was turned away. When the 'shillingies' were filled to capacity, the overflow was directed to the more expensive empty seats at no extra cost. Ultimately, these penniless youngsters became the paying occupants of the plushy stalls.

In those early years when great plays were given memorable productions, and played to near-empty houses, one begrudged such theatrical treasure trove to a thankless people. One despised Dublin for her heedlessness, Ireland for her lack of pride. Such criticism, however, was unacceptable to Christine Longford. Reviewing it all in the after years, her attitude was one of indulgence. Irish audiences had to be wooed, had to be educated, but never criticised. For Christine it was a matter of principle, carried to idolatry, that everything Irish was above criticism. Blindly, she defended the land that she had venerated since she was a child. For her, Ireland had no faults, only attractive failings, a view which Hilton Edwards might have called 'the enrichment of an English mind under an Irish spell'.

214

Her indulgence of everything Irish meant a lot of punishment for Christine. In doing what she called her duty to Dublin playhouses, she suffered much that was third-rate, banal, even slovenly. Whenever she had self-doubts, it grieved her that posterity might judge the work of Longford Productions as something less than scintillating, for she knew the reasons very well. Edward was a classicist by tradition, thereby earning himself a reputation for lack of adventure in his repertoire. While he educated Ireland classically, his standard of presentation may not always have sparkled. As Christopher Fitz-Simon has said, 'These Longford Productions had an air of rakish gentility; rarely of the first class, but always professional.' If ever his productions fell short of perfection, the fault was principally Edward's own, because too often he over-rode his directors. That was one of his failings, perhaps his greatest. For his audience, it was still a tiny sacrifice, bearing in mind the gifts he gave to Ireland, gifts that nobody else could have given, and he gave them with such *élan* and generosity.

Nowhere was Christine's forebearance more evident than in the theatre. There, through a lifetime of elected silence, she suffered quietly for art's sake, always making it appear as if she were having fun. To her, as certainly as to Edward and Hilton and Micheál, Dublin owes its Gate Theatre. She was the essential fourth part of the 'big four', time and again pouring the oil and calming the waters when the barque had all but sunk.

One must assume God made her expressly for Edward. Nothing else can explain their absolute compatability, their total mutual love, his pathetic dependence upon her, and her ever-faithful response. Their meeting, their marriage, and their life together, made a holy trinity destined to strew miracles of delight before the Irish people. Hilton and Micheál had walked in the footsteps of John the Baptist, but it was Edward and Christine who brought the hope, if not of eternal life, at least of the indefinite survival of the Dublin Gate Theatre.

Bibliography

Acton, Harold, *Memoirs of an Aesthete*, (Methuen, 1948)
   More Memoirs of an Aesthete, (Methuen, 1970)
Amory, Mark, Ed., *Letters of Evelyn Waugh*, (Weidenfeld & Nicolsonl,1980)
   Lord Dunsany, (Collins, 1972)
Betjeman, John, *Collected Poems*, (John Murray Ltd., 1972)
Brambell, Wilfrid, *All Above Board*, (W.H.Allen, 1976)
Canfield (Curtis),Ed, *Plays of Changing Ireland*, (Macmillan, New York, 1936)
Craig, Mary, *Longford, A Biographical Portrait*, (Hodder & Stoughton, 1978)
FitzGerald, Desmond, *Memoirs of Desmond FitzGerald*, (Routledge & Keegan Paul, 1968)
FitzSimon, Christopher, *The Irish Theatre*, (Thames & Hudson, 1983)
Forbes, Bryan, *Ned's Girl, A Biography of Dame Edith Evans*, (Hamish Hamilton, 1977)
Gallagher, Donat, Ed., *Essays, Articles and Reviews of Evelyn Waugh*, (Methuen, 1983)
Hobson, Bulmer, Ed., *Gate Theatre Book*, (Alex Thom Ltd., 1934)
Hollis, Christopher, *Eton: A History*, (Heinemann, 1960)
   Oxford in the Twenties, (Heinemann, 1976)
Longford, Elizabeth, *The Pebbled Shore*, (Weidenfeld & Nicholson, 1986)
Longford, Lord (Frank), *Five Lives*, (Hutchinson, 1964)
Longford, Lord (Frank), *The Grain of the Wheat*, (Collins, 1974)
Longford Productions Souvenir Brochure, 1949.
Luke, Peter, Ed., *Enter Certain Players: featuring the Gate Theatre Golden Jubilee 1928-1978*, (Dolmen Press, 1978)
Mac Liammóir, Micheál, *All For Hecuba*, (Methuen, 1946)
Pakenham, Frank, *Born to Believe*, (Jonathan Cape, 1953)
Pakenham, Mary (Lady Mary Clive), *Brought Up and Brought Out*, (Cobden-Sanderson, 1938)
Pine, Richard, Ed., *Gate Theatre Golden Jubilee Souvenir Catalogue 1928-1978*
Powell, Anthony, *Infants of the Spring*, Vol.1 Memoirs of Anthony Powell, (Heinemann, 1976)
   Faces In My Time, Vol.3 Memoirs (Heinemann, 1980)
Powell, Violet, *Five Out Of Six*, (Heinemann, 1960)
   Within the Family Circle, (Heinemann, 1976)

Seanad Eireann Debates, Vols.33,34,35
Somerville-Large, Peter, *The Grand Irish Tour*, (Hamish Hamilton, 1982)
    Irish Eccentrics, (Hamish Hamilton, 1975)
Strong, L.A.G., *Green Memory*, (Methuen, 1961)
Sykes, Christopher, *Evelyn Waugh*, (Collins, 1975)
Tremayne, Peter, *Irish Masters of Fantasy*, (Wolfhound Press, 1979)

Newspapers and Periodicals

Evening Herald, 15 May 1980; 18 Nov.1982
Evening Mail, Letter from Louis D'Alton, Jan. 1941
Irish Independent, 8 May 1978
Irish Press, 20 Nov., 23, 26 Nov., 6,7 Dec. 1940
Irish Times, The, 6 Feb. 1961; 22 Feb. 1978; 25 April, 15, 16 May 1980
Motley, The Gate Theatre Magazine, 1932
Observer, The, 12 Feb. 1961
RTE Guide, 19 June 1970
Social and Personal, April and June 1961
Sunday Independent, 5 Feb. 1961
Word, The, Dec. 1969

Sources of Photographs

Bord Failte 7; John Cowell 1, 6 (right), 11, 82, 84, 104, 111, 127, 128;
G.A. Duncan 167, 174, 177, 179; Liam Gaffney 91; Aiden Grennell
129, 164, 169; *The Irish Times* 116, 182, 185, 196, 207, 208, 210;
Northwestern University Library, Illinois 65, 66, 89, 96; Anne
O'Connor 6 (left) 73, 125; Thomas Pakenham 2, 47, 51, 61, 62, 63,
70, 120 (top and bottom).

Appendix

1936-1960

List of 151 plays produced by Longford Productions at the Gate Theatre

List of 151 plays presented by Longford Productions in the twenty-four years of their existence, from 1936 to 1960. Excluded are revivals, which were frequent in the company's repertoire, especially in the forties and fifties. This list was compiled by John Finegan, drama critic, *Evening Herald*, to whom I am indebted.

1936 — *Three Cornered Moon* by Gertrude Tonkonogy; *Youth At The Helm* by Hubert Griffith; *Ah, Wilderness!* by Eugene O'Neill; *Armlet of Jade* by the Earl of Longford; *A Bride for the Unicorn* by Denis Johnston; *Yahoo* by the Earl of Longford; *The Moon in the Yellow River* by Denis Johnston; *Twelfth Night* by William Shakespeare.

1937 — *Pride and Prejudice* by Jane Austen and Christine Longford; *The Duchess of Malfi* by John Webster; *After October* by Rodney Ackland; *Lord Adrian* and *Cheezo* by Lord Dunsany; *As You Like It* by William Shakespeare; *Cadenza in Black* by Arthur Duff; *A Month in the Country* by Ivan Turgenev; *The Uncrowned King* by V. A. Pearn and Brinsley MacNamara; *Anything but the Truth* by Christine Longford; *A Woman of no Importance* by Oscar Wilde; *Busman's Honeymoon* by L. St Clair Byrne and Dorothy Sayers; *Carmilla* by Sheridan Le Fanu and the Earl of Longford; *Youth's the Season* by Mary Manning;

1938 — *Henry IV* by William Shakespeare; *The Parson Said 'No'!* by Peter Powell; *The Pleasure Garden* by Beatrice Major; *The Absentee* by Maria Edgeworth and Christine Longford; *Saint Joan* by Bernard Shaw; *The Merchant of Venice* by William Shakespeare; *Lady Windermere's Fan* by Oscar Wilde; *Ghosts* by Henrik Ibsen; *Time and the Conways* by J. B. Priestley; *Tartuffe* by Molière and the Earl of Longford.

1939 — *The Cherry Orchard* by Anton Chekov; *The Rivals* by Richard Brinsley Sheridan; *Doctor Faustus* by Christopher Marlowe; *The Strange Lover* by Lord Dunsany; *The Golden Cuckoo* by Denis Johnston; *A Murder Has Been Arranged* by Emlyn Williams; *King Lear* by William Shakespeare; *Here's Your Uncle George!* by Peter Powell; *The Brontes* by Alfred Sangster; *Sister Eucharia* by Austin Clarke; *Everyman* a morality play.

1940 — *The Tempest* by William Shakespeare; *Asmodée* by Francois Mauriac; *Don Juan* by James Elroy Flecker; *An Ideal Husband* by Oscar Wilde; *The Devil's*

Disciple by Bernard Shaw; *The Late Christopher Bean* by Rene Fauchois and Emlyn Williams; *Sea Change* by Christine Longford; *The Three Sisters* by Anton Chekov; *She Stoops To Conquer* by Oliver Goldsmith; *The Two Mrs Carrolls* by Martin Vale; *Dandy Dick* by Arthur Pinero; *Kind Lady* by Hugh Walpole; *The Admirable Crichton* by James Barrie;

1941 — *Tobias and the Angel* by James Bridie; *The Seagull* by Anton Chekov; *Much Ado About Nothing* by William Shakespeare; *Othello* by William Shakespeare; *Mrs Warren's Profession* by Bernard Shaw; *Martine* by J. J. Bernard; *Macbeth* by William Shakespeare; *Lord Edward* by Christine Longford; *Hamilton and Jones* by Winifred M. Letts; *Le Bourgeois Gentilhomme* by Moliere; *Hedda Gabler* by Henrik Ibsen; *An Italian Straw Hat* by Labiche and Michel; *The Cradle Song* by Martinez Sierra.

1942 — *The United Brothers* by Christine Longford; *Hamlet* by William Shakespeare; *The Barber of Seville* by Pierre Beaumarchais; *Oedipus the Tyrant* by Sophocles; *Six Characters in Search of an Author* by Luigi Pirandello; *Getting Married* by Bernard Shaw; *The Watcher* by Christine Longford.

1943 — *In Good King Charles' s Golden Days* by Bernard Shaw; *Love from a Stranger* by Frank Vosper and Agatha Christie; *The Vineyard* by the Earl of Longford; *Patrick Sarsfield* by Christine Longford; *The Doctor's Dilemma* by Bernard Shaw; *A Trip to Scarborough* by Sheridan and Vanbrugh; *Double Door* by Elizabeth McFadden; *Love for Love* by William Congreve; *The Master Builder* by Henrik Ibsen; *The Avenger* by Christine Longford; *Two Kingdoms* by Aodh de Blacam.

1944 — *Uncle Vanya* by Anton Chekov; *The Bacchanals* by Euripides; *Rope* by Patrick Hamilton; *The Brontes of Haworth Parsonage* by John Davison; *The Careless Husband* by Colley Cibber; *The Earl of Straw* by Christine Longford; *King Dan* by Aodh de Blacam; *The Great Adventure* by Arnold Bennett.

1945 — *The Jealous Wife* by George Colman; *Night Must Fall* by Emlyn Williams; *Arms and the Man* by Bernard Shaw; *The Magistrate* by Arthur Wing Pinero; *The Lady from the Sea* by Henrik Ibsen; *A Midsummer Night's Dream* by William Shakespeare; *John Donne* by Christine Longford; *The Time of Your Life* by William Saroyan.

1946 — *You Never Can Tell* by Bernard Shaw; *Heartbreak House* by Bernard Shaw; *The Marriage of Figaro* by Pierre Beaumarchais; *Our Town* by Thornton Wilder; *Laura* by Gaspary and Sklar.

1947 — *How He Lied to Her Husband* by Bernard Shaw; *The School for Wives* by Moliere; *Uncle Silas* by Christine Longford; *Misalliance* by Bernard Shaw; *Volpone* by Ben Jonson; *The Dark Lady of the Sonnets* by Bernard Shaw;

1948 — *Les Mal Aimes* by Francois Mauriac; *Rosmersholm* by Henrik Ibsen; *The*

Great Magician by Pedro Calderon; *Tankardstown* by Christine Longford.

1949 — *Le Malade Imaginaire* by Moliere; *Mr Supple* by Christine Longford; *The Recruiting Officer* by George Farquhar.

1950 — *The Lady's not for Burning* by Christopher Fry; *The Paragons* by Christine Longford.

1951 — *Candida* by Bernard Shaw; *An Inspector Calls* by J. B. Priestley; *Man and Superman* by Bernard Shaw.

1952 — *Venus Observed* by Christopher Fry; *Witch Hunt* by Christine Longford.

1953 — *The Cocktail Party* by T. S. Eliot; *The Philanderer* by Bernard Shaw; *Hill of Quirke* by Christine Longford.

1954 — *An Enemy of the People* by Henrik Ibsen; *All in the Wrong* by Arthur Murphy; *The Family Reunion* by T. S. Eliot; *The Male Animal* by Thurber and Nugent.

1955 — *The Living Room* by Graham Greene; *Stop the Clock* by Christine Longford.

1956 — *The Lady of the Camelias* by Dumas the Younger; *The Uninvited Guest* by Mary Hayley Bell.

1957 — *The Dark Is Light Enough* by Christopher Fry; *Mount Lawless* by Christine Longford.

1958 — *A Broken World* by Gabriel Marcel.

1960 — *Stephen Storey* by Christine Longford.

Index

223

224